UNITED KINGDOM?

UNITED KINGDOM?

Class, Race and Gender
since the War

E. Ellis Cashmore

London

UNWIN HYMAN

Boston   Sydney   Wellington

Published by the Academic Division of
Unwin Hyman Ltd
15/17 Broadwick Street, London W1V 3FP, UK

Unwin Hyman, Inc.
8 Winchester Place, Winchester, Mass. 01890, USA

Allen & Unwin (Australia) Ltd
8 Napier Street, North Sydney, NSW 2060, Australia

Allen & Unwin (New Zealand) Ltd in association with the
Port Nicholson Press Ltd
Compusales Building, 75 Ghuznee Street, Wellington 1, New Zealand

First published in 1989

British Library Cataloguing in Publication Data

Cashmore, Ernest
United Kingdom? class, race and gender since the war.
1. Great Britain. Society
I. Title
941.085′8

ISBN 0-04-305014-X
ISBN 0-04-305015-8 Pbk

Library of Congress Cataloging in Publication Data

Cashmore, Ernest
United Kingdom? class, race and gender since the war/
E. Ellis Cashmore
p.   cm.
Bibliography: p.
Includes index
ISBN 0-04-305014-X. ISBN 0-04-305015-8 (pbk.)
1. Great Britain—Social conditions—1945-. 2. Social classes—Great
Britain. 3. Great Britain—Race relations. 4. Women—Great Britain—
Social conditions. I. Title.
HN385.5.C37 1989
306′.0941—dc19   88-19733

Typeset in 10½/13pt Bembo by Fotographics (Bedford) Ltd,
and printed in Great Britain by Billing & Sons, London and Worcester

Contents

UNITED KINGDOM?

CHAPTER 1

Introduction:
Forces of conflict

A cake to fight over

Is the United Kingdom a *kingdom united*? It is often difficult to decide when images of flaming buildings, violent street assemblies and baton-wielding police officers fiercely clashing with all manner of antagonists come stampeding across our television screens. Far from being united, the images depict modern Britain as a deeply divided society split by conflict and challenge. The main divisions have been evident in a number of events, although one stands out memorably: the Grunwick dispute of 1976, when the misfortunes of a group of workers, mostly Asian women, came into prominence. This was an isolated conflict, but one reflecting broader themes. Exploited by a recalcitrant small-scale employer who refused to recognize their claims to unionize, the Grunwick strikers stood defiantly outside the company's factory gates for over eighteen months. At times, they withstood a battering from the police and eventually they were snubbed by the unions. The chief players in the drama were working class, female and Asian – yet it was never clear in what order of allegiance. They defended their rights robustly as workers, but also as members of groups the white working class had ridiculed and despised: women and ethnic minorities. Grunwick (which is covered in more detail in Chapter 7) was a product of the most divisive forces in postwar society. Together with events either side of 1976, it

[1]

formed a backdrop against which the unity often attributed to the UK has looked embarrassingly misplaced.

The UK has an electoral system that produces governments representing only a minority of the electorate. It has a political party said to be a vehicle for working-class interests, yet consistently failing to command support from that class. It has, at a conservative estimate, three million people without work or engaged in some ersatz employment, like training schemes. It has large sections of its ethnic minority population feeling so thoroughly disengaged from 'mainstream' society that they are prepared to take to the streets violently in efforts to make their grievances known. It has women insisting that the anti-discriminatory legislation of the mid-1970s has not helped them achieve parity in any measurable sense. It has had over two decades of constant internecine violence in Northern Ireland. Unless these are to be dismissed as imaginary conflicts, Britain surely cannot, in any meaningful way, be described as a unified nation.

Or can it? When all is said and done, the UK has proved to be a remarkably stable society compared to many other European and Western nations. It has experienced disruptions, some of great severity, yet its balance of power has remained basically unmoved, its political and economic structure has been maintained intact, its central social institutions have remained as solid as monuments, and, perhaps most crucially, its basic inequalities have not only endured but been renewed. Inequality has, especially since 1980, been validated as something necessary to a society's health and growth.

This condition is not the product of apathy. Over the past forty or more years, the UK has become highly politicized, although in a way few people expected. There has probably been more involvement in the general political process since the war than at any time in the last two hundred years – involvement not on one dominant issue, such as national class conflict, but on many different community issues at all levels of society. This might have led to unity, in the sense of bringing together various groups, strengthening their political ties and cementing

[2]

their allegiance to a common sovereignty, its rules, laws and values. Or it could have worked itself out in the form of separatist tendencies. In the UK it has been both: cohesion and cleavage. This combination of cohesion and cleavage has made a society powerfully united, yet split by the demands of conflicting interest groups. People clash and oppose each other in their attempts to grab their share of whatever resources are available – 'the cake'. This is but one level of conflict. 'At another level', writes Peter Worsley, 'they recognize a common interest: in keeping the system going so that there will be some cake to fight over' (1970, p. 321).

Cleavages in Britain or, for that matter, any society derive from one source: inequality. Where there are grossly uneven distributions of power and discrepancies in access to resources, like money and housing, there are bound to be lines of social cleavage. Society divides into identifiable groups, some of which have an interest in lessening inequalities, others whose apparent interests are not served if the inequalities are reduced. Given the depth of the ravines within modern society and the trends that militate against their closing up, one might wonder why the conflicts they have triggered have not torn British society apart. One might also wonder if they will tear it apart in the future. The answer to the second question is implicit in the answer to the first: simply stated, the nature of British society is such that the conflicts have been allowed to surface. If they continue to surface and are not denied, suppressed, or diverted into other channels, then they will not be destructive of unity or lead to a disintegration of the overall structure of UK society. When conflict, in the form of protest, opposition, or open challenge, is bottled up, then positions harden and the groups pressing for change can lose faith in the ability of the system to absorb their claims.

Historically, this occurs when a social system is rigidly totalitarian and intolerant of protests; it clamps down on them, creating widespread discontent and a potential for further conflict of a more serious kind. South Africa presents a modern example of a society whose institutional arrangements – its economy, polity and culture – are inadequate to meet the demands of the country's black majority. Instead of conflict being accommodated, it is obliterated. It is not blotted out in reality, because it returns, each time with a greater ferocity and more and more blacks see it as their only recourse.

Despite the political forecasts of some who see the UK as in the throes of transformation into an authoritarian state, British society has been relatively flexible, sponge-like in its capacity to soak up challenges and wring them out, sometimes in a fundamentally changed way. There is usually a modification in the immediate conditions which bring about the conflict. This is how conservatism succeeds: adjusting strategies and ideologies according to changing circumstances, at the same time preserving power balances and primary inequalities. The disruptions are usually subdued and the tensions eased; but while the inequalities remain, so does the potential for future outbreaks. One of the aims of this book is to identify the circumstances in which conflicts erupt and to analyse why there are not more of them in Britain.

I have approached this book by way of three main divisions in British society, all sources of profound inequalities. The inequalities are structured; they have occurred with such regularity over time that they cannot be dismissed as accidental or random. They are repetitive, patterned inequalities that have been fully incorporated into the British social structure. Class, race and sex inequalities have been the three major sources of *social* conflict since the war. I stress 'social' conflict because, for purposes of this book, I do not deal with the conflict in Northern Ireland, which cannot, I feel, be analysed within the terms of reference of class, race and gender. There are, of course, elements common to all three kinds of inequality. (The Northern Ireland situation strikes me as a very special type of political conflict deserving its own form of analysis. Rather than attempt to integrate it into an already congested framework, I have chosen to keep the focus of this book on the three social divisions, recognizing that the conflicts emerging from these are as relevant to Ulster as they are to the mainland; they are overlooked conventionally because the intensity of the political struggle often appears to subsume all else.)

The book is organized in three parts, each corresponding to one of the divisions, but it will be seen that there are correspondences and links between them. For example, a comparison of class and racial inequalities would reveal overlaps. Ethnic minorities in Britain are predominantly working class and are in similar circumstances to their white counterparts. On occasion, they have shown that they also see their problems similarly. Trevor Carter, himself black, believes the 1984–5 miners' strike 'awakened a level of solidarity' amongst both miners and blacks. But where conflicts run deep, groups experiencing inequality have tended to define their problems and adversaries in different idioms; and groups that are, in an objective sense, in much the same social position tend to see their interests blighted by each other. Working-class women might see their true enemies as working-class men who insist their domestic roles stay unchanged, rather than the more abstract and intangible systems of patriarchy or capitalism. Unemployed blacks living in deprived inner cities may cite racism in their slogans, but they also blame members of the white working class for their predicament.

Conflict within unity

'Conflict' is an over-used term and one which needs sharper definition if it is to be useful. One way to approach it is by stating what conflict is not. For example, I want to distinguish 'conflict' from 'competition', in which two or more parties seek control over or access to a finite amount of the some resource and agree beforehand to abide by clearly stated principles, rules and standards; there will always be obvious winner. Struggle is an underlying condition of conflict, although not of competition. It has Darwinian connotations of a physical struggle for survival and Marxian ones of class struggle. In both cases, groups clash because their fundamental physical or material existence depends on it. Marx saw his life's work as on the same scale as Darwin's, arguing that, as all living species struggle in their relationship to their environment, humans struggle over the means of production. There is a fundamental opposition between the interests of workers and those on whom they depend for their wages. Struggle may and sometimes does bubble up into open conflict.

A useful working definition of conflict is found in the work of Lewis Coser, who in 1956 defined it as 'a struggle over values and claims to scarce status, power and resources in which the aims of the opponents are to neutralize, injure or eliminate their rivals'. Conflict, in this sense, is a type of struggle brought into the open. Its pivot may be values, perhaps of the more basic kind on which whole societies stand; or it may be resources or, more specifically, access to them. In Britain the conflict has not been over values (nor over the moral, legal and institutional system of which they are part) but over the distribution of resources. We might say that if conflicts over resources were continually blocked or frustrated, people would eventually question the values underlying the distributive process. Afghanistan, Nicaragua, the Philippines and South Africa present a few of the many cases where conflict has built up not so much over specific issues or resources, but over fundamental principles of a moral nature.

There is sense and perception in Coser's work on the consequences of conflict, and, although written in the 1950s, *The Functions of Social Conflict* remains an authoritative source of insights. I will use Coser's formula for analysing conflict to tackle the question: is the UK a united kingdom? The title of Coser's book conveys his focus; while he does not deny that, under some conditions, conflict can be destructive of unity and lead to the collapse of complete societies, it can also serve to pull societies together, morally bind their members, unify their purposes and stimulate the creation of reforms in policy. Not everybody benefits from conflict, of course, and we have to ask a further question: functional for whom? The mutual repulsion of *jati* in the Hindu social hierarchy might be very functional for the caste system as a whole, but is not especially functional for the untouchables. The open struggle precipitated by the revolutionary Bolsheviks in early nineteenth-century Russia was hardly functional from the viewpoint of the autocratic Tzarist regime. But, Coser uses the term 'function' in a rather different sense to diagnose the consequences of conflict for entire societies. He provides possible answers to the question of why societies remain stable and continuous despite the volatility that usually grows out of inequality. The UK is a society sharply divided amongst classes, ethnic groups and the sexes. Yet its social and political system has looked solid and consistent. This raises questions.

In each of the book's parts, I will answer three cardinal questions. (1) *What* have been the chief developments or changes in the areas of class, race and gender? (2) *How* have these changes affected existing patterns of inequality? (3) *Why* do those inequalities persist, often in the face of forceful attempts to eliminate them? Each part describes the main changes in the postwar period, highlighting certain signpost events that seem to show the direction of and impulse behind social change. Following this, there is, in each part, a more analytical appraisal of the extent of inequality in the three spheres, breaking down (whenever possible in measurable terms) the depth and breadth of the three divisions. For these chapters I have drawn together empirical studies to show how patterns of inequality do change, although never dramatically.

This leads logically to the third and, arguably, most important question: why? I suggest reasons why inequality has remained such a permanent feature of British society and how it continues amidst the often rampant conflict it generates. Here the focus is on (to use Arthur Marwick's expression) the 'mechanics of non-change' – the apparatus, its motions and its tendencies that keep the UK divided. One component of the apparatus is education, and I devote a good deal of my account to the sometimes opaque but always crucial role education plays in the transmission of inequality over time.

A central argument of the book is that the same apparatus that produces inequality and promotes conflict simultaneously maintains unity, a broad-based agreement on the rightness or legitimacy of Britain's fundamental social, political and economic institutions and the values on which they rest. Unity and division are more than just cohabitees; they are symbionts, interwoven, each owing its existence to the other. This is a view of unity as having its source in conflict, and vice versa: not unity versus conflict, but unity as the result of an ability to express interests and fight in their defence. Yet the fighting, however dogged and factious, has been moulded, shaped by the institutions in which it takes place (the economic and political spheres, the legal framework and the class structure). It may seem odd logic at this stage, but I will show how conflict has actually strengthened unity by reaffirming faith in the 'openness' of this system, a system that is responsive enough to allow grievances to be vented, often quite violently without punishment or suppression (although there have been exceptions, as we will see).

In no way will this be a conservative evaluation of British society. It is an evaluation of a society that is conservative. Self-preservation being one of the objectives of society, the UK has developed permanent but flexible arrangements for dealing with conflicts that do not challenge the basic values, rules or 'logic' of society. The result is an accommodating status quo that has a chameleon-like quality, adapting and repairing to suit changing times. I write this not in admiration but simply in recognition of the way conflict has been treated and inequalities have been maintained. To follow on from these propositions, the argument has to be that only a severe and prolonged conflict that strikes at the values and logic of capitalist society can hope to hasten the disintegration of the structure of inequality in modern Britain. The conflict witnessed since the war has been disruptive but not corrosive; the framework from which the conflicts have emerged has remained unchallenged.

This book should not be approached as an orthodox work of social history that charts developments and summarizes their impact. I have gathered the raw material from which historians might work, taken a hammer to it and smashed it to pieces. In putting the pieces back together, I have produced an arrangement that is, I hope, both original and provocative. Interpretations of past events may be thought of as neither true nor false; they are best judged in terms of their ability to illuminate previously obscured areas, to spark new debates or nourish existing ones and to guide future exercises with concepts and observations.

Influences

The influence of many books is evident in the text, but three works in particular have to be singled out for special acknowledgement. The idea behind *United Kingdom?* originated after reading historian Richard Polenberg's *One Nation Divisible*, a portrait of the United States split by what the author calls the 'fault lines of class, race and ethnic identity'. Developments in those areas have been of central importance in the lives of American people, Polenberg argues. While I have approached my book in a totally different way, I begin from a similar conviction: that class, race and (in this case) gender are of central importance to British people.

I have already mentioned the theoretical input of Coser's work, in which he concludes that 'conflict tends to be dysfunctional for a social structure in which there is no or insufficient toleration and institutionalization of conflict'. Coser argues that the main 'threat' to a society's stability 'is not conflict as such, but the rigidity itself which permits hostilities to accumulate and to be channelled along one major line of cleavage'.

Britain has clearly not experienced such rigidity, and it is for this reason that Alan Fox, in his *History and Heritage*, is able to argue convincingly that 'Its political and social system has been uninterruptedly in the making for three centuries, and the probability is that while minorities on both sides may be prepared in the last resort to test class relations to destruction, majorities will not.' Fox reaches this verdict after tracing the social origins of the British industrial relations system; and, while my purposes are quite different to his, Fox's argument has guided much of my own analysis. Whether this argument is credible when set against class, race and gender conflicts is something the reader will have to decide after reading the following chapters.

Part 1

CLASS

CHAPTER 2

Reform and reaction

Building the new society

'He's been the greatest union leader this century,' claimed Steve McGhee as he cast his vote in favour of Arthur Scargill, who in 1988 sought re-election as the National Union of Mineworkers' president. McGhee, a Yorkshire miner, had stuck resolutely to his picket line for the entire duration of the epic 1984–5 strike. Yet there was caution in his prognosis: 'Whoever wins the election, *nothing will alter.*' McGhee's approach was firmly in line with the working class generally: a robust and unswerving fidelity to causes, a willingness to remain solid with colleagues even when the direction of events is unpromising, but a moderating realism about future possibilities. Essentially, these three features have shaped the development of the working class since the Second World War. Working-class people have struggled to improve their material conditions; they have shown impressive solidarity in the defence of what they take to be their interests; but, when it comes to envisioning changes of scale and substance, they have fought shy.

Over the next three chapters I intend to look carefully not only at the character of the British working class but also at the structure of which that class is part. There has been change in both; there has also been stability, continuity and inactivity. These contradictory yet coexisting elements were evident in the immediate aftermath of the war, a time when 'fighting shy' sat uncomfortably amidst the radical sloganeering and abundant promises of a society in the process of transformation. 'We have to rebuild Britain to standards worthy of the men and women who have preserved it; we have to organize social services at a level which secures adequate health, nutrition and care in old age for all citizens; and we have to provide educational opportunities for all,' declared the Labour Party in a publication revealingly entitled *The Old World and the New Society* (1942, p. 11).

Despite the promises, the war brought about two factors which weighed against the probability of dramatic change in the reconstruction period. First was the unity of purpose emerging in the war period. Class-specific interests and preoccupations were, in large part, forgotten as the majority of the population pushed behind the war effort. Survival in the face of two hostile military powers assumed prime importance. This effort, successful as it was, created a second factor: a strengthening of faith in existing institutional arrangements. Britain had endured physical destruction and loss of life, but could still claim to be 'victorious' in many senses. Education, industry, the state bureaucracy, *class*: these were all components of a system that had taken an almighty ravaging, yet was still intact. After five years of fighting, it was unthinkable for many that such a system should be dismantled. There was little room for self-criticism; Britain was still in many people's eyes a 'world power' – a resilient myth that was to play its part in the racism of decades to follow.

Compromises brought about by the wartime coalition government, under Churchill, helped lift Labour's profile and lend that party credibility as a potential governing administration. The ultimate goal was to produce a *classless* society, but not by destroying the political framework. There was a widespread constituency for the view that a socialist party could launch an ambitious programme of social and economic rebuilding within the existing institutional arrangements. Wartime arrangements had been effective; a stringent state had capitalized on the unity of purpose and enforced austerity and had achieved results.

Labour's principal idea was to sustain the momentum, and

this meant minimizing what one might call the logistical changes – keeping the unity from dissolving into traditional class antagonisms and mounting modernization programmes to be initiated and controlled by the state. The spirit and machinery of the war effort were to be extended into peacetime. Events in the six years after 1945 suggested a stable equilibrium between the elected Labour government and a working class buoyed by a successful, if costly, defence of the nation and great egalitarian promise as embodied in the 1944 Education Act. The trade unions showed great confidence in Clement Attlee's government, which asked for a prolonging not only of wartime unity, but also of restraint as it set about constructing a web of health and social insurance Acts.

By 1948 what Beveridge (1944) called 'a comprehensive policy of social progress' was in motion, a process that drew little or no opposition from the Conservative Party. The beginnings of the welfare state were Labour's major (some would argue, only) initiative in this period. The nationalization of industry on a grand scale had been an article of Labour Party faith since 1918, but the Attlee administration showed little interest in such economic change. It conceded that the limited nationalization it required was to *improve* the efficiency of British industry and finance, not to change it. The government was under no pressure from trade unions to wrench the ownership of industry from private hands; they seemed content with the newly instituted joint consultations between workers and management. This aside, the basic industrial relations pattern was maintained. The question of industrial efficiency was to be answered by blending central state planning with private enterprise. For some, this was a dilution of socialist principles; for others, it was a practical step towards a mixed economy.

The British working class emerged from the war like a boxer, groggy after surviving a couple of knock-downs and grateful for the respite brought by the sound of the bell. Heartened by the encouragement of his corner, he might greet the next round optimistic of an improvement, yet with caution sufficient to

[15]

make his approach less than adventurous. The lack of any broad working-class demand for drastic postwar change simplified Labour's task. Sensible, rational and attainable revision was the objective, not a wholesale change in the control of the means of production. This was reflected both in the Labour government's practical policies and in the posture of a working class whose welfare was legally protected by the sheltering canopy of the state. The working class had glimpsed some of the potential of state control during the war, especially in areas such as taxation, wage level maintenance and nutrition policy.

Expansion in education made it technically possible to combine talent and application to lift oneself away from a deprived background and scale the social pyramid. New housing programmes promised to crush overcrowding and squalor and provide decent accommodation for all, regardless of income. Emergent leisure industries created new avenues of consumption. Added to these benefits was a new bargaining power; full employment was tailor-made for the trade unions, whose membership rose to give them formidable numerical strength and a sharper cutting edge in industries that demanded labour – and plenty of it. Ideals of a 'new Jerusalem' were suspended in favour of more immediate, pragmatic considerations.

The character and conditions of the working class made the institutionalization of class conflict possible, even desirable. Trade union leaders worked with Attlee's administration, formulating compatible aims and policies. Aware that wartime facts of life, such as food rationing, were likely to persist for a while, the unions were restrained in their aims and willing to accept limitations on collective bargaining. But the vice of austerity that held the unions began to wear loose by 1948. Minimalism and abstinence lost their grip. Conditions generally had been improved by the social reforms, and the 1946 National Insurance Act had, somewhat symbolically, abolished the last vestiges of the Victorian Poor Law and the workhouse system of relief (which had stood on the embarrassingly outdated assumption that poverty was a product of personal failings rather than social conditions). Wages had increased, but so had prices and at a faster pace. For two years after 1948, wages slipped back in relative terms; wages rose by 4 per cent, while the retail price index showed an 8 per cent increase. Government attempts to discourage wage increases met with rebuffs from the unions. While the working class' consumption of goods and services clearly rose, it did not rise proportionately anywhere near as much as the consumption of 'the rich', according to C. J. Bartlett (1977). By 'the rich' Bartlett refers to the wealth- and property-owning class of the day; the working class missed out in relative as well as absolute terms.

It is probable that many sections of the working class could sustain their resolve by thinking back to earlier depressions, but younger sections could not. As Bartlett speculates: 'Memories of the 1930s would weaken, just as the belief would gain ground that Britain did not always have to be subjected to so much government control and to so many personal restrictions on personal consumption and preference' (1977, p. 81). As well as the remnants of food and clothes rationing, high personal taxation was straining working-class fidelity to the Labour government.

Perhaps 'fidelity' is not an apposite term here, for the manner in which voters, in particular working-class voters, transferred allegiance to the Conservatives in the 1951 general election suggests that the Labour government was a convenient vehicle for expediting postwar ambitions. Such ambitions did not extend to the grand changes of a more traditional socialist vision, but to a series of practical yet imaginative steps to improve the immediate material conditions of the working class. While Labour had relied on the respect and co-operation of the unions in assembling a package of welfare reforms and rationalization plans for key industries, it could not restrain a certain impatience and restlessness born of their members' relative lack of spending power. To compound this there was the residual worry of unemployment; a revealing study by Milne and McKenzie indicated that over half of Labour supporters felt threatened by the prospect of losing their jobs

(1954). In the run-up to the 1951 general election, the Conservatives made full employment their number-one objective.

Traditional working-class allegiance to the Labour Party was shamelessly split. The 1951 election was won by the Tories with 321 seats to 295, with no mandate for drastic change. It seems that the victory was based less on a creative plan for the future, more on the weakness of a Labour government internally divided on questions of defence and the struggle to control prices. Not that the change of government signalled a departure from previous policies. Continuity was the hallmark of the new Conservative government which ushered in a period of 'Butskellism' – a compound of R. A. Butler, the Chancellor of the Exchequer, and Hugh Gaitskell, the Labour Party's leader in opposition and former Chancellor, whose eagerness to withdraw grand nationalization from Labour's manifesto drew him acclaim as a realist and criticism as a violator of first socialist principles, as we will see in the next section.

Live now, pay later

Here is how the *Daily Express* imagined the typically affluent working-class 'housewife' of the early 1960s surrounded by her consumables:

> The lady of the house should be lounging in her *jeans* and *thick-knit sweater* over her *nylon panties* and *girdle*, sipping a glass of *sherry* and nibbling *potato crisps* in her *gloss-paint* lounge with its *oil heater* and *latex-backed carpet* before taking the *roast chicken* or *fish fingers* out of the *refrigerator*, and popping it into the *electric cooker* while her man should be cleaning his *motor-scooter* from a *plastic bucket* and keeping an eye on his *wrist-watch*.
>
> (17 March 1962)

The thirteen unbroken years of Conservative government were ones in which class lost much of its activating significance, due largely to a steep rise in incomes, an opening out of home ownership to all but the lowest income groups and a sudden rush in consumer spending. Elemental inequalities remained, although extra spending power provided a great diversion from this fact. It was a period in which the working class enjoyed a relatively short, but in many ways unprecedented, burst of 'prosperity'.

From a purely economic point of view, government policy was short-sighted and self-destructive. The price of basic materials bought from abroad dropped, while the price of home-produced exports rose, producing between £400 and £500 million per annum in additional purchasing power. Home production kept rising as exports declined; hence, virtually the whole of the UK's growing output was absorbed by the home market. Industry was not, so it seemed at the time, in great need of re-equipment. This meant that reinvestment stayed low and wages high. Wage claims were usually met, so consumer demand was kept up by purchasing power. Tax relief and the availability of hire-purchase facilities made it possible for the working class to (in the phrase of the day) 'live now, pay later'.

The alleged prosperity, then, was founded – precariously, as it turned out – on an artificial cheap flow of imports, an unnervingly low export rate, a profligate neglect of industrial reinvestment and the availability of credit. In the world market, competition was weakened due to the effects of the war, although the economies of West Germany and Japan were poised to surge. In spite of the lack of long-term economic wisdom, the tangible benefits to the working class were apparent enough. Real incomes rose by 20 per cent, while prices remained stable between 1951 and 1961. Home ownership grew: in 1951 only 12 per cent of all homes were privately owned; by 1954 the figure had increased sharply to 26 per cent, and by 1959 it had reached 56 per cent. This had a political impact; as Vernon Bognador notes: 'as more and more voters were able to purchase their own houses, the swing away from Labour would be more accentuated' (1970, p. 76). A 'property-owning democracy' was how Tories described their vision, and clear moves were made towards realizing this. For those who were not able to enjoy the fruits of home ownership, a large-scale housing project of 300,000 new dwellings every year was initiated by Harold Macmillan, as Minister of Housing in 1951. Macmillan succeeded Anthony Eden as Prime Minister in 1957, when, after two years in office, ill health forced the latter's resignation.

Then, a slight murmur: in the second half of the 1950s there was some unease amongst the unions, which had been acquiescent for the last ten years. Between 1946 and 1954 an average of 2.25 million days per year were lost in industrial disputes. In 1955 this went up to 3.7 million. Frank Cousins, of the Transport and General Workers' Union, reflected on the rising affluence and the uncontrolled wage bargaining when he announced ominously: 'If there is to be a free-for-all, we are part of the *all*.' Bartlett believes that if any event symbolizes the passing of an era it was the death of Arthur Deakin in 1955 (1977). Deakin, of the Transport and General Workers' Union, had been a leading unionist during the previous twenty-five years and was an ally of the Labour government in the Trades Union Congress' (TUC) conditional wage restraint agreement in 1948. From the mid-1950s, shop stewards' influence over both management and central union leaders grew, and the authority of key individuals like Deakin was diminished. The 'new breed' of shop stewards was roundly satirized in the Boulting brothers' 1959 film, *I'm All Right, Jack*, which featured a farcical *mésalliance* between a unionist's daughter and a middle-class wimp in search of shop-floor experience. In the year of Deakin's death, a rail strike triggered a state of emergency for two weeks; the railway workers' union established a precedent for wage bargaining.

Internationally there was also something of a turning point, for in 1956 any delusions about Britain's status as a world power were smashed. Nasser's nationalization of the Suez canal prompted military action from Prime Minister Eden, in league with France. By the end of 1956 British troops had been withdrawn, the strategy was exposed, and Britain's limited international status was underlined. As the so-called national consensus began to evaporate, industrial disputes multiplied.

Macmillan succeeded Eden as Prime Minister in 1957, a year in which the phrase 'you've never had it so good' was taken out of the context of a much more foreboding speech and interpreted as 'Supermac's' blithe and blind optimism. In fact, Macmillan's intention was to prompt the question, 'Is it too good to last?' according to Bartlett (1977, p. 143). Contrary to popular views, Macmillan may well have had the measure of the industrial and economic trend, for earnings continued to rise, as did the price of consumer durables, while food prices stayed stable. Net national output had, at this stage, increased by 20 per cent since 1952. Annual wage increases had been established.

After two years of Macmillan's government 70 per cent of the nation's homes had television sets. Holidays abroad were affordable events. Between 1955 and 1959 hire-purchase debts increased by 75 per cent, giving rise to the idea that people were living on borrowed time. The balloon of affluence continued to inflate, a thing of air rather than substance. Affluence is a great antidote to class conflict in some circumstances. An end to the affluent period might have been in sight as the end of the 1950s approached, but an income-tax-reducing budget in 1959 was duly rewarded with another emphatic Conservative victory in an October general election. The Tories' approach to society and the economy looked sound, despite the mounting number of industrial disputes.

The Labour Party, in the meantime, had done itself few favours by engaging in an internal ideological argument over the issue of nationalization. According to clause IV of the party's constitution, nationalization was a central socialist doctrine. Yet within the party's leadership there was a gathering of revisionists who refused to acknowledge nationalization as ineluctable and, instead, pushed for a mixed economy with public ownership of important industries only. Harold Wilson likened the revision to removing Genesis from the Bible, though Gaitskell argued that nationalization was but a means to achieve ultimate socialist objectives, the central one of which was social equality. The debate hinged on whether the

[21]

ownership of the means of production was to be regarded as the prime target for reform, or whether socialist ambitions would be realized within the framework of an economy comprising public and private ownership. What began as an academic debate before the 1959 election broke into an internecine affair after the somewhat surprising defeat of Labour at the hands of a Tory Party not only embarrassed by Suez but having to deal strenuously with the new authority of the shop stewards.

By the time of the 1959 election the composition of the working class was in flux. Technological advance necessitated a new flank of the labour force, educated, specialized and comparatively well paid. The expansion of the white-collar sector created a new band of workers whose political affiliations were not structured by older class loyalties. The new technicians and white-collar workers constituted together between 30 and 50 per cent of a working population of 25 million. Regional differences were also emerging by the end of the 1950s; it would be a mistake to assume that working-class affluence was evenly distributed through the country, when unemployment was rising in places such as Northern Ireland, parts of Scotland and areas of the north of England. In contrast, the growth of manufacturing and service industries ensured something of a boom in the English Midlands and the South.

Also, on a regional level, new housing estates pulled families out of older working-class areas and so weakened traditional neighbourhood networks, as studies by Willmott and Young suggested (1957; 1960). Immigrant families from the Caribbean and South Asia were entering the inner cities just as quickly as whites were leaving them for places like Luton, home of the typical 'affluent worker'. Multi-occupation of dwellings and squalid conditions added detail to what was then an emergent social question: what was to be done about race relations? The inner city violence of 1958 was like rolling thunder-clouds heralding a storm that was to persist in subsequent decades. No convincing answer to the question of race relations was forthcoming. Indeed, racism was to divide the working class more effectively than any capitalist's connivance could hope to do, as we will see in Part Two.

A further dimension to the structure of the working class was added by the creation of youth. I choose the word 'creation' with care because the concept of a collection of people aged between 15 and 21, sharing distinctive cultural tastes and lifestyles and consciously promoting their difference from the rest of society simply did not exist until the mid-1950s. The advent of the 'teenager' with unprecedented spending power because of relatively high earnings very quickly provoked a commercial reaction in the form of an entire industry geared to meeting the requirements of youth and generating new demands from young people. On the supply side, records, magazines, clothes, motor bikes, dance halls and assorted gimmicks such as hoolahoops were all effectively commercialized. So much so that some felt that the entire complex called 'youth' was the product of some gigantic, commercial manipulation designed to make young people part with their money. The phenomenon of youth reached the point of self-parody in the late 1970s with the release of the Sex Pistols' *The Great Rock 'n' Roll Swindle*, a commercial film entertaining its young audiences with an elegiac tale. The victims of the eponymous swindle were, of course, the exploitable youths watching the film.

By the time of the Sex Pistols' post-punk impressions, young working-class people were on the slide towards becoming a virtual lumpen group, a social residue in the wake of mass unemployment. In the late 1950s, however, very different forecasts were aired. Some saw the five million teenagers becoming, as G. M. Carstairs put it in the 1962 Reith Lectures, 'the most vociferous agents of social change' (quoted by Ryder and Silver, 1985, p. 226). Others, like Abrams and Rose, made more considered assessments based on empirical research. 'There is among young people today a complex of barely conscious Conservative sympathies which have still not yet fully expressed themselves in overt party affiliations,' they wrote (1960, p. 58).

[23]

This interpretation of youth as 'barely conscious Conservatives' had wider application at the end of the 1950s, especially after three consecutive Tory general election wins. Questions were being asked about the working class generally: had there been significant subjective adjustments to match the changes in internal structure? One school of thought had it that being part (or at least trying to be part) of the new property-owning democracy would have consequences for working-class self-perceptions; class identity would become less of a salient feature of the make-up of many members, especially the new beneficiaries of what were previously middle-class preserves. Motor cars, telephones, television sets and, perhaps most symbolic of all, washing-machines were no longer unattainable luxuries of the rich. Measured in simple terms of material possessions, the working class now came to resemble the middle class. And so some researchers, like John Goldthorpe, speculated on the *embourgeoisement* of the worker, suggesting a 'craving for social status which thus led to a willingness, indeed eagerness, to accept bourgeois social values, life-styles and political ideas' (1969, p. 3).

The thesis was that, as members of the working class acquired the material accoutrements or trappings of middle-class life, they would drop traditional working-class views of the world in which 'them', the bosses, were against 'us', themselves. Class identity would soon dissolve, and the workers would turn into an adjunct to an expanding middle class, devoid of any radical leanings. Goldthorpe and his colleagues entitled their study *The Affluent Worker* and examined in detail car workers at Luton, an expanding town to the north of London and a 'microcosm', as a Tory politician, John Hare, described it, 'of the kind of society we are trying to create'. Other 'new working-class' satellite towns sprang up as part of a drive to disperse the older inner-city slums. The dissolution of neighbourhood solidarity they seemed to herald gave further plausibility to the *embourgeoisement* thesis. Yet Goldthorpe *et al*. found that the extent to which the working class had assimilated middle-class norms, life-styles and voting habits had been exaggerated: 'Affluence, and even residence in localities of a "middle-class" character, do not lead on, in any automatic way, to the integration of manual workers and their families into middle-class society' (1969, p. 158).

The study disclosed an interesting characteristic developed by the 'affluent' sections of the working class: instrumentalism. Class politics were regarded as marginal to the workers' collective experience, as were many of the more traditional concerns of the trade union movement. Workers approached their work instrumentally; work served as a means of getting money – money to spend on the expanding range of goods and services that were available. Customary working-class loyalty to Labour had been weakened not by an absorption of middle-class habits, but by a calculation: support went to whichever party seemed likely to do more for the workers. The Beatles captured the essence of this working-class approach when they sang the Bradford–Gordy number, 'Money': 'Money don't buy everything, it's true. But what it don't get, I can't use. Give me money.'

While the *embourgeoisement* argument as a whole was rejected, the very fact that workers became more individually acquisitive and oriented to the extrinsic rather than intrinsic aspects of work indicated that certain properties and values associated with bourgeois culture had been given some importance, more importance perhaps than at any time since the war. Affluence brought a new focus; more possessions, new environments, more money and rising expectations of the future introduced new self-evaluations. People who, in terms of their relationship to the means of production or their income level, would qualify as working class (whether 'upper', 'middle', or whatever) chose middle-class reference points. Many workers evaluated themselves as middle class on the grounds that they earned a relatively high wage, worked in a white-collar job, or engaged in leisure pursuits conventionally associated with the middle class. It has been argued that class should be defined as much by people's own assignations as by objective criteria. Arthur Marwick, for one, believes that by studying 'images of class' we are best able 'to map out a social structure which conforms with life as actually lived in the period under review, as distinct from being an abstract tool of analysis' (1982, p. 39). If this is so, then the period under review was one of middle-class growth. A great many people who, by most indices, would have qualified as working class found themselves either possessing or within striking distance of middle-class status, in their own perception at least.

The problem with accepting subjective assessments is that they may obscure the inequalities in class that are not immediately apparent to the subjects themselves. Such subjective perspectives are interesting in that they often reveal no clear appreciation of the cleavages in power, wealth and incomes that underlay the redistribution of incomes in the postwar period. The character portrayed by Tony Hancock in his radio and television series, *Hancock's Half-Hour*, captured many of the pretensions: a working-class individual living in the London suburb of East Cheam.

'You're not middle class,' derides his foil Syd James in the television episode 'The Emigrant' (first broadcast in 1960).

'Established bourgeoisie,' retorts the offended Hancock. 'We Hancocks have been here since 1066. We came over on the *Mayflower!*'

Britain was not a nation of Hancocks, but there was a sense in which many members of the working class identified with the middle class and held an image of themselves as essentially bourgeois and conservative, with a small 'c' at least and, as election results bear out, with a large 'C' in many cases.

In creating the affluent worker, the Conservatives who governed from 1951 to 1964 came near to being throttled by their own monster. Having built the creature, then sustained it with electric jolts in the form of wage increases, the Tories found it running out of control in the 1960s. Voters cared about their standard of living; when exports rose by too little and imports by too much, inflationary pressures began to make life less comfortable materially.

There was no dramatic lurch to the left. Labour regained

some credibility under the leadership of Harold Wilson and inched its way into government with a four-seat majority in the general election of 1964. The party drew 44.1 per cent of a low, 27.65 million turn-out. Wilson promised a 'white-hot technological revolution', and his persuasive public style was particularly important to Labour's campaign. More homes had television sets, and party-political broadcasts took on great significance as a result. Wilson was perhaps the first postwar political leader to take full advantage of the platform offered by the media. His image, replete with pipe and raincoat, could have been tailored for television. The Wilson image has become almost a symbol of the 'swinging sixties' with all their connotations of free spending, free loving and, generally, free living. Yet there were clearly identifiable groups which were not caught up in the swirl of the 1960s. The aged, those living in deprived regions, the newly arrived migrants: the affluent society would have held little meaning for these groups.

Worth noting here are aberrant results in Labour's successful electoral challenge of 1964. The party had good fortunes in national trends, yet suffered reversals in three West Midlands constituencies, all housing substantial migrant populations. One of the campaigns was fought on an openly racist platform by a Tory candidate, whose success actually incommoded his own party. We will return to this episode in Part Two.

A further general election in 1966 consolidated Labour's position. Wilson's government lasted until 1970; he returned to lead the country again in 1974. Inflation, mild by early 1980s' standards, had brought about a decline in working-class spending power, and this had damaged Tory credibility in the two years prior to the 1964 election. The party's problems had been compounded by the Profumo scandal. Yet Labour could still not command a mass working-class body of support. Working-class perceptions and expectations had expanded in the 1950s; the decade may have been one of economic decline in terms of growth and UK exports, but people had glimpsed themselves as part of a new middle sector which was replacing the older, underprivileged working class. The working class had become used to thick wage packets and expected them to stay thick. They did, but they just did not buy so much in the 1960s. The Tories sensed the mood of frustration as inflation took its effect, and tried through persuasion to prevent the unions becoming restive. British industrial relations were regarded as a 'mature case', which meant that a resort to law was not necessary, because 'commonsense' would usually prevail; this actually meant that trade unions were rather lifeless. But during the 1950s, union confidence had grown. Pressure to maintain high wage levels had been reasonably successful, closed shops had spread, and, as noted earlier, the power centres of the union movement had shifted towards the on-site shop stewards.

In an almost pre-emptive action, the Conservatives had floated plans for curbing the unions' power in 1958 (only a year before their election win). Labour's initiative came in setting up the Royal (Donovan) Commission on Trade Unions and Employers' Associations in 1965. Its recommendations were adopted in the White Paper *In Place of Strife*; amongst them were plans to rationalize collective bargaining, legally to protect employees from 'unfair dismissals' and to introduce the possibility of legal sanctions – an issue that provoked funda-mental union antipathies. The Prices and Incomes Board was set up in 1965, the same year in which a National Plan was published; in the following year, a key Prices and Incomes Bill was passed. This represented Labour's first attempt to manage the class on which it relied for support by introducing a statutory control over pay settlements and awards that had been reached via collective bargaining. Put bluntly, the Labour government, perhaps under pressure from the United States Treasury, tried to postpone or prevent voluntarily agreed pay increases by legal compulsion. The justification was that the UK needed internal discipline (i.e. restraint) to strengthen its role in the world economy.

The unions were not in an idealistic mood: keeping wages in line with price inflation was their principal objective. They would not aid Labour's attempts to create a framework of wage restraint. Industrial disputes generally and unofficial stoppages in particular rose to the point where they were granted 'social problem' status. In the 1965–9 period, the annual number of days lost because of strikes averaged 3.95 million, the highest since the war. Placed in an international context, the UK's record was actually rather modest; while there were a large number of individual stoppages, they were mostly short and did not involve great numbers of people. The record did not stand comparison with, for example, that of Italy, Australia, or the USA in terms of the numbers of days lost (per employee). Examined in its own context, on the other hand, the upturn in the number of strikes did represent a change of pattern.

The extent of the change came fully into view when contrasted with the preceding thirteen-year period between 1951 and 1964. These were the affluent years when the relative absence of industrial conflict seemed to reflect the underlying stability of British society. In fact, what stability there was rested precariously on the working class' ability to purchase the burgeoning range of consumer products, rather than on any secure relationship with management. The strains and hostility of class relationships were still present. They simply did not manifest themselves in industrial conflict, mainly because they were submerged under a deluge of television sets, new homes and holidays in the sun. One interpretation of the apparent passivity of the 1951–64 phase is that the working class as represented by the trade unions actually avoided confrontation, fearing that it might endanger what was, at that stage, a reasonable and satisfactory relationship with management, a relationship that had as its basis the wage packet, as the Luton studies made clear. The basic consensual agreement of this time was, like most other consensual agreements, conditional on the satisfaction of both parties, the working class and the owners of the means of production in this instance.

But unemployment began to rise, so that by 1967 the number of people without work was the highest for twenty-seven years. The pound had been devalued by the Labour government in the previous year in an effort to correct the balance of payments and deflate the economy. Income tax rose sharply, hire-purchase restrictions were imposed, and the government was barely able to suppress a scramble for wages. Ironically, in 1967, a year of straitening monetary restraint, two pieces of legislation relating to abortion and contraception were to relieve many women, especially working-class women, of difficult burdens – at least in a legal sense. The year also saw the publication of an important official report detailing the depth and breadth of racialism. We will see the significance of these two events later in the book.

The first Wilson administration went out of office in 1970, its defeat due in part to its attempts to bring the unions into a tight legal framework and so control industrial disputes by use of sanctions. It was an issue that aroused strong emotions amongst the unionized working class. Edward Heath's Tory government, which succeeded Wilson's, was also to suffer from its commitment to legislating on union practices. The Industrial Relations Act of 1971 crystallized many of the elements with which several postwar governments had grappled. In essence, the idea was to 'protect' individual rights against what was seen as the intimidating might of the trade unions. While the Wilson government was always torn over the difficult question of how far or, indeed, whether the state should intervene in industrial relations, the Conservative government of 1970–4 was sententious in its attempt and unshakable in its resolve to restore order to what it saw as a disturbed society.

The previous Labour government had recognized the need to control wage claims (as the economy looped its way up an inflationary spiral), strikes and restrictive union practices; but it also wanted to maintain a delicate equilibrium, upsetting neither the unions nor, for that matter, the rest of the population. Heath's Conservatives were less reserved. They had identified the guilty party and the victim, and now set out to rescue the individual from the tyranny of the unions, as they saw it. Besides guaranteeing the individual's right to remain legitimately outside the union movement, the 1971 Industrial

Relations Act issued new powers to the Secretary of State for Employment to regulate the rules, conduct and administration of trade unions. The legislation drew a very sharp riposte, as we will see in the next section.

More power than the Prime Minister

Heath's series of failures are legion. Confrontations with the unions, strong and united in their opposition to the government, were frequent. In 1972, in particular, the government retreated in the face of a general strike threat after the gaoling in Pentonville Prison of five dockers, who were later released as a wave of strikes spread spontaneously across many industries. In his handling of wage controls, Heath, as Richard Hyman puts it, 'appeared to *invite* confrontation' (1980, p. 70). The government's problems culminated in 1974, when, in the midst of a world energy crisis, the miners struck following an unresolved pay dispute the previous year; the constellation of factors resulted in power shortages and the 'three-day week' for business and industry. Heartened by the successes of the 'Pentonville five' and the Clydesdale shipworkers, who virtually trounced the government, the miners closed in on the Saltley coal depot in Birmingham and physically resisted the attempts of police to break up their picket. There were daily routines of violence. Some believe 1974 produced the 'greatest national trauma since the Blitz'. R. W. Johnson detected Wagnerian glints in the events which provided 'a real vision of *Götterdämmerung* in the shape of the massed crowds of burly proletarians, Arthur Scargill at their head, who overwhelmed the police at Saltley coal depot, and the flying pickets, a virtual private army against which the forces of law and order could not prevail' (1985, p. 238). The popular view was that the miners' strike brought about the downfall of the Heath government. A more analytical assessment would be that a combination of Heath's staggering misjudgement and the antipathy of the working class to his attempts to control the unions was responsible. 'Who governs?' asked the Conservatives in their election slogans. The answer was a resounding 'Not you!' And Labour returned to power, bolstered by the enthusiastic support of unions.

Heath's alarmist reaction to union pressures had proved disastrous from the Tory point of view. His appeal to the voters to give him a mandate for stamping down on union practices and continuing his attempted counter-inflationary attack was met only with a rebuttal. The conception of the individual fighting vainly against the ruthless, overbearing forces of the trade unions was not an entirely plausible one. Nor, for that matter, was writer Christopher Booker's image, though there were some who found his *Time Machine* scenario of Britain convincing (1980, p. 161). As in H. G. Wells' vision, there was an 'upperworld' of Eloi, dreamy, powerless and pleasure-seeking, and an 'underground', where the noise of machinery was deafening and from where the menacing, resentful Morlocks launched their forays to the surface to wreak destructive havoc before returning to the depths. For 'Morlocks', read workers.

Labour's response was different to Heath's. It enacted a sequence of measures, beginning with the repeal of the 1971 Act and continuing with extensions of union rights and benefits through the 1974 Trade Union and Labour Relations Act, the 1975 Employment Protection Act and the 1976 Trade Union and Labour Relations Amendment Act. The period saw a vigorous use of law in the assertion of basic human rights; for, in addition to union-related legislation, the 1976 Race Relations Act restructured the machinery for dealing with racial discrimination as established in earlier Acts of 1965 and 1968. Also, the Sex Discrimination Act of 1975 complemented the 1970 Equal Pay Act (the Equal Opportunities Commission was set up to enforce the legislation and monitor its effects). Both sets of laws attested to a growing concern over the possibility of whole groups of people, rather than individuals, being discriminated against for reasons other than their ability, or inability, to perform work tasks. The impulse underlying all these moves was to introduce the element of compulsion: to regulate and control behaviour in order to preserve legally the rights of certain groups which had been subject to unequal treatment.

The trade unions reached their apogee of power in 1976 when they were invited to become parties to a 'social contract', an arrangement between government and organized labour designed to regulate wages and prices. Food subsidies were introduced, council house rents were frozen, and many social benefits were brought in. In return, workers were asked to moderate their wage claims. To strike this corporate bargain was tantamount to the government's admission of the limits of its control over a confident and forceful working class, bristling with demands as prices continued to rise. Labour's brinkmanship in involving the unions institutionally in the political process (an arrangement to be sharply turned around by Margaret Thatcher) was sometimes masterly and at other times inept. Jack Jones, leader of the large Transport and General Workers' Union, recalled in his biography how the public saw him as more powerful than the Prime Minister (1986). A mistaken perception, perhaps, but one not to be dismissed out of hand. The unions *seemed* to have genuine influence, and the burden was on them to restrain their members; it was a case of the government's delegating to the unions the responsibility to police themselves. The TUC seemed quite willing to support limits on pay that effectively produced a fall in the real net incomes of workers.

However, while the initial agreement seemed satisfactory to all three parties – the third being the controllers of the means of production – the second phase was not so smooth. In the two years before 1979, the Labour government, under James Callaghan (who succeeded Wilson in 1976), sought a ceiling of 10 per cent for pay rises and then reduced this to 5 per cent, with exceptions for 'special cases'. The unions contested this move, and claims for 'special cases' piled up, leading to a period of intense industrial negotiation and confrontation, the 'winter of discontent'. There was little warmth in the opening months of 1979 as a politically animated union movement issued notice to

[33]

the government: 'We've held our wage claims down in the interests of the "nation". Now we've had enough of not having enough,' was how *New Society* magazine caught the import of the message, at the same time assessing the disputes that spread from industry to industry as 'anti-collective' and 'wholly selfish' (5 February 1988). The unions were no longer prepared or able to bear the restraints of incomes policy. The answer to Heath's question of 1974 had still not been satisfactorily answered in the eyes of many, and the promise to provide the definitive answer was instrumental in lifting Margaret Thatcher to power in 1979, a year in which the number of strikes reached a postwar peak.

The best form of defence

Prior to 1979 successive governments had tried, with mixed results, to involve the working class (via trade unions) in the political process, either by force or by persuasion. Persuasion had worked quite well up till 1977, when the government found ready allies, perhaps fearful of the alternative of a stringently reactionary Conservative government led by Thatcher. Yet Thatcher did rise and she was able to do so with the support – and enduring support at that – of a working class that became estranged from the Labour Party as real incomes declined. The growth of the white-collar unions, which had no traditional links with working-class radicalism, also served to dislocate the union movement from Labour affiliations. Thatcher's response was to push the unions completely out of the corridors of power and reassert the sovereignty of the government. Her determination to subordinate the unions was reflected in legislation in 1980 and 1982, which circumscribed the legality of strike action, and the 1984 Trade Union Act. Having embarrassed Labour in the 1983 general election, when 60 per cent of the union population failed to vote Labour, the Conservatives decided to regulate the internal workings of unions by legally penetrating such areas as the election of union representatives, strike ballots and political funds – measures designed, as Coates and Topham put it, to 'disaggregate unions' and render them 'toothless' (1986, p. 96).

Assisting this strategy was unemployment. As the official figure rose to three million plus, so union membership went down, and as a consequence subscriptions dropped. A quarter of all jobs in manufacturing were lost, and the public service sector was also severely affected. The confidence and strength, if not the solidarity, of the working class were, it seems, seriously undermined. Industry was tranquil, and the number of strikes and hours lost plunged to their lowest levels since the war. As Hyman contrasted the situation in the 1970s with 1984: 'Then the successful struggles of groups of workers with little record of militancy encouraged others to take action; today, each defeat discourages others from the risk of a strike' (1984, p. 225). He called the process 'coercive pacification' and added that the so-called 'public opinion' against the unions intensified during Thatcher's first four years in office. Opinion polls support this: 75 per cent of the population interviewed in the decade before 1983 believed the unions to be 'too powerful', with about 5 per cent believing they were not powerful enough. In the build-up to the 1983 general election, Conservative attempts to restrict trade union freedom were endorsed by about 72 per cent of the population.

It was against this background that in 1984 miners, incensed and threatened by the number of pit closures, mounted their epic struggle which was to become the longest strike in history. In a sense, the miners' strike of 1984–5 reflected the changing character of the broader working class. The mine union's president, Arthur Scargill, and its leadership, by avoiding a national ballot, failed to overcome regional differences or to bring the entire industry to a halt. While the leadership and several regions stuck to left-wing strategies, appealing to solidarity and working-class radicalism, other regions, like Nottinghamshire, favoured more moderate, cautious approaches. Scargill challenged his membership, and in a way the entire working class, to reveal their loyalties. In the eyes of many, the very fact that he was able to prolong the action attested to his success. But, equally, the ultimate defeat of the strike had the effect of discouraging further action, in the manner suggested earlier by Hyman. Given the pattern of the strike's progress, with increasing numbers of miners either 'trickling' or 'flooding' back to work (depending on which newspaper one read), given too the ambivalent attitude of the membership and the demoralization of the working class implied by the result, it could be argued that the strike of 1984–5 was the final great show of mass working-class solidarity and resilience. Few unions would in future have either the resolve, the resources, or the rank-and-file backing to initiate an encounter of the kind or scale of the miners' strike. Viewed one way, the strike provided glimpses of what Marxists would call 'a class for itself', a self-conscious group whose members recognized their shared position and common interests and organized themselves for action as a class. Viewed another way, the conflict showed an especially virulent fraction of the working class, and an unusually powerful fraction at that, attempting to preserve its position, or to resist a deterioration of its position, as something of a working-class élite. The miners had more of an occupational than a class consciousness, in that their affiliation was first to other miners, then to the working class.

A similar judgement could be reached about the printers who surrounded 'Fort Wapping' in East London after publisher Rupert Murdoch moved his News International from Fleet Street in 1986. Here again was a group popularly regarded as part of the 'labour aristocracy' trying to buttress immediate interests, to protect what many other, more vulnerable unions might have regarded as material advantages. Six thousand printworkers were dismissed by News International, which had recruited members of the electricians' union to run the new plant, and transport workers to handle distribution.

Actions by particular groups of workers can assume a sectionalist appearance unless circumstances permit a more general involvement. Thatcher herself extended this analysis, portraying powerful militant sectional groups of organized labour advancing their material advantages at the cost of weaker groups. The analysis, when dramatically expressed through political rhetoric, effectively encouraged a *sauve qui peut* impulse amongst the working class. And while they approached the situation from an entirely different angle, Marxist historian Eric Hobsbawm (1981) and sociologist Steven Lukes (1984) both reached the conclusion that the working class had become internally divided in new ways, sectionalism (regional and occupational) being one of them.

But is it credible to suggest such strikes are *not* class actions, but challenges by self-seeking groups of individuals? Industrial disputes do, after all, have their origins in the response to inequality, and one of the most fundamental and divisive forms of inequality is class. In Britain the conflict has not, as we have seen, taken on anything like a revolutionary quality in motivating parties to the conflict to press for major institutional changes. The crop of strikes in early 1988 was an extreme example of pure defensive action: miners protesting against the introduction of new disciplinary codes, ferrymen trying to assist sacked colleagues, nurses striking over the limited standard of care they are able to provide with sparse resources and 32,500 Ford workers walking out after a dispute over pay and production methods. This was the working class in retreat. Even the 1984–5 miners' conflict was, when all is said and done, the defensive manoeuvre of a 'first division' occupational group under threat of relegation. Having seen their pits close and their overall position in the union movement marginalized by the Thatcher administration, the miners reacted. I use the term 'reacted' because the trade unions have traditionally *defended* the interests of the working class and have only occasionally advanced them. Such a statement is not intended as an attack on the union movement; its very nature and purpose ensure that within an obstinately capitalist society such as the UK, it has remained, and probably must remain, preoccupied with equipping the working class for survival or, at best, a limited prosperity.

[37]

Exactly how limited that prosperity has been in the postwar period we will see in Chapter 3, in which the scale and change of class inequality will be revealed.

CHAPTER 3

Two gears of class

Towards classlessness . . . and back again

Social change does not move in only one direction. Imagine the
United Kingdom as a vast steam locomotive headed for its
destination, a city called Classlessness. Inside its engine, two
different gear-wheels are grinding away. The first is small and
whirrs quickly. For thirty-five years after the war, it drove the
country to the situation where many sectors of the working
class enjoyed an income and lifestyle associated before the war
solely with the 'middle' or 'upper' classes. It generated new
opportunities for an expanding portion of the population and
eliminated some of the harsher aspects of poverty by creating a
welfare state. The second gear is vast, slow and inexorable. It
is the gear of wealth, of power, of what Marxists call the means
of production. Reorganizations of the nation's occupational
structure, redistributions of income and wealth and reforms of
health and welfare have done little to interrupt the remorseless
turning of this wheel. It seems to have rotated at its own pace,
quite independently of wheel number one and regardless of the
efforts of engineers to speed it up. Since 1980 the two gears have
changed direction, driving the train in reverse.

Both gears have been turning since the war, though at
different rates. The smaller wheel refers to the material living
conditions of the population, the distribution of income, the
availability of services and the range of occupational positions
available. The large, slower-moving wheel represents the

predominant power of capital, and its motion describes the sluggish pace of changes in the established distribution of wealth and property. In this chapter I will look at the motion of both wheels, assessing the impact of redistributions of income and wealth on the class structure and asking whether or not we are significantly closer to the city of Classlessness. Those favouring the smaller wheel as the prime mover in the attempt to change the shape of Britain's class structure would have been encouraged by several trends in the postwar period. The first steps towards the classless society was taken by the Beveridge Plan of 1942; and while many insisted that such a society was of much the same status as Eldorado, Shangri-La and other mythical paradises, there was a broad optimism in both the main political parties.

'Britain has undergone one of the greatest social revolutions in her history,' concluded Robert (later, Lord) Boothby, one of the most prominent Tories of the postwar years. The 'revolution of 1945' was comparable, he argued, with that of 1832, when the middle class secured political rights. After the war it was the working class' turn to capture rights, this time of a more economic nature. Beveridge's report provided a theoretical framework for what was to become the welfare state. Between 1945 and 1951 the Labour government acted on the plan, initiating a series of reforms that drew almost unanimous political approval. Education, the National Health Service, National Insurance, criminal justice, youth employ-ment and town planning were all subjects of legislative reform designed to alleviate the traditional problems of the working class. The working class had put its faith in the Labour Party at the 1945 general election and had its trust duly rewarded. The rough edges of working-class life were chipped away by the reforms. The trade unions assisted a government committed to laying the foundations of a future classless society by muting their protests during the period of austerity and belt-tightening that followed the war. For a while, the unions voluntarily agreed to the government's introduction of a wage freeze, although the government was reluctant to interfere with personal incomes other than by taxation. To do otherwise would have amounted to 'an incursion by the Government into . . . a field of free contract between individuals and organizations', as a White Paper put it in 1947 (Cmnd 7321, p. 2). Later Labour governments in the 1960s were less inhibited about making such excursions, as we have seen.

At the end of the war, Tories and socialists alike talked of a 'social revolution' and welcomed the substantial modifications to the class system that were promised. No one wanted a repetition of the impoverished 1930s, and it was generally agreed that piecemeal reforms were insufficient guarantees. Drastic social measures were called for. Beveridge's plan supplied the necessary forethought. The Conservative R. A. Butler envisioned a 'mosaic' of social services; and while the enterprise began, as Marwick points out, as more like crazy paving, by 1950 a system of welfare had been created (1970, p. 345).

The Labour government was committed to the principle of universality: free education, free medical treatment, family allowances, pensions, insurance and subsidized housing were to be available to everyone, regardless of income or possessions. Even if Labour had not won office in 1945, it is probable that the Conservatives would have legislated on most, if not all, of these issues, although perhaps without the breadth implied by Labour's commitment to universality. Labour intended to make state services available to *all* and remove the humiliating taint of means testing. With this egalitarian flourish, the Labour government succeeded in smoothing the path of the working class, yet without seriously threatening the basic class structure.

After a straitened six-year period of austerity, when the after-effects of war kept biting and wages barely kept pace with price increases, a surge began. Real incomes grew by 20 per cent during the 1950s, and by 88 per cent between 1952 and 1976. Between 1955 and 1964 alone average pay shot up by 34 per cent. The result was an impressive rise in the living standards of many previously depressed groups, in particular the manual working class. Reports from tax authorities showed a convergence of incomes towards the middle ranges (the trend had actually begun before the war, but accelerated after 1950).

Accompanying this process, or maybe precipitating it, was the expansion of managerial, administrative and technical occupations in both manufacturing and service industries. As industries grew larger and became more dependent on technology in what some called 'post-industrial society', so it became necessary to recruit employees who were educated, skilled and adept at working without supervision. Their knowledge and expertise with regard to what was often sophisticated management and technology gained them status as a new élite occupational group, the 'technocrats'. The 'managerial revolution', as James Burnham coined it in 1945, enlarged higher working-class and lower middle-class groups to such an extent that the previous triangle-shaped socioeconomic structure came to resemble more of a diamond. The small, power-holding group remained at the apex, but a much larger middle space was now occupied by a relatively well-off working class and the middle class; the smaller base comprised a diminishing number of poor workers and unemployed. (Corresponding to this trend, there was a drop in the number of unskilled and casual jobs.) As the pyramid changed into a diamond shape, more and more non-manual workers enjoyed the rewards of their new type of labour. They earned more than manual employees, even though they worked shorter hours, received more holidays with pay and attracted a whole range of fringe benefits, like company cars, expense accounts and beneficial pensions.

The new managerial administrative class signalled the end of the old class structure for some. It coincided with the affluent period covered in the last chapter, when *embourgeoisement* may be seen to have transformed members of the working class, making them 'privatized', secluded and more interested in their homes than in their work. Private home ownership increased to 56 per cent by 1959. The more unpleasant and incapacitating elements of working-class life were removed, and working-class interests were specifically catered for. While to some this was progress towards the classless society, to others it was another instance of the unfolding logic of capitalism. The logic in this case ensured the unbroken development of a class structure cram-full of inequalities. Both arguments have some strength, as we will now see.

Lilliput

Since the war, there have been several trends to support the belief that the older class structure has been disintegrating, replaced perhaps by more of a spectrum of groups, without clearly demarcated lines between them. The equalizing trend in the distribution of incomes began promisingly, but soon faltered and was actually reversed after the election of Margaret Thatcher in 1979. Even in the midst of affluence, Richard Titmuss, writing in the early 1960s on *Income Distribution and Social Change*, detected 'more than a hint from a number of studies that income inequality has been increasing since 1949' (1962, p. 198).

Labour, in the postwar period of austerity, raised taxation to record levels and, in a context of full employment together with the institution of the welfare state, increased trade unions' bargaining power. From 1951 Conservative governments lifted some fiscal pressures towards inequality, although there was no reversal apparent in the statistics, as W. D. Rubinstein's detailed breakdown shows (1986). Higher minimum wages and continuous employment, plus a decline in family size, helped reduce the percentage of people with income below the supplementary benefit level to 5.8 per cent in the mid-1960s. Yet it was dangerously misleading to use this as evidence of the end of class inequality. While severe taxation reduced the net income of the top earners, and the working class seemed to be enjoying the fruits of the welfare state, Titmuss noted concealed changes, such as an increase in non-taxable fringe benefits – and not just luncheon vouchers! – that were neutralizing the effects of high taxes.

Rubinstein's data, on the other hand, reveal a continuous general trend towards equalization, certainly until the late 1970s, although the author believes the trend 'is broadly inherent in the contemporary British economic and social structure, and was not a function of the special conditions of the Second World War and Austerity period' (1986, p. 83). By Rubinstein's criteria, there was a 'small, but perceptible increase in household income inequality' between 1976 and 1980. The increase has been more pronounced since, as more recent figures indicate. In 1975 the top 10 per cent of the economically active population (that is, about 3.5 million people) accounted for 25 per cent of the nation's total pre-tax income. Ten years later, their share of pre-tax income had grown to 30 per cent, just 8.8 per cent less than the portion that the same group had in 1949.

The key year in the upswinging fortunes of the well-to-do was 1979, the year of Thatcher's ascension; for the next seven years, the pay of the top 10 per cent rose by 21 per cent. At the other extreme, the lowest-paid quarter of the population saw their earnings rise by only 5.5 per cent in the same period. They also saw a decline in their share of the nation's income after 1979, while the richest fifth increased their share from just over 38 per cent to almost 40 per cent. The total share of the middle fifth income groups dropped from 18.2 per cent to 17.7 per cent in the seven years before 1985. By the middle of the decade, the top 5 per cent increased their share of income to 15.1 per cent (from 12.9 per cent in 1979); this compares with the 22.3 per cent of the total earned by the bottom half (a fall from 23.5 per cent in 1979). In measurable terms, income inequality was almost as great in the mid-1980s as it was in 1949.

One ingenious way of giving these lifeless statistics some impact was devised by economist Jan Pen (1971), who visualized all members of a working population stretched or contracted to a height determined by their gross income (including social security benefits, share dividends and other unearned items). They line up according to their height (shortest first) and proceed to march in single file. In Britain it is several minutes before the marchers reach one foot high; most women and many many part-time workers are only fractions of an inch tall. Even after ten minutes they are still less than two feet tall. (The ranks of these low-paid groups have been inflated by the number of part-time workers, nine out of ten of whom are women, which rose dramatically from the early 1970s; by 1980 one in five employees were part-timers. Beechey and Perkins, 1986, estimate that this should be one in four by 1989.) After about forty minutes the white-collar workers arrive; they stand about 5 feet 6 inches tall. Because of the expansion of white-collar work since the war, it is about ten minutes before they all pass. As the march reaches its end, the heights soar. In contrast to the droves of minuscule part-timers, the final few workers are 15 or 20 foot professionals who pass in seconds rather than minutes because there are so few. Christopher Heath, a stockbroker whom Barings in 1987 paid £2.5 million a year, the UK's highest wage earner, is several hundred feet tall; and bringing up the rear is the Duke of Westminster, whose income is derived from inherited wealth and whose height, of probably 20 miles, makes him a great deal more than a Gulliver amongst the Lilliputians.

Obviously, the image does not convey the complexities of income distribution, and taxation cuts down the height of many of those at the parade's end – although since 1979 tax cuts have benefited the £50,000-plus-a-year earners handsomely, especially after 1988 when even the aforementioned £2.5 million man would be viable to a maximum 40 per cent income tax. Yet it suggests vividly the skewed distribution and the sheer disparity of incomes in modern Britain. It also lays bare the shortcomings of arguments favouring income equalization as the main instrument to end class inequality. The post-1945 equalizing trend was arrested in 1979, and the recent reversal looks set to continue, with a seemingly permanent unemployed group, a growing aged population and an increasing number of part-time workers hastening the trend.

The importance of the white-collar expansion can also be overplayed. Closely related to the 'managerial revolution' thesis, this approaches the class structure as a sandwich with a sizeable wedge of middle-range workers forming the filling that separates the manual working class from the 'upper' and 'upper-middles'. Many members of this middle group have profited from the postwar diffusion of stock control; as honorary executives, they are able to exercise effective control of corporate businesses. Although they depend on salaries, their identification with the manual working class has been minimal and they have formed a new class, whose power derives from their expertise and position in organizations.

In a sense, these new white-collar workers came to occupy a privileged position and did have a degree of control over the owners of the means of production. They possessed the know-how, and this became a very valuable commodity during the 1950s and 1960s. In another sense, they were still 'wage slaves' because they depended on employers for their livelihood. They became, in effect, a 'service class' between the middle and working classes, having rights, privileges and salaries far in excess of the majority of workers, but no material power, save that which they carried in their heads. They were bearers of the managerial revolution which transformed the occupational structure of the UK, and they gave lie to the suggestion that class polarities were sharpening. On closer examination, a distinct division was still in evidence. Those with managerial power supplemented this with share options and capital ownership, while those who resisted this strategy stayed mere managers and, effectively, part of the larger working class, albeit a well-salaried and prestigious part.

The picture offered by optimistic egalitarians was one of a plural class, rather than a classless, society: one made up of a variety of different, though not necessarily conflicting, interest groups, each defined by its access to certain levels of income, life-styles and personal possessions. The so-called 'middle classes' could be identified as 'lower middle class' (clerks, administrators, and so on), 'middle middle class' (technicians, specialists) and 'upper middle class' (top management, professionals, directors); the 'working classes' could be broken down similarly, the best-paid being barely recognizable from their lower middle-class counterparts, save for their blue collars. (In the 1980s, it might be argued, an underclass has become gradually disembodied from the rest of society and become ossified as an immobile lump at the bottom of the social scale; more on this argument later.) Certainly, this type of account squared with peoples' own perceptions and experience of affluence, particularly in the 1950s and 1960s. But there were other dimensions of inequality that were not immediately available to the senses. We will look at these next.

5:41

There is an alternative assessment of the UK's class structure, one which emphasizes the role of power and wealth. This alternative sees rather less significance in the redistribution of income, the emergence of the welfare state and the managerial revolution than in the more enduring inequalities of power. Power is contrasted to *authority*, an attribute of people within an organization, whether it be a corporation, a family or even a government; within any organization, some individuals or groups have more competence or ability than others, and this gives them authority. There has been a considerable amount of adjustment in authority relations in postwar Britain, due principally to the kinds of change mentioned previously. Yet if power is defined as the ability of holders to exact the compliance or obedience of others to their will, then change in the power structure has been slow.

Following the Labour Party writer R. H. Tawney, A. H. Halsey distinguishes between property for *power*, meaning control over other people, and property for *use*, that is, possessions that free people from others' control (1986). A person who owns some part of a commercial organization on which many others depend for a living clearly has some say, if only in principle, in how those others are able to earn their living. One who owns the land on which houses or factories stand has some degree of power over those who live in those houses or work in those factories. Halsey draws the conclusion that 'three-quarters of the British have been virtually property-less in that area which covers the central part of life and occupation . . . A minority has monopolized wealth, and an even tinier minority of that minority has monopolized property for power' (1986, p. 45). Let's examine the argument.

Wealth – or, more specifically, marketable wealth – is made up of two types of asset: first, stocks and shares (that is, capital invested in corporations or companies); secondly, property and land. J. H. Westergaard points out that 'the two overlap to the point of near identity: private wealth is not divorced from private corporate power' (1972, p. 138). Together, the two form a portfolio of considerable power, a power that can be used to influence, or control, the lives of others.

This leads us to reconsider the British class structure, switching the emphasis away from material conditions and towards the sources of influence on those conditions: in other words, wealth and power – the second gear wheel, the movement of which has been ponderously slow. Yet there has been movement none the less, and there are figures to prove this. Before the First World War the richest 1 per cent of the population owned 70 per cent of the country's total wealth. This was reduced to 56 per cent before the Second World War and to 24 per cent in 1963. By 1986 the once-great slab of wealth had been eroded to a mere 20 per cent or, put another way, the same amount owned by the worst-off 75 per cent of the population.

It is misleading to imagine the upper class sitting atop the other classes. Change in British society over the forty years following the war has made this group 'upper' in name only. By 1987 between 1 and 2 per cent of the population belonged to a resilient group of aristocrats who had seen off all attempts to overthrow them since the sixteenth century (when vast personal fortunes in the form of land were dished out to those securing the favours of Henry VIII). Primogeniture ensured a continuity in wealth and power, the entire estate passing through generations via the first-born son. The Industrial

Revolution threw up the challenge of an expanding bourgeoisie, whose rapid acquisition of wealth came through success in industry, commerce and trade. Some of the massively successful bourgeois families were integrated into the upper class and became members of the aristocracy. Since 1945 this tiny minority, which has land, wealth and income totally disproportionate to its size in the total population, has seen its power slip away. Ancestral homes have been opened to the public, grounds have been converted into theme parks, art collections have been sold off. The distinctly upper-class culture or lifestyle is still very visible to the public, so that the aristocracy appears to sit on top of the tree. But since the middle of the nineteenth century, and especially since the Second World War, the erosion of the landed gentry, as they were once called, has been accelerated by the rise of the comparatively new urban middle class. In particular, the growth of the 'consumer society' after the war provided opportunities for entrepreneurs to carve their fortunes from such ventures as advertising, retailing and services industries generally.

As well as this decline in the personal fortunes controlled by a small élite, there has been a lifting of barriers. Before 1950 more than 90 per cent of the UK's millionaires inherited their wealth. Today, by contrast, about one-fifth emerge from humble backgrounds to become self-made men or, to a much more limited extent, women, as we will see in Part Three. Not only has there been a redistribution of wealth since the war, but it is also very much easier to become a millionaire. The trend since the war has been towards an equalization of wealth and an opening up of opportunities to get to the very top. More people own homes, have access to adequate education and can become rich, provided they have the skill and application. So, in a statistical sense at least, the UK has moved towards becoming a slightly more equal society. In the 1980s the 'selling off' of British Telecom, British Petroleum and other industrial giants led to a diffusion of ownership, although the pattern suggests that low levels of share ownership have been widely dispersed, while high levels have been concentrated, a pattern accentuated after the crash of 1987.

Despite the postwar developments in the distribution of wealth, some blunt reminders of the inequality of property for power remain. For example, a relatively tiny collection of 20,000 people in the UK own much more wealth than the poorest half of the British population combined. The bottom half of the population has hardly any wealth at all, not even homes in most cases. In fact, their total wealth is approximately half that of the richest 0.1 per cent (and they number 43,000 people). The richest 5 per cent of the country, just over a mere 2 million people, collectively own a formidable 41 per cent share of the total wealth in the UK – or, put another way, over ten times as much wealth as the poorest 50 per cent, about 22 million people. In 1966 this 5 per cent élite had 56 per cent of the country's total wealth; this dropped to 52 per cent in 1971 and then to 44 per cent in 1978 (the real value of shares fell in the early 1970s); in 1980 it 'bottomed out' at 39 per cent, before edging back up to its current portion. The fortunes of both the top 5 per cent and 1 per cent groups have shrunk by about 4 per cent per year since the war, but only up to 1979–80; after that their cut of the wealth cake stayed around the same size (Inland Revenue statistics, HMSO, 1986).

True, there has been an equalizing tendency, but, as Rubinstein points out: 'the thrust of wealth distribution has been from the very wealthiest to the merely wealthy or affluent sections of the population' (1986, pp. 97–8). A grossly unequal and imbalanced structure remains. A small group of people have a lot, and a great many people have little or nothing – and have only a small chance of getting much wealth and therefore power, in spite of the supposedly encouraging news of self-made millionaires and the intention of the Thatcher administration to build a 'share-holding democracy'.

'The bulk of the population is excluded from property ownership of any substance – entirely from a share in the privately owned means of production' concludes Westergaard (1972, p. 154). Since the war the percentage of the country's population without property for power has stayed consistently above 70 per cent. The people comprising this group may have been manual or clerical workers, they may have been technicians or professionals, they may have had a decent income or lived off supplementary benefit. The crucial characteristic they have in common is the fact that they have had no independent means of support and so depended on others for their wage or salary. Once X-rayed in this manner, British society seems to comprise three main segments: first, the small aristocratic upper class, with sufficient, if declining, means to remain aloof and independent of all others; secondly, those who own substantial wealth and property enough to generate power over others; and thirdly, those whose livelihood depends on them. But, of course, there are various other groups who present awkward cases. Members of the medical and legal professions and clergy possess a great degree of autonomy and claim a special place in the division of labour. Their incomes are high enough to compare with the best-paid company directors, yet they only rarely have great wealth or exercise control over a great number of other workers. It is their independence from the owners of property and holders of power which separates them from the working class and aligns them with the middle class. Being middle class in its basic form means having no direct dependence on others for one's livelihood, although it could be argued that a great number of professionals depend on the government.

In terms of income and personal wealth (that is, property and possessions for personal use, rather than for control over others' lives), the upper echelons of the working class, or service class, are better off than a great many of the small owners. And what of these service-oriented self-employed and small business owners? They earn their living at the probable cost of long hours of work and have levels of earnings only similar to or lower than a comparable employee, as well as more anxiety, if the research of Frank Bechhofer is anything to go by (Bechhofer and Elliott, 1981). And, as Richard Brown summarizes: 'when the majority of the self-employed and employers are compared to employees doing the same sort of work . . . the general patterns of their other rewards and deprivations from work are probably very similar' (1984, p. 147). Only those with 'larger and growing

[51]

businesses where economic independence can provide incomes and material benefits markedly greater than are normally available to comparable employees' can legitimately claim to be amongst the capital-owning class. The Thatcher administration's encouragement of self-employment with tax incentives and new enterprise assistance brought forth a sprouting of new businesses, though not of the size or worth to make any appreciable impact on the distribution of wealth and power. For the most part, the small-scale entrepreneurs of the early 1980s lacked the property and equipment to make themselves more prosperous and less vulnerable than their employee counterparts.

As we approach and enter the 1990s, it has become quite plausible, perhaps even fashionable, to assert that no changes in social policy or taxation systems will make much impact on the structure of inequality. The rediscovery of theories of the 'culture of poverty' type, in which individuals' lack of motivation, apathy, or sheer pathology is blamed for their lowly position, has bolstered the New Right's opposition to redistribution or any interference with free market forces. Social mobility has affected modifications, but without altering the substantive economic inequalities (as we will see in Chapter 4). Far from being embarrassed by this, right-wing opinion has used it as empirical proof of the inevitability of class inequality and has organized its policies accordingly.

While income and wealth distribution are the chief economic determinants of the class structure, social policy and the welfare state since the war could be – indeed, were intended to be – a major force for greater equality. Social reform has to be directed at ironing out health inequalities, for example. Yet in 1980 the publication of the Black Report on *Inequalities in Health* exposed contrasts in death rates, early deaths and infant deaths. 'A child born to professional parents . . . can expect to spend over five years more as a living person than a child born to an unskilled manual household,' the report stated. As with the more measurable indices of class inequality, health took on a new aspect after 1979. Mortality in general fell, but, as the *Lancet* reported, it declined more rapidly 'among non-manual groups than among manual groups' (2 August 1986).

To repeat this chapter's opening observation: social change does not take place in only one direction. While much of the glaring social inequality of prewar years was removed in the thirty-five years after 1945, there have also been some sharp reversals since. The position of many sectors of the working class has improved, so much so that many occupants of newer occupational areas enjoy material conditions and lifestyles unimaginable before the war. On the other hand, there is enough evidence of a persistent, mortifying poverty to fill a library shelf. Beginning with a short pamphlet, *Casualties of the Welfare State*, by Audrey Harvey in 1960 and culminating in 1979 with Peter Townsend's tome, *Poverty in the United Kingdom*, the statistics showed that about 14 per cent of the population lived in poverty.

Income distribution has been modified since the war. The density of capital has also changed, but not significantly. And while the two structures can be assessed separately, ownership of capital remains a potent, direct source of income inequality in the sense that capital generates its posessors' incomes. While I used the image of a locomotive to describe Britain's advance towards more equality, a more apposite metaphor might be that of a cart pulled by an ageing mule. Income and wealth are still concentrated in the lap of a small numerical minority, which wields power over a huge majority.

The era since the war has contained the rise of the Labour Party, the construction of the welfare state, the emergence of progressive taxation and the arrival of the property-owning democracy. Yet, forty-five years after the promise of a social revolution and of transition to a classless society, Britain still has mountainous peaks and deep valleys in its economic landscape. Interestingly, the contours of the landscape are continuous; there are no major fault lines apparent. This raises the question: why has a class structure that maintains such asymmetries in power, wealth and income not been seriously challenged, at least not since the general strike of 1926? After

[53]

the war Britain entered an era in which, as Marwick describes it, 'now one interest group gained, now another, but in which there was no concerted pressure for fundamental redistribution of power, wealth or status' (1970, p. 392).

The answer to the question 'why not?' lies in two sets of forces. The first is the ability of those who benefit most from the class structure to perpetuate it and seal up their own class boundaries. They do this primarily by passing on their power to future generations and by absorbing new entrants to their ranks. As Peter Bauer comments of the *nouveaux riches*: 'the new recruits soon become indistinguishable from the class in which they have been introduced' (1978, p. 9). The second force comes from the reluctance of the working class, who do not benefit from the existing arrangements, to do much about changing them. Working-class people, especially since the war, have evinced a concern with status and material achievement, an interest in the highest living standards that can be realistically attained. Their efforts have been towards *achieving* – achieving, that is, as individuals within the boundaries of the economic and political order. They have shown little inclination to probe the validity of the institutional arrangements that permit, or even encourage, the type of gross inequality assessed in this chapter.

Perhaps the workers see the structure as stable and unalterable; perhaps they are convinced of the 'rightness' of inequality. I will consider these possibilities shortly, but first I want to concentrate on the methods employed by the owners of capital to maintain their interests in the face of attempts to loosen their grip through parliamentary means. The way a class reproduces itself from one generation to another is clearly crucial to its existence. If this process can be interrupted, the consequences will be great. Education was, for many years before the war, a target for reformers. Here was an apparatus so vicious and discriminatory in its operation that it not only maintained but deepened class divisions and, as I will later argue, perpetuated sex divisions. It was largely a matter of individual means and responsibility; if you could afford to send your sons and daughters to a school and desired to do so, all well and good, if not, tough. This made for a kind of separate development, with the children of the wealthy receiving the kind of education that in the long-term helped them retain their families' wealth and power. At the end of the war, all this was to change. At least, that was the intention.

CHAPTER 4

The mechanics of non-change

A silent revolution in education

There is a story of a senior *Sun* journalist who in 1986 passed his father every morning on the way to his office at 'Fortress Wapping', Rupert Murdoch's East London dockland centre for his News International publishing empire. The father was a member of the National Graphical Association union and stood resolutely on strike duty as his son negotiated his way through police road-blocks, razor fencing and high-speed lorries carrying newspapers from the plant. At the beginning of the dispute, the father refused to talk to or even look at his son; after a year, they had patched up their differences. The import of the story is in two areas, both of which bear directly on the assessment of class in the United Kingdom. First, the process of the son's social mobility suggests ways in which the class structure maintains its stability: by absorption and fluidity. Second, the ability and willingness of the father to challenge and protest, yet still keep his focus wide enough to compromise within a common perspective, indicates why that same structure has not been under sustained, direct attack. The reason seems to be that class conflict has been institutionalized, that is, regulated through a series of procedures that take place within a framework regarded by all as legitimate. There is an agreement over the limits of conflict.

The class structure of Britain has avoided any major fissures largely because of these two aspects, and the purpose of this chapter is to examine both of them. The two are linked by the motive of self-improvement. Individuals have built their ambitions around the goal of 'bettering' themselves, and social changes have made this actively possible. 'Nothing succeeds like success,' the saying goes; and as more people achieved more in material terms, their allegiance to the system that permitted, even promoted, their achievement strengthened. Later, I will consider the apparent reluctance of the working class to forge a policy of direct attack on the established order of power and property. But my immediate task is to describe how the class structure stays 'open' and encourages mobility without ever losing its basic shape.

The journalist son of the trade union father in the Wapping anecdote was an embodiment of the meritocratic ideal: a grammar-school boy of working-class origins – his father being a skilled manual worker – who had allied effort to intelligence and boot-strapped his way up the occupational ladder. He had lived in his family's council house as a boy; by 1980 he owned his home in Bushey, Hertfordshire. Socially mobile and personally ambitious enough not to let traditional loyalties interfere with his progress, he was the type of person for whom the 1944 Education Act was designed.

'The notion that schools and colleges can change the world around them is an illusion,' argued Dahrendorf in his essay *On Britain*. 'Educational institutions are much more likely to reflect the world about them' (1982, p. 46). This would not have been a popular idea at the time of the passage of the 1944 Act, which was hailed as the fulcrum of great social changes. It came into being amidst an atmosphere of promise; the impoverishment and uncertainty of the war years were over, and people could look forward to a time when the limits imposed by class would diminish. The atmosphere is captured in Fred Schepisi's film *Plenty* (1985), its title signifying the abundance of opportunity people thought lay before them.

The first step was to guarantee all children of whatever background a compulsory free education. At the age of 11 or

12 the pupil would move from a primary school to a form of secondary education which would continue until the child was aged at least 15. Children would sit an 11-plus examination administered by their local authority, and the results would have a bearing on whether they were to attend a prestigious grammar school or a less desirable secondary modern. Existing alongside grammar and secondary moderns, which were non-fee-paying, state-funded institutions, were older and generally more prestigious private grammar schools supported by direct government grants (not via local authorities). A fourth sector, the independent or public-school sector was not affected by the new legislation, so that the likes of Eton, Winchester and Harrow continued to draw fee-paying recruits from the aristocracy and middle class. Although its intention was certainly not to reflect the country's class structure, the Act established a structure of sorts, with the independents continuing to draw their small and exclusive clientele from the wealth-owning élite, the direct-grant schools accommodating the children of the middle class, the state grammar schools attracting a mixture of middle-class and upwardly mobile working-class pupils and the secondary moderns taking the rest of the working class. Research by Floud, Halsey and Martin in 1957 confirmed this.

Establishing a national programme for free education had been the Labour Party's aim since 1920, though the architect of the 1944 Act was R. A. Butler, himself a Tory in the wartime coalition Cabinet. In broad terms, however, the thrust and ambition of both national parties were in alignment, and there was agreement over the trends that needed to be encouraged. Public expenditure, particularly in the crucial sphere of education, needed to be stepped up. And it was: in 1940 secondary education in England and Wales absorbed 19 per cent of total expenditure; by the end of the decade this had risen to 27 per cent.

The National Insurance and National Health Service Acts of 1946 kept up the momentum started by Butler's legislation. The wartime coalition ended when Labour came to power under

Attlee in the year after the Butler Act. By 1948 a further series of acts were added, but the Education Act was intended to assume centrality in the attack on inequality. Provision of and access to education for all classes created, theoretically at least, equality of opportunity. All had more or less equal chances of becoming well off and successful, regardless of the class of their parents. It was meant to be a decisive leap forward.

In fact, it was less a leap, more a shuffle, for at least the first five years. Inadequate school buildings, lack of equipment and staff shortages militated against any kind of progress, although by the middle of the 1950s the number of pupils staying on until the age of 17 was double what it had been before the Act. Less encouraging were the figures for stayers-on when expressed as a percentage of the total age group: 7.9 per cent in England and Wales and 9.1 per cent in Scotland (where a separate but essentially similar provision to the Butler Act had been added in 1945). So, although extra public money was invested in secondary education, it benefited only a small minority of the young population. In tertiary education, too, money allocated for university places reached only the few select. The Labour government had expanded the power of the University Grants Commission in 1946, and within ten years universities derived nearly 70 per cent of their income from the government. By this time the country's university population was just below 90,000, with about 75 per cent receiving public grants.

Over the next twenty years, expenditure on education in real terms doubled, outstripping the expansion of the Gross National Product, the cost of the National Health System and consumer spending. University, further and adult education were the sectors most favoured with public money. In a further spurt, the 1964–70 Labour government under Wilson began creating comprehensive secondary education in 1965. Comprehensive schools were intended to end the segregation between selective grammar and secondary-modern schools, which still served as a reminder of a class society. In 1970 the creation of the Open University made higher education possible for those engaged in work or rearing families. The move followed the

Newsom and Robbins reports of 1963 and 1964 which examined secondary and higher education respectively; both highlighted the disadvantageous position of working-class children in education. The school-leaving age was raised to 16 in 1974, and Certificate of Secondary Education (CSE) examinations were introduced.

Ironically, it could be argued that the extra money served to reinforce the very system it was supposed to undermine. Resources for the development of further and higher education were used disproportionately by young people from middle-class backgrounds. As an illustration, at the end of the war 41 per cent of university places were taken by students who had been privately educated at school. By 1972 this had been reduced to just under 30.4 per cent: a sizeable percentage nevertheless, especially when one considers that the independent sector accounted for only, at most, 6 per cent of the country's schools. This is but one extreme example of the way in which government finance in tertiary education was appropriated. Halsey summarizes the overall effects of the postwar expansion in further education thus: 'in spite of a slight tendency to more equal investment in the school education of children from different classes, the development of further education more than counterbalanced this equalizing effect because it was concentrated on middle-class children' (1986, p. 40).

Tertiary education has taken on increasing importance since the war because there has been what Anthony Heath calls a 'silent revolution of certification', meaning that paper qualifications, though not an automatic passport to fortune, give their bearers bargaining power in the job market (1987, p. 14). Entry to universities and polytechnics was dependent on public examination results. As Robert G. Burgess put it: 'The higher the social class, the smaller the percentage without qualifications' (1984, p. 102). Statistically, working-class children improved in their examination performances after the war. Indeed, between 1910 and 1960 their attainment improved tenfold (compared to a 2½ times improvement for middle-class children). The problem is that, as fast as the working class increased its share of qualifications, so the demands of the job market rose. As they got more GCE A-levels, the plum jobs needed degrees; as they got more degrees, the jobs wanted higher degrees, and so forth. More qualifications have therefore not necessarily improved the working class' chances in the job market. Having studied the 'class inequalities in educational success', Heath calls them 'chameleon-like' in that they 'reappear in a new guise but fundamentally unchanged as the educational environment changes around them' (1987, p. 14).

In spite of these shortcomings of educational reform and the failure of some of the more idealistic schemes of the 1944 Act, the evidence of our senses tells us that education has benefited the working class in many respects and that class has become more of a moving vehicle than a stationary receptacle. There is, after all, such a thing as social mobility; well-qualified, ambitious people can *move* upwards from one class to another. Some of the most extensive research into the ease or difficulty with which people move and the power of education in assisting this has been conducted by Halsey.

The anodyne effect

Let us surmise that the printer's son in the story at the beginning of the chapter was born in 1950. Had he been born in similar family circumstances twenty years before, his chances of rising from a manual working-class background to a well-salaried white-collar job would have been considerably less. More likely, he would have stayed in basically the same social position as his father.

The efforts of Halsey, Heath and Ridge to assess the amount of movement between social positions over a period of time is captured in the title of their book *Origins and Destinations* (1980). Halsey's conclusion is that the UK, far from being a sealed-in class society, is relatively open. Just under half of his sample had moved class positions, and the middle class appeared to be quite a porous group, with two-thirds of its members seeping in from working-class origins.

Two further points need to be noted. One is obvious: although the chances of working-class children escaping their lowly positions improved, their chances of getting into the middle class were not nearly as good as those of children from middle-class homes; it was easier to stay in the middle class than to climb there. Another reason why working-class children were able to raid the middle class was that the middle class itself expanded; as we saw previously, the expansion of senior managerial jobs created more positions for working-class children to move into. Some would argue against this with evidence of the country's 4,000 millionaires who have emerged from working-class origins.

But this is a less significant statistic than those presented by Philip Stanworth, who found the boards of the largest financial and industrial organizations studded with men from public schools and Oxbridge. He found this to be a growing trend since the war. The opening out of state sectors and the increase in redbrick, or modern, universities have improved the chances of working-class children of reaching expanding top management positions. But adds Stanworth 'Whether or not they will be successful in gaining access to the boardroom in anything but small numbers is doubtful . . . schools which educate between 2 and 5 per cent of British children usually provided 60 to 80 per cent of those holding elite positions' (1984, p. 261). There has been social mobility since the war, but there has also been social stasis, a lack of movement in certain areas. In particular, there has been little flow from the working class into élite positions. The main tributary for these has been the independent school system, whose effect on the class structure has arguably been more decisive than the upward movement of the working class. For this reason, the independent sector deserves some attention.

Stanworth demonstrates that, in industry, finance, Parliament, the civil service, the judiciary, the armed forces and even the church, there is a top drawer of individuals who share a remarkably similar educational background: independent school followed in a great many cases by Oxford or Cambridge universities. 'Despite a recent broadening in the recruitment of specific elites', argues Stanworth, 'they remain dominated by persons from privileged social backgrounds' (1984, p. 261). David Boyd's research in the 1970s reached broadly similar conclusions (1973). It is interesting, and perhaps revealing, how independent schools have been excised from most of the major debates on education since the war. With the exception of the Fleming Committee Report and Newsom's Public Schools Commission *First Report* of 1968, which recommended assisted places, the independents were hardly considered – a surprising omission when one considers the origins and destinations of their pupils. The Assisted Places Scheme, introduced in 1981, permitted a maximum of 5,500 pupils annually selected on merit to attend independents with their tuition fees paid wholly or partly by the state. Before this, direct government grants had made it possible for achieving working-class children to attend selected independents. But prohibitively high fees of around £6,000 a year (late 1980s prices) have otherwise warded off all but the upper and middle classes and, according to Irene Fox, the 'service class', whose members all 'share in common the fact that they are clearly beneficiaries of the system of capitalism and therefore likely to remain loyal to its fundamental tenets which have served them so well' (1984, p. 49). I will argue shortly that the mere prospect of becoming a beneficiary has, in some senses, kept many sections of the population 'loyal'.

In 1951 the independent school population was 564,000, or 9.2 per cent of the country's school population. Thirty years on, it had declined to just under half a million (6.2 per cent). By 1986 it was back up to 6.7 per cent. Over the same period the independents' share of the total number of pupils staying on for A-levels slid from 40 to 20 per cent. As a result, competition for university places hotted up. The independent schools rose to the competition and gradually increased their share of the total number of pupils attaining three or more A-levels. By 1981 they were providing an impressive 29 per cent of the total, an achievement made possible by many features, including low teacher–pupil ratios, excellent study conditions and better resources. (A survey of independent schools' spending on books, for example, revealed that state secondary schools spent only 36 per cent of the amount private schools did in 1984–5; this represented a drop from 44 per cent in the previous twelve months.) The grip on Oxbridge places continued into the late 1980s, despite the incursions of maintained school pupils from 1944.

The Labour Party sometimes openly opposed the independent schools, one of its prominent ministers of the postwar years, Anthony Crosland, identifying them as a cause of class inequality. It puzzled Crosland why his party sunk so much energy into questioning grammar schools and yet remained, as he put it, 'so indifferent to the much more glaring injustice of the independent schools' (1956, pp. 260–1). As Secretary of State of the Department of Education and Science, Crosland in 1965 introduced the Public Schools Commission and issued it with a brief to devise a way of integrating independent and state sectors. The commission offered a scheme which was subsequently appraised and then shelved. In 1973 Roy Hattersley, then Labour's Shadow Minister of Education, issued a new warning that he would abolish independent schools, given the chance.

Crosland's critique of the independent school system was launched in the 1950s but remains valid today. Revisions to the state sector have supplied more equal educational and, ultimately, occupational opportunities for those of working-class backgrounds. But they have been largely irrelevant to the class structure. As we have seen, this has been maintained uninterruptedly, and the role of the independent schools has been pivotal. If Stanworth's figures are to be accepted, public schools take in a small minority of upper- and middle-class pupils and lubricate their passage to universities and then to influential positions at the top of the social hierarchy. The formula is recycled when those at the top afford their children the same 'start in life'. The mobile minority who clamber to the top from humble origins are 'absorbed' so that they become 'loyal' to the system that has operated in their favour.

As their name implies, independent schools do not depend on another authority for their existence and validity; at the time of the 1944 Act, they were under obligation to no one and despite the creation of the Assisted Places Scheme they have stayed that way. Crosland called them 'the strongest remaining bastion of class privilege', and they have not weakened since the 1950s. For 'class' we might easily read 'male' and 'white'. (A study by myself and Carl Bagley in 1985 revealed that no independent school in England or Wales recognized the need for multicultural education or the provision of any form of education designed to reflect the changing ethnic composition of British society. In some cases, headteachers held openly racist views. The probable destinations of pupils being educated in such an atmosphere are positions of power and privilege in government, industry and the civil service.)

Generation after generation, they facilitate a route to the top for children whose parents are already there or thereabouts. Independent schools uphold the UK's class structure. In this sense, the lack of change in the independent sector is immeasurably more important in the transmission of class inequality than any amount of change in the state system. The future incumbents of positions of power are in all likelihood now walking the cloisters of Merchant Taylors' or Rugby. There is no secret about the fact that privilege begets privilege, but the manner in which the upper middle class has kept its stranglehold on the key powerful positions in spite of equalizing forces tells us something about its special resilience. Numerically, the numbers passing through the public schools are not great. But then again, the numbers of those with access to wealth and power are not great either, yet they are the ones with the control.

Classes are often quite impervious to educational change and have a tendency to reproduce. There are three main methods to secure class reproduction, one pointed out by the National Child Development Council, which concluded that a child is imprinted with class during the first five years of his or her life, a phase before the formal education process begins. No amount of education can erase the stamp of class on aspects of the child's behavioural development and ability, the head researcher, Ronald Davie, argued after studying 17,000 children in the 1950s. Another method involves an indirect tactic: that of supplying the child with ample study facilities, a stimulating home environment and the motivation to succeed at school and after. Thirdly, a child can be placed in the kind of fee-paying institution that is beyond the means of the working class, or in a suburban school where favourable teacher–pupil ratios guarantee more careful nurturing at crucial stages of the child's intellectual development. Good schooling is generally a precursor to qualifications, which in turn secure places at prestigious universities.

Heath writes of yet another method: 'The *direct* influence of social origins – whether through patronage, nepotism, inheritance or some other mechanism – on occupational attainment has declined, but simultaneously its *indirect* influence via the educational system has increased' (1981, p. 191). The influence of this educational pedigree on ultimate destinations is clear enough. Added to this is the recognition that education is geared to middle-class requirements in terms of language, values and authority arrangements. The 'direct' mechanisms, which Heath believes have declined in influence, involve the naked transmission of wealth and hence power; but allied to the 'indirect' and 'imprinting' methods, they form a powerful instrument for ensuring the permanence of the class structure, in defiance of educational policies intended to have the contrary effect.

Small wonder then that many writers have isolated education as a target for criticism. Not only can it never negate social inequalities, they would argue; it actively contributes to the maintenance of them. In 1972 Young edited a collection of essays tellingly entitled *Knowledge and Control*. The volume raised a number of doubts about the whole purpose of compulsory schooling, suggesting that the educational system reaffirms general inequality. The contention here was that educational institutions have been established and run by groups in power who want to preserve a system that has served their best interests, and not to have it disrupted by future generations. Attempts to use schooling to reduce class inequalities were regarded as limited, inappropriate and futile. The structure of the curriculum, the ways in which class determines access to knowledge and the processes operating to reproduce class divisions – all features of postwar Britain, as we have seen – have not been materially affected by the educational reforms since 1944.

This was a much more sombre image of education than the one favoured by proponents of educational change as an agent for equality of opportunity. The latter can argue that the UK's educational reforms have bitten into the significance of class as a determinant of a young person's future. This is certainly true, but not across the board. The reforms have reduced the significance of social background for much of the working class by facilitating a degree of social mobility and this has had what Alan Fox calls 'a valuable anodyne' effect (1985). Fox continues: 'the equal opportunities ostensibly offered by the educational system and the market place make inequalities of outcome appear to be the necessary result of individual talent and effort on the one hand, or of ineluctable economic forces on the other' (1985, p. 424). The comforting illusion of main chance disguises the way the upper and middle classes have prolonged their stay at the top: by affording their offspring education at selected establishments or by co-opting into their ranks the socially mobile, who in turn can take advantage of the system. Britain's educational system has been an ambiguous blessing: it has given the impression of change and opportunity, whilst perpetuating rigidity and closure. In the process, it has nourished faith in the country's capability for rewarding talent and effort. This has greatly influenced the ambitions and aspirations that people regard as legitimate and attainable – with consequences for the entire class structure, as we will now see.

Dazzled by the bourgeois ideal

'Must Labour lose?' was a question many political commentators and researchers were asking in the early 1960s. More than a decade of Tory rule and no sign of working-class enthusiasm for the kind of major reform only a socialist government would undertake raised problems. Various explanations of the working class's apparent devotion to Conservatism came from academic sources. McKenzie and Silver believed that workers had attitudes of deference, an exaggerated respect for individuals of higher status than themselves (1968). W. G. Runciman showed that Tory-voting workers were generally those who considered themselves members of the middle class, quite regardless of their actual class position (1966). Frank Parkin inverted the problem, believing that Conservative voting had become the norm and working-class Labour voters were the 'deviant' group to be explained – those living in solid working-class communities that afforded them some insulation from the 'pressures of the wider society' (1967).

Although it did not destroy the validity of the research findings, the answer to the question 'Must Labour lose?' was actually 'No'. Wilson's narrow four-seat victory in 1964 broke the seemingly unbreakable. While the size of the majority seemed practically to rule out any ambitious plans, it did not subdue Wilson, who told the population, 'We must start a revolution!' Three years later, even his political *alter ego*, Edward Heath, agreed: 'Britain needs a revolution' (quoted in Marwick, 1970, p. 462). A major transformation of British society was anticipated, by both government and governed; the trade unions were to be integral to this process. 'When Jack Jones and Hugh Scanlon, with very left-wing records, were elected to run the two biggest unions in 1967–68, the "terrible twins" were seen as agents of a new revolutionary era,' writes Anthony Sampson; but 'Twelve years later they appeared as guardians of moderation: Jack Jones was the saviour of the Labour Party, and Scanlon was Lord Scanlon' (1982, p. 61). The mooted revolution had gone flat. The unions had in 1976 signed a 'social contract' with the Labour government, setting out the terms of an incomes control policy. By the end of 1979, Thatcher was in office.

Talk of revolution then seemed laughable. What had begun

with socialist rhetoric in the mid-1960s ended, after twelve or fourteen years, with a confirmation of Conservative control. The transformation actually turned out to be a phase of discontinuity. It was a phase when the 'British disease', a 'virus' associated with industrial action and overbearing trade unions, was thought by some alarmists to be afflicting society's institutions. The trade union movement's strength and its capacity for collective action suggested more working-class power than at any time since the war. Yet slow economic growth, combined with an inflationary business cycle, rising unemployment and internal political changes, precipitated something of a crisis. The unions tumbled from grace, their powers snatched away by an assailant Conservative government. So back to the original question: must Labour lose?

Not only has the working class helped return successive Tory governments to power, it has affirmed the legitimacy of the existing economic and political system. Over the past two chapters, I have described how the working class has failed to exert pressure for a fundamental redistribution of power, wealth and status. Following this, I looked in more detail at how these resources have been distributed over the years since the war, noticing in particular the glacial pace of change in the distribution of income and wealth. In the first part of the present chapter, I began to uncover what Marwick calls the 'mechanics of non-change', isolating reforms in education, the illusion of equal opportunities and the recognition of social mobility as moving parts. For class inequalities to persist, something else is needed: a common perspective shared by all classes.

Despite any reservations about the extent and potential of social mobility, such a common perspective *does* exist. As we noted, it enables analysts such as Halsey to describe, albeit reservedly, the UK as a 'model of constant social fluidity'. The ability to move from one class to another, or at least from one occupational income group to another, has become a valued feature of British society since the war. Coser believes that this type of situation reveals something about the quality of relations between classes: 'In societies in which upward social mobility is institutionalized, in which achieved rather than ascribed status dominates, hostility between various strata is mingled with a strong positive attraction to those higher in the social hierarchy, who provide some models of behavior' (1968, p. 36). This has some relevance to Britain. The origins of the hostility–attraction combination lie in the period of the Industrial Revolution when an urban working class had to be instilled with the discipline and recognizance required of an effective labour force. Resentment and sporadic revolts were stilled by the use of authority backed by violence in the early nineteenth century, after which a strategy of continued concessions was employed. Workers' protests were followed by piecemeal reforms, such as the Workmen's Compensation Act 1897, the Unemployed Worker Act 1903, the Trade Groups Act 1909 and the National Insurance Act 1911. Alan Fox's historical study shows that by 1880 Britain had developed a compromise between organized sections of the working class and the ruling class, a compromise involving mutual recognition of the conditional legitimacy of collective bargaining conducted in a political and economic framework that protected power and property from any challenge from below. The result was a 'mature' but inert society with no scope to restructure class relations (1985, pp. 124–74).

Fox notes the importance of an 'imperialist consciousness', one facet of which was the 'acceptance of responsibility for improving the condition of the lower orders'. (1985, p. 233). This impulse helped shape the context in which the working class developed, a context of ever-improving material conditions and expanding 'opportunities in education, industry, and elsewhere for individuals of lowly origin to ascend the ladder' (1985, p. 233).

The motive came not only from the generosity and finer spirits of the ruling class and the emergent bourgeoisie, but also from the expedient tactic of conceding limited reforms and permitting certain groups to rise to 'better things'. Here we find the nucleus of social mobility. The strategy had far-reaching consequences for working-class character and disposition.

Working-class leaders, while trying to build solidarity amongst their followers, were, as Fox puts it, 'also dazzled by the bourgeois ideal of "bettering oneself" '. Individuals could better themselves, but would have to pursue this improvement within the existing institutional framework; so the process involved, if only by default, supporting the status quo. Radical thrusts were constantly blunted by 'incorporated' elements of the working class who accepted the existing political arrangements, including the police, education, the role of the state, the distribution of income and wealth and the class structure.

This process of incorporation took on a new aspect after the First World War. The experience of war produced a new kind of social cohesion created and sustained by a unity of purpose and an acceptance of difference. The working class, according to Dahrendorf, 'created its own social world which was unique in many respects, though some elements looked like a mirror image of the values of those on top' (1982, p. 74). This suggests a complement to Coser's concept of 'models of behavior' and Fox's 'bourgeois ideal'. There was, it seems, a symmetry between the aspirations and values of the working class and those of the middle class. The way in which they were brought to life in the working class was through collective efforts; but the aim was historically derivative of the middle class: self-improvement, or 'bettering oneself'.

Far from seeking 'to turn things upside down', as Dahrendorf puts it, the working class accepted the legitimacy of the existing system and proceeded to work inside its limits. As we have seen, the British working class has generated a robust solidarity that is as broad as it is deep in its opposition to 'management', the owners and controllers of capital. It has not opposed the actual structure that permits one group to own and another to labour; it has not created a vision of an alternative system, or a method for overthrowing the present one. While it might have disagreed fiercely with distributive details, the working class has accepted the essence of capitalism as legitimate. Legitimacy derives from persuasion, not from force; it is invaluable to the class structure (indeed, to any system of inequality). The

[71]

mingling of hostility and attraction implies that underlying certain forms of inequality there remains a respect, even deference, for the system of government. As we will see in the following section, the working class has shown more interest in working through the system than in confronting it.

Interest in the system

The evidence presented in Chapter 1 certainly matches this evaluation. At the same time, however, the evidence indicates long and severe conflicts, often over specific issues, but sometimes relating to concerns affecting the entire working class. There are three plain facts about such conflict. (1) It was generally regarded as an inevitable feature of an unequal society comprising 'haves' and 'wants'. (2) The conflict was not repressed but was always contained and resolved through prescribed institutional processes – what Westergaard calls 'a series of compromises which defines not only the means and procedures of conflict, but also the area of the conflict at any given time' (1972, p. 140). (3) There has been a commitment to the rules that govern the conflict or to the basic values that underlie specific values and interests. Workers have played what James Hinton describes as 'an accommodative game compatible with the bourgeois social order' (1986, p. viii).

What's more, far from being destructive of unity, the conflict has acted as a unifying agent. This brings us to another component in the process of 'non-change'. The idea of having rights implies a facility to criticize, challenge and, if necessary, fight in defence of one's interests. It is a notion closely linked to liberty and, as such, has been a guarded preserve of the British working class. People have had the right to rise up against low wages, lack of food, bad conditions, racialism, sex discrimination, nuclear armament and virtually any issue that they have felt affects their lives in a negative way. Challenges of this nature are perfectly congruent with the ideology of an 'open society'. Sometimes the challenges have been stifled (the Peterloo

Massacre of 1819 being the outstanding example) but in the twentieth century they have usually concluded in a negotiated settlement. So, in avoiding the dogma and tyranny characteristic of less flexible regimes, the UK has sustained a political climate in which dissatisfied or disaffected groups can express their grievances in the anticipation that some improvements will come about. Conflicts are resolved by negotiation more than by force: causes are debated, solutions are discussed, policies are offered. There is unity precisely because the conflict is allowed to come to the surface.

There is no contradiction here, for a system that guarantees the right to challenge also secures its members' faith in its ability to absorb that challenge and so enhances its own legitimacy or 'rightness'. The result is something similar to what the nineteenth-century social theorist Emile Durkheim perceived as a unifying morality that allows for the meshing of diverse groups, some with viciously opposed interests, yet all bound by feelings of obligation and belonging. In the UK, every fresh protest has appeared to affirm the openness and the democracy of the system and so to solidify the underlying cohesion, or accepted morality. This helps explain why for almost fifty years since the war, and maybe for 250 years before that, mainland Britain has managed to avoid violent political upheavals and to sustain a continuous internal stability, whilst at the same time maintaining a divisively unequal class structure. In summary, the common perspective has its sources in the working class' acceptance of 'bettering oneself' as an ideal, in the perceived legitimacy of economic and political arrangements and in the possibility of conflict being expressed openly.

Abiding images of the working class at the end of the 1980s might include the unemployed teenager drifting about the inner city, or the redundant miner from South Wales, but most members of the working class have since the war seen their living standards rise markedly. The middle class has, of course, benefited disproportionately from the same trend. Nevertheless the fact remains: employed workers are not crippled by deprivation; they enjoy a formerly middle-class lifestyle and they harbour, as I have argued, middle-class aspirations. The spread of private home ownership, bringing with it more autonomy and choice, has accentuated the bourgeois ideal of bettering oneself and has reduced the force of more collectivist ambitions. The 1980s, in particular, have seen the signals of the 'new realism', with videos, cars, holidays abroad and share ownership dominating the ambitions of the working class. This has not prevented the working class from keeping its essential characteristics: the source of its income is wages (or social benefits, or a combination of both); the level of its income is low; and the individual influence, responsibility and power of members of the working class are small and nugatory. Rises in net personal income are generally balanced by cuts in health, education and transport provision. The bulk of the working class, however, does not share the squalor, insecurity and hopelessness of the poor elderly or the unemployed teenager.

'New realism' in the working class seems less a dramatic shift than a continuing tendency: avoiding what might be regarded as more idealistic socialist visions and beginning from the attempt to solve practical problems as people experience them (rather than as others suggest they should be experienced). The working class has in general demonstrated no penchant in acting other than to survive or prosper. Its members have, for the most part, absorbed the values of individual advancement, progress on merit and personal freedom. The unions' attempts to oust blacks and subjugate women are aspects of its defensive strategies. They have not tried to replace existing values with alternatives based on collectivist or class principles. Success and failure have been defined ultimately in the individual terms; the methods for achieving one or slipping towards the other have been accepted, even though they may work systematically to the detriment of the working class as a whole.

There are powerful forces of conservatism within the British working class. They emanate from the longing to preserve working-class autonomy, to maintain individual liberty and to protect material possessions – all properties derived from bourgeois worldviews, it could be argued, but properties that nevertheless have greatly influenced the working-class response to inequality. There has been conflict, violent conflict in some instances, but usually of a containable kind. Conflicts, particularly those since the war that have been articulated through the trade union movement, have been about pragmatic issues, not ideals. The working class has consented to accept the system and play by its rules and, in return, has exercised its right to protest. There has been little evidence of struggle over matters other than immediate practical interests. And, in its role as the chief vehicle for furthering or, as this analysis would have it, tenaciously defending working-class interests, the union movement has reacted to change rather than precipitated it. So it has not seriously challenged any of the dominant social or political assumptions and arrangements, nor pushed for any transformation that would require massive state intervention and a levelling out of class inequality.

The unions have attained undeniable material improvements, making possible better housing, clothing and diet and an assortment of valuable conditions relating to work. At the same time, their ability to deliver has reinforced the commitment of the class they represent. The working class has an interest in the system, even if it is a far smaller interest than it believes.

Whether or not one chooses to recognize the unions' role positively, as an agent of the social cohesion that has characterized the UK, or negatively, as an instrument of working-class stagnation or even repression, is a matter of perspective. Yet it is still a stubborn fact that the unions have reflected working-class concerns, and these have focused on occupational rather than on broader class interests. The working class has not seen its condition, past or present, graphically in terms of power, exploitation and control over the means of production. Nor has it regarded its future as involving a colossal confrontation of labour against capital. Only a few have implored the working class to link its material circumstances with this wider struggle and perceive itself as belonging, in the final analysis, to a genuine class of people and not an aggregation of individuals pursuing their own interests, bettering themselves. Nowhere can we find the British working class' complete transcendence of pragmatism; at no time can we discern a full ideological commitment to change, inspired by a vision of a new set of institutional arrangements. At very best, we find such a commitment and vision in a few isolated individuals, popularly depicted in the media as megalomaniacs or communist demagogues.

Ideological commitment and belligerence have not been among the prominent qualities of the working class, then; but other qualities have been notable and these bear on Parts Two and Three of this book. In particular, the stout nationalism and respect for country so evident in the working class have flourished in an atmosphere of relative affluence in which it has not needed to rethink its posture. Class has not been a motivating quality in the same way as nationalism has. The quick and excited mobilization of sentiment during the Falklands War gives some flavour of this. Call it xenophobia, a hatred or abhorrence of those defined as 'outsiders', or call it simple patriotism. Either way, the British working class has manifested an insular interest in itself – as 'British', that is, not as 'working class'. Such a preoccupation sweeps across class boundaries. The working class has been reluctant to identify fellow Britons as its enemies even though they might occupy a position on the 'have' side of the means-of-production equation. Working-class people have been more comfortable, it seems, in regarding non-British 'have-nots' as their enemies, as we will see in the following chapters.

Part 2

RACE

CHAPTER 5

The solution that started a problem

Shouts and whispers

'In quite a few instances, we have been successful in changing ships from coloured to white,' announced the assistant general secretary of the National Union of Seamen. 'White men should be carried in preference to coloured.' He was addressing his union's annual conference at Liverpool in 1948. One of the conference themes was 'the colour question': specifically, how to keep black seamen off British ships. There were at the time about 10,000 blacks in the United Kingdom, many resident in Liverpool, working on ships or at ports. The union resolved to set up committees at main ports for the purpose of vetting 'coloured entrants to the country who claim to be seamen'.

The ruling set in motion a series of physical attacks on blacks, culminating in three nights of violence over the August holiday. According to Peter Fryer, two thousand people attacked a hostel for black seamen, who were forced to barricade themselves in (1984, p. 368). Further offensives on clubs and hostels followed, and street battles went on, prompting police intervention. 'The general impression appears to be that the police took action which they thought would bring the disturbances to a close as quickly as possible,' writes Anthony Richmond, 'which, in their view, meant removing the coloured minority, rather than attempting to arrest the body of irresponsible whites who were involved' (1954, p. 103). Effectively,

[79]

the police joined forces with the white attackers and set about intimidating blacks, either through physical beatings or through arrest, or both. After the violence had subsided, a police spokesman was quoted as proclaiming: 'There isn't any colour question in Liverpool.'

Fryer believes that 'Present in the overture were *all* the themes that the next generation of black people in Britain were to know so well in their daily relations with police' (1984, p. 371). Although he does not actually specify these themes, we can safely assume he means that the motive behind the attacks was racist; blacks were criticized and abused for allegedly snatching work from local whites (there were also parallels of sexual jealousy). Police, sharing the common prejudices towards blacks, were of little use in protecting them and sided with whites in the attempt to restore order. And when matters were brought to court, the state ruled in favour of the whites, sentencing the blacks for an assortment of offences such as obstructing the police. Over the next three chapters we will test the validity of Fryer's claim, beginning by describing migration and settlement and, more decisively, the white reaction to them. Chapter 6 asks how unequal a society Britain has been for ethnic minorities and why. The answers to these questions lead to an account of the conflict that has been provoked by racial inequality.

The Liverpool episode happened just two months after the arrival at Tilbury of the *Empire Windrush*, which brought 492 work-seeking Jamaicans to British soil. The 22nd of June 1948 is popularly regarded as the starting date for the postwar migration to the UK and, because of this, it marks a historic date for race relations. The disturbances at Liverpool, on the other hand, are frequently forgotten. In the forty years following the arrival of the *Empire Windrush*, Britain's black population grew at an exceptional rate. After the initial rush of migration from the Caribbean, there began a surge from South Asia (comprising India, Pakistan, Bangladesh and Sri Lanka). By the end of the postwar job boom in the mid- to late 1950s, the number of people from the Caribbean and South Asia in the

UK was estimated to be 200,000 or 0.5 per cent of the total population. This had increased tenfold by 1988, when about 5 per cent, or 2.6 million people, were of New Commonwealth origin or descent. Over half of this minority were born in the UK.

Opponents of those who in the 1970s pressed for the repatriation of New Commonwealth migrants would often point to the fact that much of the initial migration more than twenty years before had been prompted by British employers. Under the 1948 Nationality Act, citizens of Britain's colonies and ex-colonies were granted UK citizenship and were free to travel to, work and reside in Britain permanently if they wished. The postwar worker shortage encouraged British industry to look abroad for fresh sources of labour, and it found a willing and available supply in the Caribbean and South Asia. Some organizations, like London Transport and the British Hotels and Restaurants' Association, went as far as operating recruitment campaigns in the West Indies.

Some explained the mass migration by reference to the attractive job opportunities in the UK's industrial cities which acted as a magnet. Others pointed to the disincentives of staying at home. In the Indian subcontinent, millions found themselves homeless and jobless after national independence; flood, famine and poverty were established features of life. The cost of living in the British West Indies almost doubled during the war, leaving large-scale unemployment and no supporting social security system. The USA's McCarran–Walter Act of 1952 closed off a possible migration option for many with its restrictions, leaving West Indians with little choice apart from the country they sentimentally called 'the motherland'. All the studies of the day supported the idea that Caribbean migrants regarded their UK citizenship with some pride and regarded themselves, in genuine sense, as British.

The migrants had little difficulty in finding employment, because there were serious shortages in many areas of industry. It was a period when, as one works superintendent put it to researcher Peter Wright, 'you couldn't get an armless, legless

man, never mind an able-bodied one' (1968, p. 42). Strange as
it seems from the vantage-point of the 1980s, the 1950s were
times of a sellers' market; people who had labour and skill to
sell were able to exercise some selectivity in their jobs. 'You can
sack me if you want to,' says Albert Conroy, a young
draughtsman in Stan Barstow's novel, *A Kind of Loving*, set in
the 1950s; 'I'm taking me talents elsewhere. I shan't have to look
long either; there's plenty of firms crying out for blokes' (1973,
p. 118).

Between 1944 and 1950 a part of the country's labour
requirements were met by 175,000 European migrants, mainly
from Poland, Germany and the Ukraine. The arrival of 492
Jamaicans in 1948 understandably aroused little concern, yet it
did not escape the attentions of a government working party
set up in 1948 to examine the possibilities of employing the
'surplus manpower of certain colonial territories'. The committee urged great caution in recruiting colonial workers, a
statement echoed by the Home Office during the following
year. The Labour Cabinet requested Prime Minister Attlee to
look further at the situation, with a view to introducing some
element of control; while European migrants were not seen as
problematic, the visibly different entrants from the New
Commonwealth were regarded as a potential tax on Britain's
capacity to absorb.

In the event, economic considerations overrode all others,
and suggestions of restricting the influx were dismissed. The
fears of a short-lived boom followed by a dire recession and a
surfeit of unwanted labour persisted, particularly amongst
trade unionists and some Labour politicians. A Royal Commission report of 1949 acknowledged that colonial migration on a
mass scale would meet some of the needs of industry, but would
also impose strains on housing and social services. On a cultural
level, the commission raised some interesting points about the
compatibility of the host and migrant populations and the
ability of the new groups to assimilate. Its conclusion was that
only migrant groups of 'good stock' should be encouraged.
While certain Labour MPs did not necessarily subscribe to this

argument, they still saw a need for immigration checks on colonials in the future. A Cabinet committee announced in 1951 that 'coloured persons' might be subject to control at some stage. Migration from South Asia had barely started at this point; it rose sharply after 1954. Not that the actual presence of 'coloured persons' was seen as the essential problem. Both blacks and Asians have a long and often distinguished presence in British society. In the mid-sixteenth century, black valets and manservants were taken to Britain to serve the planter aristocracy. Thousands of West Indians served in the Second World War effort, either in the Royal Air Force or in war factories, and as seamen they had travelled to and from British ports, often settling in sizeable ethnic communities. South Asians played a prominent role in public life and moved smoothly in the upper echelons of society. But when the sheer numbers of Caribbeans and Asians in the UK built up to an unprecedented 400,000, then doubled in one year, a problem of cataclysmic proportions was envisaged by some, especially after street violence seemed to herald its beginnings.

The pattern of violence witnessed in Liverpool in 1948 reappeared a decade later, this time in the Midlands city of Nottingham and the London district of Notting Hill. St Annes Wells Road was a part of Nottingham where around 2,500 blacks and 600 Asians lived in the late 1950s. From 1957 ethnic-minority groups became targets for sporadic unprovoked attacks. Unrest in the area took a new turn when, after eighteen months of being victims, a group of blacks fought back and for ninety minutes staged a street battle with local whites. The response was swift. Within a week thousands of whites took to the streets, chanting, 'Let's get the blacks' and 'Let's lynch 'em' (Fryer, 1984, p. 377). The media, alerted by the previous week's episode, were ready in force to cover and perhaps even promote, according to some sources, the first 'race riot' for a decade.

At Notting Hill, *Sturm und Drang* had been in the air for some years. In 1954 a house occupied by a West Indian family had been petrol-bombed. Racialist attacks were commonplace. Often, they were encouraged by fascist organizations that were active in the period. The League of Empire Loyalists (formed in 1954), in particular, had rushed into a void created by the melting of the Tory Party's hard right wing into the consensual politics of 'Butskellism'. Other groups, like the White Defence League under Colin Jordan, circulated anti-black leaflets around Notting Hill. 'Coffee coloured monstrosities' were being supported by the National Assistance Board, the leaflets stated. 'Material rewards are given to enable semi-savages to mate with one of the leading civilizations of the world' (quoted in Walker, 1977, pp. 33–4).

Such messages reached a receptive public in Notting Hill. The district was populated by working-class people packed into old, squalid and overcrowded properties and often exploited and harassed into paying extortionate rents by landlords like Peter Rachman, whose physical methods of ensuring payment earned him notoriety. Notting Hill was a depressed area, feeling the effects of the recession that followed the boom years.

Most of the incidents in the early 1950s involved a core of violent adolescents who were amongst the most impressionable and manipulable elements of the population. Certainly, they were impressed by the new youth culture that was finding its way from the USA to Britain via rock 'n' roll music. The teds, or teddy boys, were the first of what was to become a procession of postwar youth subcultures. The connection between organized fascist groups and youth subcultures was to be given renewed relevance in the 1970s with the arrival of the skinheads. Teds had featured in a number of almost ritualistic assaults on blacks prior to the major incident which took place in August 1958. It began with a night of violence in which six blacks were badly beaten. Nine white youths were later imprisoned. By the end of August, brawls and racialist attacks were quite regular, and in September a crowd of hundreds of white youths went rampaging through the streets, while the police retreated, offering no effective opposition.

These two incidents reflected a wider and growing unease.

The violence spread throughout the country, with teds figuring prominently in a series of attacks that continued for the next several years. During that time, migrants were blamed for a variety of social evils, including a decline in housing standards and a rise in unemployment. The classic scapegoating process was in gear, with blacks and Asians spuriously attributed with the cause of problems which were, in objective terms, nothing to do with them. In a revealing passage about the teds, Paul Rock and Stanley Cohen wrote that 'There was enough latent hostility to make the object of the Ted's aggression irrelevant', meaning that, with a diminishing job market and a corresponding drop in living standards compared to the immediate postwar period, unrest was increasing, especially amongst young people released from the ties of National Service. 'As it happened, the object – a coloured racial minority group – was visible and very relevant' (1970, p. 314).

What made them relevant? Some analysts trained their eyes on the economy. Migrant workers were drawn in as an auxiliary workforce, used basically to support a buoyant economy. Native workers, confident and satisfied with real wage rises (after 1950) and their improving material conditions, saw no apparent threat in the guise of the new additions to the workforce. Points of stress that did appear were in the inner cities, where migrants struggled with each other and with a residual class of poor whites for housing. When the dole queues began to lengthen, people who were once looked at as workmates were, by some alchemy of perception, transformed into competitors for jobs.

In such situations, it is less convenient for people to trace the source of problems to structural changes in the economy; more convenient to place the burden of responsibility on a strikingly different and identifiable group. Once the source had been found, then everything fitted into place, and that group could be assigned responsibility for any other problem – housing, poor social services, even 'taking white women', a common theme of the time. 'A film of the time, *Sapphire* (1959), directed by Basil Deardon, dealt with the emergent racial conflict. A police superintendent investigating the murder of a woman who had passed herself off as white, but was in fact "coloured" [to use the movie's term] comments, "Given the right atmosphere, you can organise riots against anyone: Jews, Catholics, negroes, Irish – even policemen with big feet" ' (quoted in Hill, 1986, p. 88). While white workers were earning more money, working under better conditions and claiming more prestige, migrant workers were reasonably satisfied to lurk at the cellar level of the occupational hierarchy. After all, the conditions of famine, chronic unemployment and sometimes civil war they had left behind were appreciably worse than the conditions they had to endure in the UK. At the time, Birmingham might have seemed like paradise compared to Kingston or Karachi. Blacks and Asians were still over-represented at the lower end of the income scale and were generally under the subjection of whites.

Britain's first large survey of race relations took place between 1960 and 1967. While its conclusions were expected by many, it did nail down, in a systematic manner, the full extent of racialism. 'There is racial discrimination varying in extent from the massive to the substantial,' wrote the eventual report's author, W. W. Daniel (1968, p. 209). The experiences of 'black and brown immigrants' were demonstrably worse than those of white immigrants from, for example, Poland or Cyprus. They were excluded from certain jobs and houses for no reason other than they were presumed to belong to a different and, in some fixed way, inferior racial group. ('Racism' refers to this presumption, or belief; 'racialism' is the discriminatory action that follows when it is put into practice.) The implication of the report was not that racism and racialism had suddenly sprung up in the aftermath of the 1958 events, but that they had held a pervasive presence in British society, at all levels in all aspects, for many years. As Ruth Glass observed in 1960: 'The trouble-makers of Notting Hill acted out tendencies which were latent in all social strata'. In her memorable phrase, 'They were shouting what others were whispering' (1960, p. 146). The shouts became louder, and academics, politicians and the media listened attentively as racialism became enshrined as an officially recognized social problem.

If the 1958 outbreaks were the first from street level for ten years, there was no shortage of debate inspired by racism at political levels. Some have even argued that politicians, in introducing racist immigration policies, caused racial antagonism where it would not otherwise have existed. Paul Foot, for example, believes that instances of racialism were exceptional and that whites' reaction was kind and helpful (1965). This is not a view I find convincing, and my reasons will shortly become clear. But we must still recognize the influential role played by politicians, and this subject will occupy the rest of the present chapter.

Building the race relations industry

As early as the 1940s questions about migration were being raised in Parliament, although, as we saw, the Labour administration resisted any attempt to control the inflow. The return of the Conservatives to power in 1951 promised no significant shift in policy, even if one voice, that of Cyril Osborne, grumbled. Disease and crime were being brought to Britain by blacks, Osborne argued. He demanded health checks and an extension of powers of deportation. Despite having little support in Parliament, Osborne and his colleague Norman Pannell, MP for Kirkdale, in 1948 persuaded the Conservative Party's Central Council to pass a resolution in favour of immigration control. The Labour opposition too had its proponents of control, particularly John Hynd, of Attercliffe, who in 1954 called for a restriction of the right of entry of 'coloured colonial immigrants'.

There were two main difficulties for all supporters of control. The first was simply that the 'coloured' immigrants were holders of British passports and legally entitled to entry; any attempt to tamper with this freedom of entry would have been a violation of their citizenship rights. The second was that industry needed their labour. It was tacitly agreed by politicians of all parties that racialism – or, as it was known, 'the colour bar' – did not exist in the UK on anything like the scale in the USA, where in 1954 the *Brown v. Board of Education* decision started desegregation. At the same time, there were occasional acknowledgements that the pressure on housing resulting from migration to the cities might lead to tension. As early as 1953 Labour's National Executive Council (NEC) had invited an academic, Kenneth Little, to submit a memorandum on racial discrimination. In 1955 the NEC published a short report arguing for the establishment of organizations to oppose discrimination and examine the problems unique to the migrant population. Months later, the London Labour Party expressed worry over 'the intensification of present problems'. While these statements were being prepared, there was enough activity in the House to suggest at least a recognition that racialism existed. From 1953, Labour MPs Norman Sorenson and Fenner Brockway began a persistent campaign to pass anti-discrimination laws. Their Private Member's Bills failed virtually every year up till 1964.

At this point, the trade union movement was undecided. Trade unions have traditionally played a racist role with respect to migrant workers, regarding them as potentially cheap labour, frequently unorganized and liable to drag down wage levels. Historically, the argument has some justification. Unions have often reacted quite violently, a classic instance being the anti-Chinese agitation of United States labor unions in the 1860s. There was a certain ambivalence about British unions' position in the 1950s. On the one hand, they wanted to secure the livelihood of their members; on the other, they needed to assert unity and working-class solidarity regardless of skin colour. The ambivalence was illustrated in Roy Baker's 1961 film, *Flame in the Streets*, in which a union official is opposed by both unions and management for supporting the promotion of a black colleague.

It would be difficult to maintain that the violence of 1958 actually signified the beginning of racial conflict. Sure, the eruptions were the first serious mass disturbances since 1948, but the extent of debate and concern over the 'colour bar' seems to indicate that strain was already there, even if it was not legally recognized as a 'social problem'. Equally fallacious is the belief that the migrants were disappointed, resolutely optimisic, or acquiescent. It is interesting that in the disturbances little attention was given to the retaliatory action, especially of blacks. Hopelessly outnumbered as they were, many blacks mobilized, some, as Fryer notes, making pre-emptive strikes on fascist organization headquarters. The struggle against racialism did not always escalate to overt conflict, but, from 1958 especially, ethnic minorities were increasingly prepared to probe, challenge and confront the more obvious injustices they saw before them.

There were two approaches to the problems raised by the riots of 1958 and their aftermath. One was to take notice of the calls of Brockway and implement some form of legislation to prevent racial discrimination. The other was to limit the numbers of colonial migrants entering the UK (between 1956 and 1960 the net migration from the New Commonwealth was just under 200,000). The first option went against the grain of the Conservative government's philosophy in which the values of free enterprise and the avoidance of state compulsion were propounded. The second, as suggested before, involved compromising the citizenship status guaranteed under the 1948 Act. Confused, but keen to do something positive, the government tried both approaches, first limiting migration, then passing anti-discrimination Acts. In a way, the one contradicted the other.

Immigration control had been considered by the government in 1954, when the ferocity of opposition to it deterred its progress. But, Britain was forced to reappraise its position in global terms. The *faux pas* over Suez in 1956 was a major international embarrassment that undermined Britain's pretensions to be a world power. So perhaps it no longer needed to play such a central part as host to Commonwealth populations. The obstacle formerly presented by industry's needs was by now gone; labour shortages were no longer acute

– indeed, unemployment was taking over as the main economic headache. As the debates over immigration control unfolded, a formula became clear. According to this formula, the problem to be solved was racialist disturbances. The solution was reached via the simple proposition that if migrants were not here, then there would be no antagonism. This applied not to all migrants, but to those who were recognizably different and easily earmarked for attention: colonial, 'coloured' immigrants, in other words. Although the term 'race' had not entered into the debates, it lay buried in the subtext, so that, as Miles and Phizacklea argue, 'the question of "immigration" was inextricable from "race" ' (1984, p. 40).

The mood of the times favoured control. According to a Gallup poll of May 1961, 73 per cent of the population wanted migration curbed. Their wishes were satisfied in the following year when the Commonwealth Immigrants Act withdrew the right of entry from Commonwealth citizens unless they held one of three types of voucher. 'A' vouchers were granted to those with a confirmed job, 'B' to those with qualifications or skills that met a special need in the UK and 'C' to those considered on individual merits, such as service in the British armed forces. While the Act looked to be a rational and considered response to the economic situation, it was not quite so. Ceri Peach's work (1968) shows how selective controls were unnecessary, because migration had up to that stage been self-regulating, rising and falling according to the number of job vacancies. In any case, the 1962 Act did not cover migrants from the Irish Republic, so it would seem that economic considerations were not really paramount.

The 1962 Act marked the start of the 'numbers game', as it was called, since the abiding concern of politicians, the media and the majority of the white population was with the actual numbers of New Commonwealth immigrants entering the country and not with the quality of the relations between settlers and native whites. Once the element of control had been instituted, successive pieces of legislation eroded the legal rights of blacks and Asians to enter the UK. The parliamentary consensus over the numbers game was demonstrated in 1965, the year after the ascension of Labour under Wilson. The Labour MP Roy Hattersley declared: 'Without integration, limitation is inexcusable; without limitation, integration is impossible.' He was speaking on his party's White Paper which, amongst other things, favoured extending the controls on entry from the Commonwealth. Integration between ethnic groups in the UK might have been the ultimate goal, but the means to achieve it were to limit the presence of blacks and Asians, the assumption again being that the problem was one of sheer numbers. Part III of the White Paper accepted that the UK was a multiracial society and recommended the creation of a new National Committee for Commonwealth Immigrants (NCCI), designed as a clearing-house to assist the absorption of migrants 'without friction'. One of its functions was to advise the government, and to this end the NCCI appointed a series of panels focusing on such issues as education, employment, housing and health. Michael Banton, in his essay *Promoting Racial Harmony*, reflects on the limitations of the White Paper: 'Despite the sentiments expressed in Part III its tone was overwhelmingly negative and its emphasis on the need for controls helped feed the very anxieties about immigration that the controls were meant to allay' (1985, p. 46). The government's policy, he contends, 'encouraged the belief that immigration caused problems'.

Between the 1962 Act and the White Paper, which abolished the 'C' vouchers, a new central character in the numbers game had emerged. His name was Peter Griffiths, and in the 1964 general election he overturned a safe Labour majority in the West Midlands constituency of Smethwick. His opponent, Patrick Gordon-Walker, was a member of the Labour Shadow Cabinet and a politician of some stature. In the 1950s Gordon-Walker had advocated control and upheld a 'colour bar' in his constituency, but in 1961 he had opposed the Commonwealth Immigrants Bill. Griffiths' device was crude but evidently effective. Addressing the predominantly white working-class constituents – who, while not worried by unemployment, were anxious about housing shortages and problems associated with multi-occupation – he told them: 'If you want a nigger for a neighbour, vote Labour.' They didn't. Gordon-Walker was ousted with an almighty swing of 7.2 per cent to the Conservatives. The national trend was 3.5 per cent to Labour, which won the election. Griffiths's was, in the political vernacular, a 'dirty campaign', but it worked away at British fears and thumped home its points by repeating them over and over. Migrants were a threat; they must be kept out. The malignant design of Griffiths's 'warning' was to be replicated in a less crude, but no less effective, form two years later when Enoch Powell began his hectoring.

The physical bullying of 1958–9 might have subsided, but the undercurrent of racialist rage was still present. It was becoming an actual or potential source of contention and disorder at the workplace, if not in the streets, and it therefore had to be regulated. The 1965 White Paper officially recognized the need for some legal framework for race-related matters. Hattersley's remark provided a start, and a Bill was drawn up. The Race Relations Act of 1965 outlawed discrimination on the basis of 'race, colour, or ethnic or national origin' in 'places of public resort', such as restaurants and transport services. The Act also provided for the Race Relations Board to receive complaints about alleged offenders and seek voluntary settlements where prima-facie cases of discrimination existed. It had no powers to initiate investigations. The Act was quickly followed in 1966 by the important Local Government Act, section 11 of which provided local education authorities that had 'substantial' concentrations (later specified as 2 per cent) of immigrants with financial assistance. This piece of legislation remained the major source of funding for all subsequent educational initiatives, including specialist additional staff and multicultural pro-grammes. The spending was at no time guided by a coherent directive from central government.

Nineteen sixty-seven was a key year in the recent history of Britain. We will see in Part Three how a number of reforms regarding sexuality, abortion and contraception came into being in that year. W. W. Daniel's report on *Racial Discrimination in England* (1967), which put the extent of racialism as somewhere between 'the substantial' and 'massive', was also published. It exposed several glaring gaps in the existing anti-discrimination law, particularly in the areas of employment, housing and the provision of services.

In a way, the report mortified the government, which recognized that any extension of the law would be unpopular amongst a white population shown conclusively by the report to be racialist. But if it failed to respond positively to the new findings, it would contradict its commitment to assist integration. The concept of integration was defined rather well by the then Labour Home Secretary, Roy Jenkins, in 1966: 'Equal opportunity, accompanied by cultural diversity, in an atmosphere of mutual tolerance.'

As if to compound the government's dilemma, events in the United States were being regarded by some as a harbinger for the UK. Riots in the Watts district of Los Angeles in 1965 had sparked off a series of black uprisings in cities all over the USA. Coming so soon after the Nottingham and Notting Hill disturbances, and the Sharpeville massacre in South Africa in 1960, these events seemed to signal global unrest amongst blacks and whites. Prime Minister Macmillan had in 1960 talked of 'the winds of change' blowing across Africa and the world. Mindful of the developing situation, the British replaced the 1965 Race Relations Act with a 1968 version, this time modelled quite closely on its US equivalent. It enlarged the scope of the previous law to cover the areas highlighted by the 1967 report. The Race Relations Board remained a reactive agency, empowered only to respond to complaints and not to prosecute. The law required proof of deliberate acts of distrimination by and against individuals and was thus helpless to control what later became known as institutional racism, where there was no culpable villain, only a widespread pattern of discrimination operating in organizations.

It was not until 1976 that the anti-racialist legislation was amended, and this time the stimulus was a survey conducted in the 1973–4 period. Broadly, the survey set out to answer a set of questions: how effective had the 1968 Race Relations Act been in reducing racialist practices in employment and housing and what was the impact of racialism generally on the material living standards of ethnic minorities? The researchers found that 'there has been a sharp decrease in the extent of discrimination in the field of housing' but that the liberal pretensions of the 1960s were now no longer tenable (Smith, 1977, p. 312). Despite its proscription by law, racialism was still extensive, the report concluded; and the attempts to eliminate it through legal measures were clearly not effective. The Race Relations Board was seen as an ineffectual piece of machinery, processing only 150 complaints in the whole of 1973, while tens of thousands of instances of racial discrimination were estimated as taking place.

Parliament tried to meet both sets of complaints, making the 1976 Act an instrument more of education than compliance and fashioning a new agency, the Commission for Racial Equality (CRE), to supersede the old board. Discrimination was declared unlawful (as opposed to illegal), and victims were provided with redress by way of compensation. The law covered practices which, whatever the intentions, were shown to have a disproportionately adverse effect on ethnic minorities. This followed in the footsteps of US law, at this stage, moving in the direction of trying to provide equality of opportunity rather than ferreting out specific cases of racialism.

The CRE integrated the functions of the Race Relations Board with those of the Community Relations Commission, which was an advisory body erected by the 1968 Race Relations Act which operated without any conspicuous success at local and national levels (it had taken over from the equally ineffectual NCCI). The amalgamation brought forth a new organization with functions of enforcing the law and promoting good relations. Some felt the two were best kept separate. But while race relations laws had pattern as well as a certain pith, their purpose was seriously invalidated by the ever-restrictive immigration controls that seemed to spring up as reactions to every twitch of racist nervousness.

The retreat from the principles of 1948 had begun in 1962 and been extended in 1968, largely as a result of a panic over the impending inflow from Kenya of Asians holding UK citizenship. Labour Home Secretary James Callaghan completely capitulated to popular demands in rushing through what has been described as 'the first incontestably racialist law to be placed on the statute book'. The 1968 Act ensured that only those British passport holders with 'substantial connections' with the UK had an automatic right of entry. 'Substantial connections' meant having at least a grandfather born in Britain; this qualification could usually be met by white passport holders from Australia, Canada, New Zealand and Rhodesia (now Zimbabwe), but not by most Asians from Kenya, despite their equivalent passport credentials. Premier Wilson's insistence that the criteria for exemption were geographical and not racial looked rather implausible, particularly to Asians already resident in the UK. The image of the 'coloured' migrant as a threat was actually validated by the government with this pivotal piece of legislation. The Act may well have appeased a white population fearful of the coming of 95,000 Kenyan Asian passport holders. Its anxieties had been masterfully stretched by one Conservative Shadow Cabinet member, Enoch Powell.

Literally mad: Powell

'We must be mad, literally mad,' warned Powell in 1969, 'to be permitting the annual inflow of some 50,000 dependants, who are for the most part the material of the future growth of the immigrant-descended population' (quoted in Seymour-Ure, 1974, p. 104). In the days following Powell's first speech on this issue, a Gallup poll was conducted, showing as many as 96 per cent of the adult population to be aware of Powell's views.

Powell chose his moment carefully. During the 1950s and early 1960s he lent no support to Osborne or other early advocates of control, and in 1965 he said nothing about tighter restrictions even when helping A. D. Holmes draw up plans for a repatriation programme. Powell's constituency in Wolver-hampton was barely ten miles from Smethwick. They were parts of a region that had seen a 0.6 per cent swing to the Tories in contrast to the national trend in the 1964 election. Three of the five Conservative gains could be attributed to 'racial backlash', according to D. E. Schoen in his analysis of *Enoch Powell and the Powellites* (1977). Powell spoke with some conviction when he urged limitations on the Kenyan Asians. 'Those of us living in the Midlands . . .' he prefaced his remarks, suggesting, with every justification, that he was articulating the sentiments of the majority. The *Colour and Citizenship* survey (Rose, 1969) showed that immigrants were seen as threatening by at least 60 per cent of the population.

Five days after Powell's plea for more restrictions, the Labour government brought in the appropriate controls. Yet within four months Powell was elaborating metaphors of 'the River Tiber flowing with much blood' to convey what he felt the future would bring. Whether or not Powell and the consider-able publicity he received were instrumental in creating, or at least helping foster, racism, or whether they just gave voice to what the majority was already thinking, is open to doubt. In any event, the remarkable working-class support given to Powell leaves no doubt at all about his popularity. Some trade unionists, traditionally Labour supporters, publicly committed their loyalty to this Tory politician. Powell certainly added shape, clarity, credibility and, most significantly, legitimacy to racist ideas.

Sacked by his party leader from the Shadow Cabinet, Powell continued to berate the government for shrinking away from Draconian immigration controls. He delved into his box of metaphors once more in 1970. 'The explosion which will blow us asunder is already here,' he proclaimed, 'and the fuse is burning.' Now the only option remaining was mass repatri-ation. 'Race bomb will blow us apart,' announced the headline of the Labour-supporting *Daily Mirror*. The outrageous nature of Powell's warnings and proposals was enough to ensure saturation publicity, but the widespread support and popularity he enjoyed need more explanation. Powell's own view would have been that the working class was demoralized by the lost empire and the demise of National Service, with its standards of discipline and authority that were reflected in the whole society. Migrants symbolized this loss and Powell expressed a reaction, a search for a bygone age. There is also the possibility that, as the effervescence of the 1950s and early 1960s went flat, self-doubt and introspection replaced material satisfaction. Class party loyalties were already in doubt amidst the relative affluence and a convergence of party policies. Politics, it could be argued, was growing remote or coming detached from the electorate. This might be supported by the drop in voting turn-out from 79 per cent in 1959 to 72 per cent in 1976.

Powell arrived as a 'man of the people', alienating both his own party and the government with his acerbic critique and outlandish proposals. Yet, despite his obvious visceral appeal, he was still regarded very much as a character in a drama; the drama itself, its plot, setting and production were not under fire. As Schoen observed: 'the growth of general disillusion-ment has not been accompanied by a basic questioning of British political institutions. People apparently feel that their institutions have not been working properly, but they are not willing to abandon them' (1977, p. 279). While the solidity of the political system was not shaken, resentment and animosity against the migrant population ran high; the disenchantment, not just with parties, but with management, became manifest with industrial unrest (as we saw in Part One).

Against this background, a beleaguered and narrowly elected Conservative government under Heath enacted the 1971 Commonwealth Immigration Act which effectively ended all primary immigration from the New Commonwealth (that is, the admission of heads of households rather than dependants). Together with the race relations laws, it tapped out a coded message to blacks and Asians: we're doing all we can to ensure your right to exist legally as equal citizens in the UK; but, as our immigration laws make clear, we don't want any more of your kind here!

Under the 1971 Act, only those who qualified as 'patrials' did not need work permits to work or settle in the UK. The net balance of traffic over the next several years showed Australia, Canada and New Zealand as those countries where patrials were most likely to be found. A Treaty of Accession between the UK and the European Economic Community, also in 1971, allowed patrials the benefits of EEC member states. Patrials were not liable to deportation and enjoyed full civil and legal rights. This legislation coincided with the close of what Banton refers to as the 'liberal hour', when the tone of discussions was set by white liberals in positions of influence. Powell's decisive move in 1968 had precipitated a change in tone, and by 1971 the character of debates about race relations became totally illiberal.

Between 1972 and 1979 the neo-fascist organization known as the National Front gained infamy with its unashamedly racist platforms. It proposed an extraordinary theory of history according to which a vast Zionist conspiracy was at work, encouraging mass migration as a way of diluting the 'pure races', until a future arrived when only the Jews would retain the biological purity and could assume mastery over the world. The NF now called for an abrupt end to immigration and an involuntary repatriation of black and Asian residents of the UK, who were in any case only puppets of the Jews.

For the most part, the NF could not translate its notoriety into electoral support, although it had its moments. In 1974 it supplied sufficient general election candidates (ninety) to command television campaign slots; and in 1976, in combination with another extreme right-wing group, it took 44.5 per cent of the vote in a local council by-election in Deptford. It could also add to its achievements a creditable showing in a Stetchford, Birmingham, by-election in 1977, when it pushed the Liberals into fourth place. But the NF's electoral accomplishments perhaps disguise its genuine success, which came at street level, where it was able to mobilize large sections of working-class youth and powerfully motivate them to rally, protest, march, or just intimidate ethnic minorities. I have analysed this peculiar association between NF dogma and the 'skinhead mentality' in another book, *No Future* (1984); here I want to note the wave of racism that animated particular sections of the population in the 1970s.

The NF's message caricatured Powell's, and there were similarities in the events that underlay the rise of each. If Powell traded on the Kenyan Asians, the NF used the Asians of another African country, Malawi, with comparable effect. Early in 1976 a small number of Asians migrated to Britain from Malawi as a result of restrictive measures taken by the Malawi government. The Asians, who travelled to the UK as non-patrials but under quotas stipulated in the 1968 Act, were temporarily accommodated in hotels shortly after arrival, prompting newspaper headlines such as 'Scandal of £600-a-week Asians' and 'We want more, say the £600-a-week Asians'. The NF attracted most of its support in local elections at the time in those areas where it was anticipated the Malawi migrants would head: Leicester (where the NF averaged 16.1 per cent of the vote), the West Midlands (17.6 per cent) and parts of Yorkshire (10.9 per cent). Elsewhere, NF results were not so good; but, as Zig Layton-Henry points out: 'They showed how powerfully the media could inflame popular prejudices over coloured immigration and how, when those prejudices were aroused, quite large minorities of the electorate were prepared to vote for extreme right-wing candidates' (1984, p. 99).

A popular explanation for the sharp descent of the NF after 1979 was that its central imperative was adopted and incorporated into major party programmes. Even the urbane Jenkins, to whom so much was owed for his steadiness of liberal vision in the 1960s, saw in 1976 'a clear limit to the amount of immigration which this country can absorb'. There was a grisly complementarity between this and another remark made in the same year, this time by Kingsley Read, a one-time NF member, who, commending the racialist murder of Gurdip Singh Chaggar, said: 'One down, one million to go.' A much more celebrated political announcement came in 1978, a year before her election, when Margaret Thatcher spoke of the dangers of being 'swamped' by 'those coming in'.

The national character

The appointment of Thatcher as Prime Minister brought with it what Martin Barker has called 'the new racism', meaning that the political rhetoric and action of Conservative governments after 1979 were geared to the notion of a 'way of life' that was threatened by 'outsiders' (1981). This notion formed a sub-structure supporting many of the philosophies and actions of government over the following decade. Tory politician William (now Lord) Whitelaw had publicly introduced the notion, and Barker quotes him: 'We all know that the principles of the fair and tolerant society which we seek to uphold will be undermined if individual fears are allowed to grow' (1981, p. 13). No reference to racism here, of course, but a cloaked warning about limits. 'Many genuine people, entirely free from any racial prejudice, want reassurance,' Whitelaw continued.

The idea that there were genuine fears about losing a British way of life, Barker argues, worked as a bridge between apparently innocent descriptions of what was happening and a theory of race. Possessing a way of life, feeling it is under threat and wanting to defend it: on the surface, these sentiments contain no reference to racism; they have nothing to do with disliking foreigners or ethnic minorities, or discriminating against them. They do, however, have the potential to impose boundaries around 'us', the insiders, which also serve to keep out 'them', the outsiders, or at least those outsiders who are not prepared to work flat out at adopting the alleged 'way of life'. Barker's account was written before the Falklands War of 1981. This was an occasion for expanding the 'way of life' notion into a much grander affirmation of nationalism. 'The people of the Falkland Islands, like the people of the United Kingdom, are an island race,' Thatcher insisted. 'Their way of life is British.'

Whereas Barker sees the new racism making a break with what we might call the 'old racism' – which he never actually defines – Robert Miles sees much more continuity. The Conservative Party legitimated and incorporated racism as it was voiced 'in the bus queue and the workplace', but in a way that was not explicit, according to Miles (1987). It succeeded in this project by linking race to nation. Although Miles does not cite him, Reginald Horsman provides an historical analysis of the complex, jumbled 'hodgepodge of rampant, racial nationalism' and shows how biological notions have underpinned nationalist tendencies that have no obvious connections with biology. He quotes from the *Edinburgh Review* of January 1844: 'Of the great influence of Race in the production of National Character, no reasonable inquirer can now doubt' (1981, p. 60).

Miles believes that British politics has, in its own way, updated this type of argument. 'Racism is in the lining of nationalism,' he writes; it gives old ideas new meanings. The main old idea is race, and the new meanings are found in identity, culture and nationality. Three moments in the first reign of the New Right under Thatcher illustrate this. The first is the Falklands War itself, an occasion for buffing up anachronistic images of Britain as 'the nation that had built an empire and ruled a quarter of the world', as Thatcher described it in a successful attempt to revive a belligerent patriotism (quoted in Barnett, 1982, p. 150). In ruling a quarter of the world, imperial Britain also managed to enslave 15 million Africans and many more millions from South Asia, as well as completely wiping out vast portions of the Australian Aboriginal population. In recalling the age of imperial greatness, Thatcher brought into force the Falklands factor, which was to exert a sizeable influence on her election to a second term of office in 1983. The episode came 25 years after Suez and 45 years after the Second World War. This suggested to Anthony Sampson that 'older British values and attitudes were still lurking close to the surface, as if the war and empire had happened only yesterday' (1982, p. 431). Could the 'national consciousness' be likened to the human brain, he asked, 'divided between the fore-brain which can calculate and reason, and the primitive hind-brain which reacts only to simple stimuli and dangers? If so, the Falklands brought the old brain back to the forefront.' Barry Troyna and myself in *Introduction to Race Relations* (1983) stressed the resilience of the colonial mentality in the face of rational argument and measured debate; it has been an outlook quite beyond mere prejudice. The Falklands episode abroad added fresh substance to the colonial mentality at home, and the British sense of superiority was enhanced by the famous victory.

Nineteen eighty-one was a watershed year in more ways than one, as we will see. The Tory government had, in the preceding years, committed itself to a tough line on immigration, particularly in regard to secondary migration. The idea was to stop the flow of spouses and fiancés. The right of abode and settlement was available to citizens, who fell into three categories under the terms of the 1981 British Nationality Act. British citizens were those with close personal connections with the UK, having parents or grandparents born, adopted, naturalized, or registered as citizens. Citizens of British territories had their status by virtue of their own or their parents', or grandparents' residence in a dependency. British overseas citizens were those who did not fit into either of the above categories, who lived abroad in places like Malaysia and Hong Kong but had no close connection with the UK and could not pass on citizenship rights to their children.

Shadow Home Secretary Roy Hattersley opposed the Bill on the grounds that citizens of New Commonwealth origin whose children were born abroad might lose their automatic entitlement to citizenship. This would adversely affect many of his own Asian constituents in Birmingham who might have their children educated abroad. The residential qualification for marriage partners also posed problems for women who were waiting to enter the UK. He insisted that being born in the UK should properly entitle a person to citizenship automatically. The Bill underwent revision at its second reading, but basically it tightened up immigration control by creating hard-and-fast rules for citizenship. No reference was made to race or ethnic group, but the Bill aroused the anger of Asians who saw the consequences: geographically divided families who could not reunite because some members could not fulfil the new citizenship requirements.

Not surprisingly, the 1981 Act lost the government a great deal of confidence amongst ethnic minorities whose connections were with New Commonwealth countries. This was the cause of some concern because the ethnic vote was becoming an increasingly important one; turn-out improved with every general election, and at the 1981 Greater London Council elections Asian and Afro-Caribbean votes were exceptional and therefore contributory to the Labour win. The government's response in the 1983 general election campaign was to run a now-famous advertising poster featuring a young black man, arms folded, legs akimbo, dressed in a business suit. 'Labour says he's black. Tories say he's British', read the copy. Again, nationalism was being hammered out. As with the 1981 Act, which was intended as the final word concerning who was and who was not British, the campaign drove home the nationalist message. Ethnic background, skin colour, culture – none of these were relevant in the 1980s; what *was* relevant was national identity. In other words, as Layton-Henry detected, the assumption was 'that New Commonwealth Immigration is largely over and that the crucial issues concern the integration of the second and third generations and the need to forge new bases of loyalty and legitimacy to integrate black Britons' (1984, p. xv). My disagreement with this verdict is over the term 'integration', which seems inappropriate. More accurate would be 'assimilation', since the campaign, with its visual of a young black executive, suggests very strongly that ethnic minorities should discard their ethnic character, forget their culture and all the distinguishing features that have vivified their communities and become an upwardly mobile part of the British nation. Being British, in this rendition, is instead of, not as well as, being an ethnic group member. Acquisition involves loss.

This was known as the 'colour-blind' approach in the 1960s. The advertisement's text captured it perfectly: 'With the Conservatives, there are no "blacks", no "whites", just people'. One might be tempted to reply that there manifestly *are* blacks and whites, who want to be recognized as such without necessarily inviting conflict. It went on: 'the British

Nationality Act . . . gives full and equal citizenship to everyone permanently settled in Britain'. The divisive implications of this for many families are obvious.

The Falklands, the passing of the 1981 Act, the 1983 poster campaign: three moments in the early 1980s, each an occasion to elevate a strong, muscular conception of nationality and nationalism, each chock-full with unspoken racism. The major absence in all of these events was any hint of the possibility of diversity; nationalism was a transcendent force, thundering over all other interests, perhaps even destroying them. Thatcher's government considered the endless factious debates of the 1960s and 1970s tiresome. The 1980s were to be a time for the stiffening of backbones. 'Our people, our race' were under threat from Argentinians, from the descendants of populations over which Britain once ruled and from those who saw blacks as 'blacks' and not 'people'. Almost every issue, not only those concerning ethnic minorities, was keyed to the idea of nation, itself obscurely wrapped around the concept of an 'island race'. How close this seems to the 1949 Royal Commission's reference to migrants 'of good stock' who were welcomed as settlers only if they 'merged into' the host population (quoted in Miles and Phizacklea, 1984, p. 24).

Government policy moved swiftly through its liberal hour, when laws were enacted and agencies created, and into a chastening and unyielding period. Despised and ridiculed as the race relations industry, as it is called, has been, at least it had the advantage of being created to solve the problem of integrating an ethnically diverse population. With the ascendancy of reactionary over liberal approaches, the preferred goal became to absorb all groups within the single, homogeneous nation; diversity was not to be tolerated any more than necessary.

No one seriously doubts that what goes on at the level of government policy has some impact on how race relations are experienced at street level. Policy since the war has been marred by an unwillingness to accept the desirability of New Commonwealth migrants and their offspring. Anti-discrimination legislation has established a framework as a way of control, or influence, behaviour and to protect the best interests of ethnic minorities. But much of its effect has been undermined by a set of immigration controls that have sent a very different message both to minorities and to the white majority. We will shortly look at how those messages were interpreted and what responses they gave rise to. But, next, we must answer some questions about the effects of racial discrimination since the war and about the reasons for its persistence.

CHAPTER 6

Making sense of racism

Immobility

It is 1950 and you are invited to offer a forecast on the future of race relations in Britain. Figures suggest that migration from the Caribbean and South Asia is rising. Your immediate reaction might be to look for precedents. Over the centuries, the British Isles have accommodated all manner of persecuted refugees, religious minority groups and an assortment of settlers, including Huguenots, Flems, Jews and Irish. All have been successfully assimilated or 'absorbed' into the mainstream culture and have become socially indistinguishable. On this evidence, it might have been plausible to speculate on a further assimilation, blacks and South Asians being progressively accepted by British society and, in time, being able to make inroads economically, socially, even politically. This would have been a somewhat roseate view. The reality turned out to be much grimmer. The presence of blacks and South Asians in the UK was not at all marked by their progress, but by their lack of it. There have been three main features of the UK's black and South Asian population: social and geographical immobility; educational underachievement; and dislocation from the criminal justice and political systems. In this chapter we will examine each of these, closing with an explanation of why the features have proved so resistant to change.

New Commonwealth migrants in the late 1940s and early 1950s quite naturally settled in areas where there were prospects of work. The South-east and the Midlands were metal-manufacturing centres, and northern cities had textile industries. Ports like Cardiff housed sizeable populations of migrant seamen who had settled in the UK after the war. At the onset of the postwar migration, the settlement patterns accurately reflected the job opportunities available to migrant workers, who were clearly hopeful of a lucrative stay in Britain, possibly followed by a return to their country of origin – as many studies of the time indicate. The pattern was fixed for the next forty-odd years; 56 per cent of the black and Asian population remained in London and the South-east; 23 per cent in Birmingham and the Midlands; 16 per cent in the cities of the North and North-west; and 4 per cent in South Wales and the South-west. There was virtually no dispersal of the migrant population, and even within this pattern there were further concentrations: for example, in the Brent and Haringey areas of Greater London, and Handsworth and Wolverhampton in the West Midlands, where well over one-third of the population were New Commonwealth born or descended. A Department of the Environment report showed in 1976 that 10 per cent of the census enumeration districts housed 70 per cent of the black and Asian population; in these districts, migrants comprised 20 per cent of the population. By contrast, some areas were virtually untouched by migrants: vast portions of East Anglia, Mid-Wales and the north-east of England. So, although the New Commonwealth population remained a numerically small (if growing) minority, its presence was made apparent by its visible concentrations in particular areas of the country.

During early phases of settlement, migrants were forced by circumstances to find accommodation in some of the least salubrious parts of the cities, 'zones of transition', as Rex and Moore called them in their study of Sparkbrook, Birmingham (1981). Sparkbrook became a kind of model for other inner-city areas where migrants, with no access to council accommodation, crowded into deteriorating nineteenth-century lodging houses, many of which had been condemned as unfit for occupation. The migrants lived in such circumstances primarily because they could not afford much better, but also because of discrimination in the housing market, because whites refused to sell or lease to 'coloureds', or because of 'redlining' (building societies' policy not to allow mortgagers properties in some areas). There is also what might be called the comfort factor: migrants huddled together to assemble a type of social support system.

Forty years on and matters had, as one might expect, improved. More Caribbeans were eligible for council housing, and, by the 1980s, over 45 per cent occupied local authority accommodation. Asians too qualified for housing lists, of course, though the trend was for them to buy houses and flats; their use of council housing was only a third of the national average of 30 per cent.

Yet the actual distribution of blacks and Asians in the housing sector reveals only part of the picture, because, as a Runnymede Trust publication stressed: 'It is clear from a number of studies that West Indian and Asian people tend to live in lower standard housing than the rest of the population' (1980, p. 73). Part of the Trust's argument centred on access to three basic amenities: a fixed bath or shower, plumbed hot water and an inside toilet. 'A greater proportion of black [and Asian] people live in housing with poor amenities than white people,' the Trust concluded (1980, p. 73). More multi-occupation of dwellings was found amongst black and Asian families. The proportion of overcrowded households was also greater for blacks and Asians than for whites.

For the moment, I am not concerned with the mechanisms which brought this situation about, merely with the geographical profile and housing conditions of blacks and Asians in modern Britain. Basically, the UK was highly segregated in the 1950s, with migrants and their offspring residing in very specific regions of the country; all available modern surveys point to stasis – the segregated pattern remained. Home ownership increased amongst South Asians, while Caribbeans became predominantly council tenants. Although there were visible exceptions to the rule – for example, Asians living in suburban middle-class areas – research in the 1980s indicated that migrant families generally occupied poorer-quality housing than their white counterparts, even allowing for the fact that overall 'there has been a change for the better', as the Policy Studies Institute (PSI) recorded (Brown, 1984, p. 68).

Where you live depends largely on what you can afford, and what you can afford depends on what work you do. Proximity is also a factor: nearness to work means less time and money to spend on travelling to and fro. Migrants, in the postwar years, headed for the areas most fertile in job opportunities and readily took the work most available. Many became engaged in the heavy manufacturing and textile industries. Frequently, they were prepared to become what were, effectively, ancillary workers, tending to occupy the positions not wanted – or, indeed, needed – by local whites, who were prospering from the job market's widening choices. As industry prospered and expanded, whites were able to step up, leaving the new arrivals to take the left-over jobs, which were mostly undesirable, low-paying and with few chances of occupational advancement. After the 1950s there were many modifications in the employment of migrants and their offspring, but by and large they stayed rooted in the least desired, unskilled, manual positions or, as was increasingly the case in the 1980s, out of work entirely.

Having been recruited originally to plug holes in the job market, black and Asian workers might not have been expected to stay fixed at what Douglas Glasgow calls 'the cellar level', in 'menial, low-level, manual jobs' or 'a somewhat higher category of unskilled employment' (1980, p. 77). In fact, they did not lift themselves – or, more accurately, were not allowed to lift themselves – too far away from the cellar level. Asians, in particular, as Ralph Fevre's study shows, were all but locked into the textile industry's undesirable positions (1984). Fevre's quantitative analysis of West Yorkshire's woollen industry plots the course of Asian workers' progress since the war. Arriving as 'cheap labour', they came to constitute the majority (up to 65 per cent) of the industry's workforce; as many as one in four of Bradford's Asian workers, as against one in ten of all workers, were employed in wool textiles at the end of the 1970s. Large numbers of them worked nightshifts at low hourly rates of pay. The general conclusion was that the position of Asians in the northern wool textile industry had not improved significantly since the days when they were first drawn to the UK, and that their alternatives to this type of work were limited.

Fevre's study is not intended as a microcosmic view of the general situation, but there have been many other surveys of the employment position of blacks and Asians that reveal similarities. The volume edited by Braham, Rhodes and Pearn in 1981 concentrated on 'the experience of black workers' and it collected a number of articles, all of which emphasized the difference between 'the pattern of black [and Asian] employment and that of the British population as a whole, and the extent to which black [and Asian] workers remain concentrated in the type of unskilled and semi-skilled jobs for which they were initially recruited in the 1950s and 1960s' (1981, p. 92). In the 1980s the vast majority of former New Commonwealth workers found themselves in low-status, unskilled positions in the textile and clothing industries, engineering and foundry works, hotels, hospitals and transport services.

Although it should be treated with the caution customarily reserved for across-the-board statistics, the median figure for white males' weekly earnings in the 1980s was about £20 higher than for black males and £18 higher for the Asian males. White women tended to earn £4 more than Asian women, but usually £3 less than black women. 'On average, white men earn substantially more than black men, whereas there is little difference in the case of women,' reported the PSI (Brown, 1984, p. 167).

Two sets of factors have threatened to break up the employment patterns. The first is the effort of many minority group members to become either self-employed or business owners. This is especially marked amongst Asians. There is nothing unusual about this, of course: Jewish minorities have built an entire tradition of entrepreneurship out of being excluded. Pushed out of the main areas of work by hostile, prejudiced employers, they simply began working off their own initiative. Chinese minorities in both the UK and USA have done similarly, acquiring for themselves a reputation as 'middleman minorities'. Ownership of a business enhances people's sense of independence and self-esteem and has been an obvious goal for minority groups, especially those disparaged by the majority of society.

After the influx of Asians from Kenya (in 1968) and Uganda (in 1972), Asian-owned businesses seemed to spring up in virtually every city where migrants had first settled. Rags-to-riches stories of dispossessed Indians, ejected by Idi Amin, clawing their way back to prosperity in the new land of opportunity were commonplace. But the commercial success of Asians was more image than reality. Certainly, there was a rapid rise in Asian-owned small businesses in the early 1970s, and by 1982 about 18 per cent of Asian men and 14 per cent of Asian women were self-employed. Most such businesses remained small and vulnerable to changes in the market – more like *My Beautiful Laundrette* than the Murjani jeans company. In a sense, Asian businesses were not dissimilar to other forms of migrant work. Asian shops, for instance, were generally opened up in those inner-city areas vacated by whites; their growth was not seen as a threat to white retailers, but rather as a continuation of Asians' role as replacement labour. Asian-owned enterprises were concentrated almost entirely within specific communities, giving rise to a sort of commercial segregation. This restricted the scope for expansion and made it difficult for them to penetrate bigger markets. Writing to *New Society* in 1978, researcher John Cater reported: 'Just as Asians are restricted to residual residential space in provincial cities, they are predominantly restricted to economic opportunities voluntarily relinquished by the host community' (9 March 1978, p. 565).

Evidence on the efforts of Asian and, to a much more limited extent, black businesses (about 7 per cent of black men were self-employed in the mid-1980s) was collected by Ward and

Jenkins (1985). Their general conclusion was that in the 1980s, despite the illusion of great success, Asian businesses were marginal, relying on a limited, segregated market. In addition, because they have been predominantly secondary rather than primary producers (that is, outside sectors such as heavy manufacturing, car making and oil production), Asian entrepreneurs have had only a reduced chance of expansion and little exporting potential. Despite this, in the 1980s an increasing number of blacks and Asians were generating their own employment opportunities, perhaps as much out of necessity as choice. Unemployment was often the only alternative. The 'alternative economic system', as Braham, Rhodes and Pearn call it, provided employment for only a minority, however, and the majority continued to seek work in 'the "majority" economy, with all that implies' (1981, p. 95).

By the latter part of the 1980s vast numbers of blacks and Asians were affected by unemployment. For a variety of reasons, migrants and their children have been more susceptible than the population as a whole to the effects of economic recession or decline. When unemployment rates shot up, blacks and Asians were the first to be affected. In 1974 the unemployment rate for both white and minority groups was around 4 per cent, although there were statistics showing that young black people and black women suffered slightly more. By 1982, when the PSI conducted its third major national survey, the white unemployment rate had risen to 13 per cent for men and 10 per cent for women, while for blacks the equivalent rates had risen to 24 and 16 per cent respectively, and for Asians 20 per cent for both. 'The survey shows that the rate of unemployment among black people at this time of very high general unemployment is much higher than among white people: about twice as high among West Indians and about one-and-a-half times as high among Asians,' the report's author, Colin Brown, concluded (1984, p. 174).

For school-leavers, the chances of finding a job, irrespective of background, were uniformly bleak after the onset of the Thatcher administration in 1979. For young people of Caribbean and South Asian origin, the position was especially dire. Unemployment struck hardest in particular regions, mostly inner-city areas. Malcolm Cross and his research team reported on Birmingham, where in the 1980–1 period registered unemployment amongst black youths rose at twice the rate for young people in the city as a whole (Cross, Edmonds and Sargeant, 1982, p. 3). In the Brixton area of London, in the year following the 1981 riots, unemployment amongst young blacks aged 19–24 rose by 71 per cent (*Sunday Times*, 4 April 1982). Bradford, a centre of dense Asian concentration, was surveyed by Campbell and Jones, who recorded 72 per cent of South Asian youths without jobs twelve months after leaving school; this compared with 31 per cent of school-leavers as a whole in the city (1982, p. 51). If we translate these local patterns into national trends, the unequal effect of youth unemployment is revealed. As the CRE observed: 'The overall change among the unemployed aged under 18 in Britain for the 12 months to January 1980 was a *reduction* of 2.4%; the *increase* among ethnic minorities was 7.3%' (1980, p. 14).

In 1983 the Youth Training Scheme (YTS) replaced the Youth Opportunities Programme (YOP), itself a response to the problems posed by the lack of work opportunities for young people. After a year of operation, the National Youth Bureau investigated YTS and discovered that employers were using the scheme as a probationary period for trainees (1986). Effectively, the chances of a black teenager getting a job were dependent on landing a YTS place with a potential future employer. But, the Bureau reported, this was precisely the type of place young black and Asian people could not secure. Young blacks tended to end up on Mode B schemes, based in skill centres or community projects, rather than the more desirable Mode A schemes. The Bureau's research showed that, in outer Birmingham, only 2 per cent of white trainees at the craft and technical level were on Mode B schemes in 1984, whereas 8 per cent of blacks were. At the semi-skilled and remedial level, 13 per cent of white trainees were on Mode B compared with 27 per cent of blacks. In the inner city, the disparity was more marked; 10 per cent of white trainees and 32 per cent of blacks were on Mode B.

The Bureau's report drew on research from elsewhere in the country, highlighting particularly how even a high level of qualification (especially amongst Asian females) was often not enough to get a young minority person a job in a Mode A position. Young blacks and Asians were often treated as if they had 'special needs', the report concluded, adding that the only 'special need' they had was to be judged by their qualifications, skill and aptitude, rather than by their skin colour. The research confirmed the findings of many other investigations into the transition from school to work. Studies by, amongst others, Hubbuck and Carter (1980), Lee and Wrench (1981), Jenkins (1982) and Troyna and Smith (1983) all found that colour had a powerful impact on the chances of success in the search for a job. Its impact, the surveys found, was independent of the educational qualifications of candidates. A separate body of research found that black schoolchildren were achieving less than their counterparts. Such results might have been dismissed as due to language difficulties in the 1950s and 1960s, but by the 1970s the issue was of sufficient importance to form the focus of a government inquiry.

Halal meat and fish fingers

In 1975 Alan Little published the results of a London-based research project, which revealed poor performances of black primary school pupils in all areas of the curriculum. Two years later, a government White Paper reaffirmed this and recommended the setting up of a special committee to look into the education of ethnic-minority groups, with particular reference to Caribbean children. In 1981 the interim report of the committee, under the chairmanship first of Anthony Rampton and later Lord Swann, provided even more conclusive evidence of the 'underachievement' of black children. For example, only 3 per cent of black school-leavers obtained five or more higher grades (A–C) in GCE O-level and CSE examinations, compared with 18 per cent of Asian and 16 per cent of other leavers. There was a similar trend in the pattern of A-level results; 2 per cent of black pupils gained one or more A-level passes, 13 per cent of Asians and 12 per cent of others. These data supported a growing number of isolated studies on black educational achievement. Sally Tomlinson reviewed 33 such studies and found 26 to show black children scoring lower than whites in tests and examinations or being over-represented in schools for educationally subnormal (ESN) pupils (1980). The final report from Rampton was published in 1985 and 'officially' recognized what academic studies had been pointing to: black children as a group consistently achieved less at school than their peers. The findings, combined with the results of work on job searches, suggest that in the late 1980s young Asian males – but not females – tended to be as well qualified educationally as whites but, because of difficulties securing positions with training programmes, less qualified vocationally. Asian females had fewer qualifications than white females. West Indian youths held less educational and vocational qualifications.

Multicultural education (Mce) represented an attempt to break this cycle of underachievement. By the 1970s the adequacy of education itself was in question. Mce subsumed a variety of beliefs, policies and practices, all geared to broadening the content of curricula and the awareness of teachers. My own research indicated that, despite a virtual unanimity amongst local education authorities on the desirability of Mce programmes, only a minority had put them into practice by 1987. The resistance to educational change came from various sources, and three incidents in the 1980s highlight some of them.

The views of Bradford headteacher Ray Honeyford propelled him into what almost turned into a crusade against Mce. He expressed his views in the *Salisbury Review*, a right-wing magazine, in 1983 and 1984. Basically, they were that the poor school performance of blacks was a result of family background and of the teachings of 'left-wing political extremists' and 'well-meaning liberals and clergymen suffering from a rapidly dating post-Imperial guilt' (1983). He resisted the introduction of Mce at his school, which had a majority Asian enrolment. Parents protested, stopping their children from attending the school and eventually forcing Honeyford's resignation.

Parents also withdrew their children from another school, again in Yorkshire, this time in 1987, but their motives were very different. At Dewsbury parents boycotted another school with a predominantly Asian roll. Rumours circulated that Muslim and Hindu festivals were celebrated, the standard of English was low, and halal meat was served for lunch. It so happened that the school was Church of England, held Christian assemblies, had a traditional curriculum, used only English and included such delicacies as fish fingers and steamed pudding on its lunch menus. Most of the parents involved in the boycott were white and knew little of the school, apart from the fact that it was 83 per cent Asian. But this was sufficient for them to want their children transferred to a nearby school without such a large Asian population. The situation was tailor-made for supporters of separate schools – Muslim, Hindu, Orthodox, Jewish, etc. Honeyford had recommended these, and his view found support in the Bradford-based Muslim Parents' Association. Both, in their incongruous ways, opposed integration and attempts to approach this via education.

There were those who regarded the London borough of Brent as a serious enemy of integration because of its anti-racist education, which equipped pupils with a knowledge of such weighty issues as power and racism. In June 1986 Adrian Parsons, the director of education, unexpectedly resigned amidst controversy over Brent's alleged 'positive discrimination' in trying to fill key posts with ethnic-minority personnel. Later that year Maureen McGoldrick, a primary schoolteacher, was suspended after allegedly stating in a telephone conversation that she did not want any more black teachers at her school. A governors' inquiry cleared her, though this failed to satisfy many, including the Black Teachers' Collective. The case crystallized tensions in Labour-controlled Brent. Some accused the council of extremism in scapegoating McGoldrick, while others believed she represented a racist presence that undermined educational progress. All these cases show the kind of brick walls changes in education have been likely to run into.

In the three major areas of housing, employment and education, blacks and Asians were immobilized despite over forty years of 'progress'. We might add to this some related observations. Blacks are two or three times more likely than whites to be committed to a psychiatric hospital under the Mental Health Act, for example. Less measurable than this, but no less real, is the problem facing aspiring black capitalists, who have enormous difficulties in securing loans to finance their ventures. (Asians have gone as far as creating their own ethnic credit unions.) The Roman Catholic Church's response to some of these issues was attacked by its own advisory group, which accused the church of militating against the interests of its black members in a 1986 report entitled *With You in Spirit?*.

Imaginary equations

Ruptured with ethnic inequality as most areas of society were in the 1980s, there were still those who maintained that the criminal justice system operated autonomously and impartially and remained unaffected by the kinds of racist influence that seemed to abound elsewhere. Sceptics had for many years suspected that black people, especially black youngsters, were treated more harshly than their white counterparts when they either broke the law or were suspected of breaking the law. The repeal of the 1824 Vagrancy Act, or 'sus' law, in 1981 was accompanied by intense debate, most of it centring on the extent to which blacks were arrested and convicted under this Act. In Lambeth, where the Act was frequently invoked, about 75 per cent of those arrested during the 1977–9 period were black, according to George Greaves (1984, p. 66). This was an exceptionally high figure, and Brian Roberts' more general analysis indicates that blacks usually constituted between 40 and 47 per cent of 'sus' arrests, still a high figure considering their proportion of the total population – less than 2 per cent (1982, p. 103). The controversy over 'sus' was primarily over the use of the law as a means of persecuting young blacks. The law's replacement did not, according to official figures, reduce the sizeable numbers of blacks stopped, arrested and convicted. In 1985 the PSI published the results of a five-year research programme which had been initiated by the Metropolitan Police. Part of the report's findings were that, whereas about 6 per cent of London's population 'look black', blacks (not Asians) represented 20 per cent of people apprehended by police officers (Smith and Gray, 1985, p. 389).

Virtually every fresh set of statistics in the 1980s revealed that blacks were hugely over-represented in street crime and criminal attempts. Interpreting the trends is not the immediate concern; the reader must set them in the context of the surrounding chapters. Suffice it to say that, while some commentators simply accept that blacks are more prone to engage in crime, others try to explain this by reference to the poverty and unemployment that beset the black community, and still others believe that black youths are subjected to more intense levels of surveillance and are falsely attributed with criminality by the police. Whatever the reasons, the crime figures show blacks as persistent offenders.

John Pitts reviewed some of the evidence, finding it questionable (1986). He quotes Scotland Yard's assistant commissioner's figures for 1982: 18,763 robberies, 10,399 committed by 'coloured assailants'. In bringing together the research, Pitts is able to conclude that blacks – for many reasons, including racialism – are given extra attention by the police, and this in itself generates further offences (sweeps and stops, for example, prompting street confrontations). Black defendants in crown court were two to three times more likely to receive custodial sentences than whites. Blacks were substantially less likely to be offered the option of probation than whites, nor were they very likely to find their way through the system to intermediate treatment. 'The disadvantages they confront are cumulative, and when they fall foul of the juvenile criminal justice system, these disadvantages appear to accelerate their progress towards the correctional institution or the prison', writes Pitts (1986, p. 141). This process carries on. Black youths represent about 3 per cent of the prison population, even though they are only 0.7 per cent of the overall 15–19-year-old population (that is, their presence in prison is over 4 times larger than chance). The figures seep into the 'common sense' of personnel in the criminal justice system, who formulate what Steven Box, in his *Recession, Crime and Punishment*, calls 'imaginary equations': 'black = crime' and 'unemployment = lazy = black' are two of Box's examples (1987, p. 167). After this point, the control net is widened, and more blacks are trawled in, thus maximizing their chances of winding up behind bars.

If blacks as offenders command the attentions of the police, as victims they do not. The PSI reported a 'reluctance' of police to act energetically in investigating racialist attacks; and, of course, blacks and Asians were much more likely to be victims of such assaults than any other groups. Stories surfaced that victims of attacks were not only ignored by police but also badly dealt with by housing authorities when they tried to obtain transfers. In one case in South London in 1986, Southwark Council set up a top-level inquiry into the reasons for the delay in processing the transfer request of an Asian family who had been intimidated. Even after the tenant's wife had been raped, the authority was needlessly slow in considering the issue (*New Society*, 31 October 1986).

These and other issues led, not surprisingly, to the opening of an ethnic divide in criminal justice, with black youth in particular seeming to be severely dealt with by the system. One police response was to mount recruitment campaigns in inner-city areas, although in 1987 black and Asian police officers were still few and far between in the force; it was as if the police were trying to entice minorities to join an institution which the latter believed was, in many senses, their antagonist.

The same could be argued of the British political system. Blacks and Asians have tended since the war to eschew their legal right to participate fully in politics. Actual numbers of black and Asian voters have increased, but the percentage turn-out prior to the 1987 general election was, as Muhammad Anwar's study shows, rather poor, dropping as low as 13 per cent for Asians in some areas (1986). Major attempts to mobilize the ethnic electorate have had little success, perhaps suggesting a lack of commitment to the political system as a whole and to parliamentary candidates as individuals. There have been a number of parliamentary candidates from ethnic backgrounds, most of whom stood for the main political parties, others who have stood as independents. In 1924, Shapurji Sakatvala was elected as Communist MP for Battersea North, London. After his success, there were no more until 1987 when four ethnic MPs were elected.

I opened this chapter by quoting a Seamen's Union official who wanted blacks excluded from work in areas covered by his union. His exhortation to keep blacks off British ships might be accounted for by blind prejudice. It was, after all, 1948, and the prospect of a sharp rise in the number of 'coloured' seamen could have caused some initial alarm. Forty years later the same kind of reaction is more difficult to explain. True, no one in the 1980s was campaigning for special treatment for whites; they would have been liable to prosecution under the various race relations Acts of the 1960s and 1970s. But the actual practice of exclusion had still not disappeared. As the various studies cited in this chapter have shown, blacks and Asians lived in worse-quality housing in less desirable areas and with different systems of tenure to whites. They worked, in the main, in unskilled or semi-skilled manual jobs in very specific sectors of industry and on average earned less than whites. No doubt this prompted many Asians from the 1970s to initiate their own enterprises, which for the most part have remained small-scale. Unemployment hit the entire population, but it hit hardest at blacks and Asians, especially school-leavers of Caribbean descent; in many areas of the country where there were large black communities, such as Handsworth and Lambeth, young job hunters out-numbered job vacancies by as much as forty to one. When they managed to escape the dole queues by getting placed on YTS programmes, black and Asian youths tended to get stuck on the Mode B schemes which carried little hope of a permanent job. At school, the picture appeared rather promising for Asian children, who performed comparably with their white peers, but horrifying for black children, who consistently achieved little of significance academically. There have been substantial demographic changes in the black and Asian population, but such changes have not been accompanied by anything resembling corresponding material improvements. If anything, it could be argued that some sections of the black population, the 16–24 age group for instance, are actually worse off than their counterparts of thirty or forty years ago.

The purpose of this section has been to provide a descriptive profile of the black and Asian population's position in modern Britain. The more analytical question remains: why have they not made progress? Is it because they have not been allowed to, or because they have not been motivated to? There have been an assortment of answers to this, one of them captured cruelly but with the ring of authenticity by writer Andrea Dunbar in the 1987 movie *Rita, Sue and Bob Too*. 'I can't help being a Paki,' says Sue's Asian boyfriend to her drunken father, who counters with tinpot reasoning: 'Yes, you fucking well can!' We will probe the sources of this insidious logic in the final section of this chapter.

Logic of racism

There is a misleadingly simple answer to the question of why blacks and Asians continue to sit on the disadvantaged side of Britain's ethnic divide: *racism*. One word, a frequently misused one at that, disguises a perplexing series of social, psychological and, some would insist, biological processes that combine to produce firm-set divisions. Few people disagree about the consequences of racism; the previous section has covered merely a few instances of them. In the British experience, blacks and Asians, despite their efforts, continued to labour with an inferior status to whites in all the main areas of society. Quite often politicians have placed the burden of responsibility for inferior status on the alleged inadequacies, disabilities or motivations of the victims. Social scientists, by contrast, have reversed the search for the causes of racial inequality and found possible answers in historical and social factors.

The issue of racial inequality and the conflict it invariably fostered were by no means confined to Britain in the postwar period. In Nazi Germany, Jews were labelled an inferior race and subjected to genocide. Black–white relations in the USA were a persistent source of turbulence eighty years after the abolition of slavery. A complete separation of whites and 'non-whites' was legally enshrined in South Africa's constitution in 1948 with apartheid.

Various United Nations organizations, particularly Unesco, began to take an interest in the problem of racial inequality and conflict after the war, seeking the counsel of biological and social scientists. Central to Unesco's concerns was the bedevilling concept of race. After 1950, it issued a series of statements, the main thrust of which was that the concept itself had extremely limited analytical value in explaining the causes of inequality and conflict. Race was more akin to a myth than a scientific fact, Unesco argued. It rejected the attempt to classify human populations according to hereditary, physical characteristics; race had no scientific validity. All the world's population were descended ultimately from common stock, and what biological differences there were could be attributed to evolutionary and environmental influences and not permanent, fixed traits. In other words, what are popularly regarded as racial differences are, at source, environmental and therefore cultural differences.

While the race concept may have been regarded as redundant as a tool of science, it was not nearly as readily discarded in the popular imagination. The belief that the world's human population is divisible into discrete biological categories called races and ranked in some hierarchical system persisted long after Unesco had tried to undermine it. Racism was elaborated into a set of meanings and evaluations about groups labelled races and usually regarded as inferior. The classic racist strategy was then to create conditions under which the labelled group – for instance, blacks, Asians, or Jews – could do little else but act out the roles defined for it by the racist.

The biological interpretation of race had been under fire from US academics for some years before Unesco's pronouncements. Three influential postwar studies had offered theories to explain 'racial conflict' without resort to biological criteria. Before the war, the Swedish academic Gunnar Myrdal had been commissioned to conduct a research project, the results of which were published in 1944. Rejecting biological ideas about the inevitability of conflict, Myrdal predicted, somewhat optimistically, that there would be change, but it would be slow and painstaking and involve bringing the treatment of blacks in line with the ideals of the US republic. In this way, society would move out of what Myrdal described in the title of his 1,300-page tome as *An American Dilemma*: the discrepancy between society's libertarian ideals of freedom and equality for all and its manifestly unequal treatment of blacks (1944). The contradiction between theory and practice was, in essence, the dynamic or motive force of racial conflict. Myrdal built on an earlier analysis of black–white relations using the metaphor of the caste system, whites and blacks being sealed into two ascribed castes.

Another offering, in effect a critique of Myrdal, was by O. C. Cox, who regarded racism as a capitalist device to divide the US working class. It was convenient for the bourgeoisie to sit back and let members of the working class fight amongst themselves over what were basically non-issues. While working-class blacks and whites were busy venting their hostility on each other, they were too preoccupied to challenge the class that was their genuine enemy. So racism consumed working-class energies and deflected anger away from the capitalists. Racism was an epiphenomenon of economic relations, that is, a secondary symptom of capitalism, and not a cause of conflict. The conclusion to the 'race problem' would be found, according to Cox, in the transition to a classless society (1948).

Many others disagreed with Cox's view that only wholesale social changes would lead to the dissolution of racism. In principle at least, the work of Theodor Adorno and his colleagues pointed to a way in which psychological factors could eliminate prejudice. Hostile beliefs and attitudes against certain groups are held because they fulfil personality needs, argued Adorno *et al.* (1950). People with an 'authoritarian personality' would not only tend to be prejudiced against 'outgroups'; they were also likely to be obedient towards authority and hold inaccurate stereotype images of others which were *idées reçues*, accepted ideas rather than products of first-hand experience. Adorno *et al.* traced the origins of this personality type and prejudice to childhood experiences in highly disciplinarian families. As a child, the possessor of the eventual authoritarian personality would be insecure, dependent and respectful of parents. In adulthood, his or her hostility would be directed against a range of minority groups, including Catholics.

This research into the 'authoritarian personality' provided a new way of understanding the conflict that was, at that time, affecting the US South. If conflict was not the inevitable outcome of natural propensities, then, theoretically at least, it could be modified. The problem in locating the cause of the phenomenon in a particular personality type was that this did not help identify exactly what needed to be changed in order to reduce conflict, apart from family circumstances.

After the publication of the study's conclusions in the 1950s, social scientists tended to move the emphasis away from unconscious childhood conflicts towards pressures and influences in the social context. This kind of approach seemed highly suited to the British experience of the period. People, it was thought, picked up prejudices against 'outgroups' from others with whom they identified. These others could have been parents or peers; either way, the individual felt a pressure to conform with the standards of others. So, if a person grew up in an environment in which all those unfamiliar people with black skin – the 'dark strangers', as Sheila Patterson described them in 1963 – were considered uncivilized and believed to eat cat food, then he or she would feel pressure to align prejudices to conform with the generalization. This worked independently of any available factual information or direct experience. The comforting aspect of this perspective, at least from a policymaker's view, was that, in time, prejudices would break down as whites interacted more frequently with blacks and Asians and come to realize that their prejudices were exactly what the name implies: opinions formed prior to experience, based on false or incomplete information. People would divest themselves of prejudice and in future base their relationships on first-hand knowledge of others.

Working in tandem with this would be an assimilation process. Migrants would bring their own customs, values, beliefs and life-styles with them; but they would gradually discard many of them, becoming similar to the 'host' community. British society, it was thought, would absorb the newcomers in much the same way as US society would, as a 'melting pot' in which groups pooled their distinctive characteristics to produce a new amalgam. The prevalent view of the postwar period was that migrant groups would mix and eventually resemble whites. Assimilation, where it does occur, is rarely a matter of choice, and the pressures on migrants to fashion their cultures to suit the new environment have been rather similar to those that incline the bigot to prejudice: the threat of sanction. What redefinition there was on behalf of minority groups was largely a response to racism, or, more accurately, racialism – the action.

On both sides of the Atlantic, events shook the credibility of the assimilation theory. Ethnic minorities that were considered, certainly by many US academics, to be disappearing into the melting pot began to stress their heritage and an ethnic revival

[125]

spread throughout the USA. Blacks, chicanos, Puerto Ricans, Asians and native American Indians were amongst the most evident ethnic minorities. In particular, in the 1960s blacks used ethnic affiliation, in their case African roots, to promote mass violent action. There was no equivalent violence in the UK, but the signs were that migrant groups were not enthusiastically dropping their cultures and becoming as 'British' as their passports indicated. Nor were whites revising their original prejudices. Job advertisements stating 'vacancy – whites only need apply' were quite commonplace in the late 1950s. The UK counterpart to Myrdal's study was *Colour and Citizenship*, commissioned in 1962 and published in 1969. The report stayed with the 'dilemma' problematic but included the observation that Britain's problem lay with a small minority of authoritarian personality types who were intensely prejudiced. When measured against later research, its finding that most of the white population were 'tolerantly inclined' reveals its staggering limitations.

If Cox's theory found little favour when first published in 1948, it gained relevance in the UK after the 1958 disturbances in which whites, anxious about the increasing number of New Commonwealth migrants entering the country and the decreasing number of jobs available after the postwar boom, began a series of physical assaults on visibly different 'outsiders'. Psychologists influenced by the 'authoritarian personality' school had warned of scapegoating, the mechanism through which people shift the responsibility for their personal misfortunes and frustrations onto other, frequently defenceless groups. Historically, Jews and blacks have been popular scapegoats, shouldering the blame for almost everything from the economic decline of whole societies to the escalation of crime rates, whilst in reality having little or nothing to do with them. Cox, in keeping his focus on economic relations, could explain the scapegoating by reference, as always, to the connivance of capitalism. Instead of seeking solutions to their problems, in this case job scarcity, in the wider economic system where they really lay, white members of the working class grasped at immediate and tangible symbols of their anxiety. If there were, say, one million people out of work and an equal number of migrants in Britain, then a simple equation could be created. The way in which the propositions followed the premiss might have been flawed in terms of formal logic, but this failed to detract from the popular power of the 'imaginary equation': 1 million unemployed = 1 million migrants. Removal of migrants = 1 million more jobs. QED.

Cox was less interested in the psychological nuts and bolts of the process than in the function the outcome served for the capitalist system. The symmetry of it all lay in the fact that workers were again at each other's throats, leaving the capitalists as beneficiaries. His brand of Marxism may have been crude by modern standards, but at the time Cox theoretically reoriented race relations, and his work provided a useful starting-point for subsequent debates.

Basically, those debates concentrated on the question whether racism and racial conflict were, as Cox suggested, by-products of an economic system or, as many other theorists argued, independent forms of stratification. Those taking the first position analysed the race issue as derived from the economic or productive system – in particular, class relations. The alternative was to examine race relations or, as they later came to be called, ethnic relations (to steer clear of biological connotations).

Both traditions agreed that an account of racism in the UK should begin from a deeper historical perspective than an analysis of British society since the war. Racism, at least in the form recognizable in the 1980s, had its origins in the ideologies and racial typologies that were often invoked to justify the open exploitation of colonial times. The great imperial powers of Europe began their conquest and colonization of vast portions of the world in the sixteenth century, expropriating the land and labour of native peoples. Although their material domination was rarely in doubt, their enslavement of other populations posed problems when set against avowed Christian ethics, especially the one pertaining to all people being equal before

[127]

God. Racism, to a large extent, eased the contradiction, offering a vision of the world in which some segments of the human population were not quite as human as others and could not legitimately be as entitled to the full range of benefits available to the superior races. The superiority of white Europeans over darker-skinned races was held to be demonstrable: they had better military and technological resources with which to assert their dominance and impose their authority. Racist beliefs, which were often elaborated into fully fledged ideologies, were a perfect match for colonial expansion. The ideas combined with the historical conditions and came to exert an influence of their own.

By the postwar period, the European empires were in a state of dissolution. The granting of India's independence in 1947 symbolized, in an almost apocalyptic manner, the end of Britain's empire. Yet racist ideas have inertia, lasting long after the material conditions in which they grew have disappeared. In the words of John Rex: 'Once a racist ideology emerges as a means of justifying opposition, conflict or exploitation, it can take on a life of its own and begin to operate as an additional factor, determining the nature of group boundaries and promoting group conflict' (1983, p. 198).

Prejudice and racism may reside in the mind, but they have their origins in specific social and historical conditions, not purely psychological ones. Beyond this, however, there has been little agreement. Trying to spell out the precise nature of the relationship between racist ideas and material conditions has proved an uncomfortable job. Returning to Rex, we find one of the more noteworthy attempts to provide a theory to account for the bewildering diversity of ethnic inequalities (1983; 1986). His empirical research with Robert Moore back in the 1960s gave rise to the concept of 'housing classes' which were distinct from classes in the more conventional economic sense. The inner city of Birmingham, where Rex and Moore conducted their study, experienced a struggle over accommodation, and different groups in the housing market had differing degrees of access to the accommodation. Blacks and Asians had only limited access. The Rex–Moore model saw the city as kind of proving-ground, with a power struggle over housing between competing ethnic groups, who constituted housing classes. One of the theory's implications was to redefine the orthodox conception of class to include non-productive spheres; in other words, conflict was produced not necessarily by work or work-related experiences – as some Marxists would want to argue – but by groups' power in the market, in this case the housing market.

Racial inequality and conflict on this account were not derivable simply from relationships in the productive system, work. Marxists, as one might anticipate, took exception to this approach, offering instead a theory of racial conflict in which priority was given to a society's economic structure. Capitalism, according to this view, is about the economic exploitation of those who do not own the means of production. In societies that have experienced the large-scale immigration of different ethnic groups, this exploitation is played out through racism. In other words, ethnic groups are for the most part members of the working class and therefore subject to exploitation. Some writers, like Robert Miles (1982), went so far as to call them 'class fractions' to denote their separation from the main body of the working class, while others preferred 'underclass', suggesting a social position somewhere below the principal strata of society. Sectional class interests are expressed in terms of race.

The late 1980s produced many versions, all avowedly based on Marxian concepts, but few agreeing on the precise nature of the link between racism and the capitalist economy. Cox's somewhat 'vulgar' comprehension of the link was discarded, though some, such as A. Sivanandan (1982), described an instrumental relationship, racism existing more or less because it was functional for capitalism. Others, dissatisfied with such accounts, inverted the orthodox emphasis, arguing, with Paul Gilroy, that ' "race" can no longer be reduced to an effect of the economic antagonisms arising from production, and class must be understood in terms qualified by the vitality of struggles articulated through "race" ' (1987, p. 28). In contrast to many other Marxian analysts, Gilroy offered the idea of 'reciprocal determination' between 'race' and class, neither being a fixed category of people, but each having potential as an organizing, even unifying agent in conflict situations or 'struggle'. Gilroy saw them as fluid, changeable, but always related. Unlike early formulations which reduced racism to an aspect of class antagonisms, this argument approached racism and class conflict as relatively autonomous features of society with a high degree of elasticity. Racism can act back on the economic system and does not just function as an instrument of it.

This gives us a useful reference point for understanding the development of race as a major division of British society. In no sense is it plausible to analyse the issue as separable from the work sphere. One's relationship to the means of production, to repeat a point made in Part One, is crucial to one's material circumstances, decision-making capacity and, therefore, life chances. Blacks and Asians have in the main been workers rather than owners, or more recently owners of small-scale companies with a major dependence on larger ones. The patterns of conflict of interest have their origins in issues of work, though they are orchestrated as racial or ethnic issues.

Whites have often adopted racist ideas and selected courses of racialist action because these were the rational means of pursuing their own material interests. From the viewpoint of a white who feels insecure because of the entry of ethnic groups to his or her neighbourhood, being racist is very logical, a point which I emphasized in the title of my book *The Logic of Racism* (1987). Racism is not a fraudulent method of justifying prejudices, but a genuinely felt and intellectually reasoned response to material circumstances. If you live on a council housing estate and believe your market position is weakened by the growing number of ethnic minorities on the housing department's waiting list, then your thoughts about blacks and Asians will be different from those of a company director whose only concern over the race issue is about the employment regulations government legislation has introduced. The legislation which entails a compulsion to adhere to new norms of conduct may be anathema to a person whose material success has been founded on a *laissez-faire* approach to life. As a person's housing position is, in turn, related to what they earn and how they earn it, both sets of responses can be traced back to economic relations.

Assuming, as most academics now do, that race is best understood as a label slapped on groups to help restrict their mobility and facilitate their exploitation, we need to explain why whites attached the label to blacks and Asians. Here we invoke the legacy of imperialism or the 'colonial mentality': racist ideas, like footprints in cement, remain long after the person first responsible for them has left the scene. Whites have infused racism with new vitality by attaching its relevance to changing ethnic situations since the war. It has acquired particular relevance in times of economic crisis, although racism has at times operated as a force quite independently of economic considerations. Yet racial conflict does have its source in economic conflicts. It can be made operative by any number of factors, many seemingly not connected with the economy; it can also affect the productive system. Bonding together and identifying collectively as a group united by common cultural, rather than specifically economic, interests does not close off a group's potential impact. Nor does it mean that the group is not engaging in a class action; the relationship of the group's members to the means of production may very well mean that class interests lie at the source of the action, while cultural interests energize it.

Disputes over the best ways to theorize race relations have reached a pitch of what Rex calls 'theological intensity' since the war, and it is my purpose merely to select insights and propositions that will help guide the account of the race in the UK. Having constructed a profile of the structural position of blacks and Asians relative to whites in modern Britain, and concluded that there is a sizeable ethnic division in need of explanation, I have looked at some of the significant attempts to understand this. Especially interesting have been the attempts to spell out the exact nature of the relationship between

[131]

race and class. Any account must begin with some explanation of the emergence of racism; and whilst acknowledging that there is an innate human propensity to select and favour those thought to be kin, the criteria on which that selection has taken place have been influenced by historical, economic processes, the most important in this context being the colonial expansion. Out of this period grew various theories purporting to justify the exploitation and oppression of other groups crudely labelled as races. The colonial mentality has undergone many modifications, but the basic premiss of white superiority has survived and continues to be given fresh relevance.

The relevance of race is seen more clearly at times of economic strain, although there is no hard-and-fast relationship between the two. Racism and the racial conflict it usually engenders have their source in economic spheres; the shape they take often conceals this. The Cox-inspired theories of class and race, important as they were in reorienting thought immediately after the war, seem rather dated and mechanical in viewing racism as reducible to class relations. More promising is the trend towards seeing class and race as linked but in a flexible, indeterminate way, allowing for the possibility that race issues can operate independently of economic factors while recognizing that the productive system is ultimately the *primum mobile* of racial conflict.

The purpose of using theory is not to be at its mercy, but to employ it as effectively as possible in order to illuminate, to comprehend, to make some sense. Racism has often been exasperatingly difficult to make sense of. Sometimes it strikes the observer as sense*less*. Often it strikes the victim like a plastic baton. Sometimes it *is* a plastic baton, especially if the receiver was one of those engaged in the violent conflict of the early 1980s. The conflict was amongst a spectrum of ethnic responses. So far, we have concentrated on the origins, development and effects of racism. But those affected do not simply soak it up like sponges; they often volley back. How and with what consequences? The answers are in Chapter 7.

A quiet fire

Straight to rage

One of the few orthodoxies in race relations is that the period following the arrival in Britain of the ss *Empire Windrush* was one of relative calm. Research in the postwar period claimed that, while racialist practices were widespread, migrants were, in some emotional sense, attached to their 'motherland' and were reasonably content with their position. Studies from such scholars as Ruth Glass (1960), Sheila Patterson (1963), R. B. Davison (1966) and Ceri Peach (1968) gave rise to an image of the typical 'dark stranger': optimistic in the first instance, devastatingly disappointed at reception, but often sustained by an unsubstantiated faith in Britain and a vague ambition to travel back to the country of origin, hopefully enriched after a prosperous spell of work. This was 'the myth of return', as it is often termed (so-called because the return was often only a myth, and the migrants settled permanently). Whites' hostile feelings were generally unrequited. Migrants, the research suggested, were insecure and demoralized, but revealed no antagonism and sought only the opportunity to adjust to the new environment.

Then, as if tearing down purdah, Asian women stepped forward to uncover a starkly different picture of race relations. Place: Grunwick Processing Laboratories, North London. Time: 1976. Subject: racialism in the workplace, at first; turning into the firm's refusal to recognize trade unions. Grunwick has been singled out as something of a 'turning point in terms of race and trade unionism' by Gloria Lee (1987, p. 148). As well as undermining the stereotype of black and Asian workers, especially females, as not interested in union activities, it forced the union movement itself into recognizing the 'race issue' – an uncomfortable experience.

As many as 90 per cent of the non-unionized firm's mail-order department staff were East African Asian women. Gentle, quiet, subservient: these were all qualities popularly associated with Asian women. In the busy summer months of 1976, students supplemented the Grunwick labour force. Devshi Bhudia was told to supervise some students; he asked for more pay for the extra responsibility. The mail-order departmental manager, Malcolm Alden, suggested they discuss the matter later and gave Bhudia additional work. This took place against a backcloth of compulsory overtime and resentment amongst workers. Bhudia refused to perform the additional work and was dismissed. Three fellow workers resigned in protest and, after leaving the plant, stood with Bhudia outside the main gates. The other key player in the drama was Jayaben Desai, an Indian woman, who stormed out after a confrontation with Alden, in which she allegedly told him: 'You are not running a factory, but a zoo. In a zoo there are monkeys who dance and lions who can bite your head off!' Seeing herself as one of the lions, she joined the others in seeking the support of trade unions for their protest. Their action sparked a walk-out by other Asian workers, complaining of racialism by management. Grunwick stuck adamantly to its policy of not allowing unions in the company, and this stirred further walk-outs.

Apex, the white-collar union, appealed to the Grunwick management to recognize the workers' grievances and the legitimacy of their strike. After meeting with a rebuff, Apex decided to recognize all the strikers and make their action 'official'. Strike pay was granted. Brent Trades Council also supported the strikers.

Over the next several months, the Grunwick dispute developed like one of the countless photographs processed at the plant: changing from hazy cloud into a series of sharply defined images, available for all to see as the mass media homed in. Whether the unions' motives stemmed from genuine solidarity or opportunism is open to interpretation, but they sent delegates to enlarge picket lines that were often over a thousand strong. The police responded in comparable numbers. On one day, 20,000 people assembled to demonstrate.

By the summer of 1977 the unions' support had begun to recede, prompting some commentators to criticize the 'regressive role' they played (Alexander, 1987, p. 123). Others, like Sivanandan, called them 'unusually supportive' and enthused about the alliance of unions and ethnic minority workers (1982, pp. 126–31). Weakened by declining support, however, and with their resources and resolve strained, the strikers called off their action in August 1977. There had been a total of 550 arrests, at that stage more than at any dispute since the 1926 general strike. It had prompted the government to set up a Court of Inquiry on its way to becoming what Ramdin calls 'an historic dispute' and while there was no obvious lineal connection between this and later ethnic protests, Grunwick clearly signposted a direction for ethnic minorities: away from low-profile frustration and towards open confrontation.

If Grunwick was the turning point suggested, it was more symbolic than actual. Not that this diminishes its importance; it merely places it in context. There is no question about its grandness of scale and its impact in dramatizing the problem of racialism in industry. But it did not spring out of an ideological wilderness. For the impulse behind it had been at work in various ways for some sixteen or more years before. Even as early as the 1950s there is evidence of admittedly small and ineffectual groups organized by migrants with the aim of defending members from the more obvious forms of racialism.

Even before this time, it seems facile to suggest that no conflict entered into blacks' or Asians' relationships with whites. Migrants may have expressed sentimental links with the UK and shown no animus, but there are latent as well as manifest elements within a relationship. Despite the avowed commitment to their 'motherland' Britain, the migrants featuring in the studies of the 1950s and early 1960s expressed deep disillusionment. They simply did not expect racialism to operate in the way it did. Early on, little open conflict was initiated by ethnic minorities possibly because they felt a bond, however fragile, and wanted – or, for practical purposes, needed – to preserve it. Nevertheless, as Coser reminds us: 'The absence of conflict in itself does not indicate the absence of feelings of hostility and antagonism and hence the absence of elements of strain and malintegration' (1968, p. 82).

Strain and malintegration: Coser's terms aptly convey the relations between migrants and what we might generally call white society in the decades following 1948. Dilip Hiro described what the typical black person's response would have been like in the period: 'He tends either to evade the white man or be aggressive and truculent towards him' (1973, p. 17). The same would go for the South Asians who followed the Caribbeans. They withdrew, not always voluntarily, into their own specific sectors of the inner cities, introducing a new cultural slant to the enclaves, which were later called ghettos. Alternatively, they decided to confront what they saw as the source of their problems and struck up an aggressive posture, sometimes modelled on US black politics.

There are few graphic first-hand accounts of the experiences of migrants in the postwar period. Hence writers have tended to rely on the body of empirical work produced by modern researchers. Yet the impressions of people like the afore-mentioned Hiro, Wallace Collins (1965), Chris Mullard (1975), Beryl Gilroy (1976) and, in particular, Remi Kapo (1981) provide a different interpretation. Here the views converge with those of people like Glass and Davison in some respects, but diverge in others. The rejection, the outright racialism, the unabashed physical and verbal abuse are all documented, yet the reaction to them is not one simply of passivity or, to use Hiro's term, evasion. In the alternative accounts, racialism did not bring on disappointment, or the despair that inclines the subject to seek invisibility in the ghettos. Many migrants did take that option, and the rapid growth of the inward-looking Pentecostal churches with their emphasis on salvation in the 'next life' seems to demonstrate this. But let us take Kapo's analysis. He acknowledges that 'Before 1962, Britain's blacks existed insensibly in a cloud of tolerance . . . "Don't rock the boat" . . . it was a belly habit' (1981, p. 9). Yet for his own part: 'I was shocked into race reality at a time when labelling anyone "coloured" denoted inferiority . . . I skipped anger and went straight to rage' (1981, p. 16).

The 'moral crucifixion of black people', as Kapo calls it, obviously did not affect all blacks in a uniform way. We must allow the possibility that tolerance, or evasion, coexisted with rage and hostility. But it strains credibility to suggest that a deep feeling of enmity did not flood the entire black and South Asian community. Every subjective account points to a brazen and hurtful racism manifested in all aspects of life. Examples range from Beryl Gilroy's schoolteacher colleagues, who referred to her openly as 'wog' or 'nignog', to Wallace Collins' beatings-up and knifing at the hands of aggressors who asked: 'You niggers, why don't you go back to the jungle?' Such events hardly contribute towards quiescence: suppression, perhaps. Those who retreated to their own enclaves stifled their dismay, thinking optimistically of the return home, or of the improvement of relations that the passage of time might bring. They would surely not merely accept the racialist abuse without harbouring some caustic resentment, if not the rage to which Kapo refers.

The prevalent image of the migrant in this period derives from either the mild-mannered Hindu, nodding obligingly and taking the racialist medicine with a smile, or the stoic Pentecostalist, unflinchingly absorbing the pressure in this life with the conviction that salvation awaits God's elect. But can there seriously be much doubt that a fierce, if underlying, enmity exists in virtually any situation where party A regards party B as inferior and party B, powerless and pushed to the margins of society, is called 'wog', 'nignog' and a few other choice names. The spirit that reared at Grunwick was alive in the years before, though it was underpowered and lacking in focus. It was a quiet fire, but it burned all the same.

When the twisting stopped

We can gauge the depth and scope of racialism in the first twenty-odd years after the war from a number of events. Mayhem had broken out in British cities in 1958, when whites uncorked their anger against their unwelcome neighbours and workmates. The 1962 Commonwealth Immigrants Act had, as Kapo puts it, 'blown the guts out of the mother country hallucination' and 'rendered unthinkable the psychic idea of a peaceful black, brown, and white rapport in the near future' (1981, p. 10). Two years later, racists could toast with champagne the astounding upset victory of Peter Griffiths in Smethwick in the general election. In 1967 the first Political and Economic Planning (PEP) study into the issue revealed a many-sided racist figure of monstrous proportions, spreading its influence throughout all areas of society. Within a year of the study's publication, Enoch Powell was able to mobilize large sections of the working class with his simple, often nostalgic and always sinister messages layered with doom.

The 1958 disturbances no doubt reminded ethnic minorities of their physical vulnerability when confronted by large numbers of belligerent whites. Small ethnic organizations, moderate in tone and modest in ambition, grew as a result. The 1962 Act reminded them of their political vulnerability, and the response this time was a loose collection of blacks and Asians. By the time of the Act's passage, at least three ethnic organizations of significance had evolved. The Indian Workers' Association (IWA) began with Kapo's 'don't rock the boat' approach, but developed more militancy, perhaps reflecting its confidence in the system's ability to absorb its pressure. In Birmingham, the Co-ordinating Committee Against Racial Discrimination (CCARD) and, in London, the Conference of Afro-Caribbean Organizations (CACO) both made their

presence felt with mass meetings, protest marches and demon-
strations. CACO, in particular, had political connections,
especially with the Movement for Colonial Freedom, led by
Fenner Brockway MP, who pressed for reform during the
1950s.

The 1962 Act, according to many views, was crucial in
signifying to the ethnic population the collective attitude of
whites. Only the year before, tireless pro-control campaigner
Cyril Osborne had declared that 'this is a white man's country';
and, while Osborne was regarded as a maverick, the Act seemed
to embody his sentiment. 'Racialism was no longer a matter of
free enterprise,' Sivanandan concluded, 'it was nationalized'
(1982, p. 12). This had the effect of converting the collective
actions of migrants from what Sivanandan calls 'settler politics
– petitioning, lobbying, influencing political parties' – to an
ethnic struggle, in which interests, loyalties and commitments
were more sharply drawn. Two developments in early 1965
seem to illustrate this. In February, following a visit to the UK
by the US civil rights leader Martin Luther King, a federation
of Asian and black organizations announced itself as the
Campaign Against Racial Discrimination (CARD – as distinct
from the earlier Birmingham-based CCARD). The same
month saw the visit of King's radical *alter ego*, Malcolm X, who
had struck out against the soft-pedalling, non-violent civil
rights movement and advocated militant, black power policies.
He too inspired a British movement, the Racial Action
Adjustment Association (RAAS), headed by the Trinidadian
Michael de Freitas, also known as Michael Abdul Malik. RAAS
exemplified Hiro's 'truculence': it was fiercely aggressive
compared to CARD, which, like King's movement, took a
gradualist approach to integration.

'Stop twisting and hit back,' de Freitas bade his followers in
1965; 'Our last name is Black' (*Observer*, 4 July 1965). This may
sound fairly unexceptional by modern standards, but it was
spoken, as Obi Egbuna notes, 'at a time when it was considered
the climax of absurdity to call a "West Indian" African . . .
[when] the easiest way to get thrown out of the "respectable"

[139]

black meetings was to walk in with a Black Power badge pinned on your jacket' (1971, pp. 17–18). Egbuna himself was responsible for creating a second national organization sub-scribing to a black power philosophy. His mentor was Stokely Carmichael, who in July 1967 addressed an audience at the Dialectics of Liberation Conference. Disappointingly for many neophytes of the then emerging women's liberation move-ment, which had (in the USA at least) drawn encouragement from black power, Carmichael displayed a crude contempt for women. By the time of Carmichael's visit, black militancy had surfaced in a dispute at a Courtaulds mill at Preston, Lancashire, and this was the other main development of the period.

In May 1965 Courtaulds' management tried to make Asian employees work different shifts for proportionally less pay. Three hundred Asian workers claimed racial discrimination and staged an unofficial strike. De Freitas and RAAS pledged their support. The strong suspicion was that white workers and unions had colluded with management. Similar dealings were also rumoured to have been behind disputes at other factories, although it was not until the 1970s that the connivances were laid open by disputes at Mansfield Hosiery and Imperial Typewriters. These incidents, together with Grunwick, 'revealed the entrenched positions adopted by white employers, white workers and the trade unions towards black workers,' according to Ron Ramdin. 'Black workers' grievances challenged the unrealistic containment of conflict in certain industries. Moreover they challenged (and in some cases proved) racism at all levels of the industrial structure' (1987, p. 269).

So, by the time of Carmichael's fortuitous visit, conflicts were blasting through industry like geysers. The American Black Panthers' leader's arrival was, as Egbuna puts it, 'manna from heaven'. Egbuna's organization, the Universal Coloured People's Association (UCPA), had as its formal aim 'the establishment of separate educational, political and economic institutions and the encouragement of pride in the separate ideology of the black man' (as defined by Hiro and Fay, 1967,

p. 8). Carmichael was deported, and four members of UCPA were indicted under section 6 of the Race Relations Act for allegedly inciting 'racial hatred'. In the same month de Freitas was accused of the same offence in a speech at Reading, for which he was imprisoned for one year. Over the next several months Egbuna and two others were arrested and charged with conspiring to murder white police officers. Egbuna received a three years suspended sentence. In the same period of 1967 CARD held its third annual convention, at which a motion was tabled that the organization's white officials be replaced. The motion was carried but failed to command the two-thirds majority necessary for a constitutional amendment. The convention was highly controversial, the meeting being adjourned after allegations that various factions had sent bogus delegates to inflate the black vote. Members dissafiliated, many moving to RAAS, leaving CARD, as Sivanandan puts it, 'to its more liberal designs'.

Further signs of the growing confidence of blacks and Asians came in industries where issues such as poor pay and working conditions and cultural questions (about, for instance, the right to wear turbans or to pray at work) sparked off disputes involving ethnic workers. The West Midlands, in particular, was an area of great ethnic unrest. The Indian Workers' Association intervened on several occasions. Conflicts at this stage were piecemeal, and it would be misleading to see each as a stage in the progress towards a forceful and effective ethnic unity. Still, the conflicts continued to build. The UCPA was especially effective in linking up with many diverse organizations and fighting cases ranging from industrial problems to physical violence, of which there was an outbreak in the late 1960s, due largely to the 'paki-bashing' habits of skinhead youth. Events gathered pace in 1970 when Asian groups took to the streets to protest at the lack of effective police protection from skinheads. Young black people became involved in several abrasive exchanges with the police, the most spectacular centring on the Mangrove restaurant in Notting Hill, a meeting place for black political circles. Police raided the restaurant on several occasions and arrested nine suspected activists. A demonstration protesting against the arrests escalated into a violent confrontation which in a way presaged later events. The 'Mangrove nine', as they became known, were acquitted, but police surveillance of militant black centres continued. The episode has been called the 'high water-mark of Black Power'.

Despite the martyrizing effects of the arrests and imprisonments, black power never achieved in Britain anything resembling the unity and collective purpose of its United States counterpart. There was never an ideology to knot the different organizations together, nor the network of communications necessary to maintain continuity. In terms of content, the only common thrust was that blacks and Asians were being systematically denied an opportunity to participate in society on equal terms with whites. Some groups saw the problem in whites' prejudices; others saw the source of malevolence in an overarching system of domination controlled by and in the interests of whites. Between the two, there were countless variations.

The elliptical movement of black power had virtually completed its course by 1971, a year in which a new Commonwealth Immigration Act was introduced. By contrast, support for set-piece industrial disputes involving blacks and Asians multiplied. At Loughborough, Nottingham, Leicester and elsewhere, strikers made their symbolic and practical point: blacks and Asians not only had to struggle as part of a class against employers; they also had to work as an ethnic group to overcome the lack of support or even racist hostility of their fellow workers, including trade unionists. In all these disputes, the approach of the strikers was dogged and duplex: they fought two elements in their struggle, class and race. And, in so doing, they were able to reveal the breadth and depth of both divisions.

There was also a subtler expression in the efforts of black power militants and ethnic-minority strikers. Each instance of open conflict suggested a willingness to demand rather than request, and a confidence that the system might be able to accommodate at least some of those demands. After all, demands are rarely issued where there is absolutely no chance of some of them being met. The crack-down on black power militants at the end of the 1960s had emphasized the limits of acceptable struggle. Organizations like UCPA had what Mullard calls 'transformative' (rather than just 'progressive') ambitions that were clearly not assimilable (1985, p. 201). But, in other instances of conflict, particularly in the workplace, there was a common element: a framework of norms and regulations governing the struggle. And each instance reaffirmed ethnic-minority confidence in the available institutional framework's adequacy in processing protests and 'progressive' demands. Each instance of conflict enhanced the critical spirit that was to endure in later generations, as we will see next.

Love and political revelation

By 1976 the more apparent and recognizable forms of racialism were under the control of legislation and the various agencies charged with its enforcement. Talk was not of racial 'discrimination' and 'disadvantage' but of *institutional* racism, a concept so elastic that it defied existing policies. Institutional racism could not be isolated; only its effects could be charted. Whether you actually believed it existed or not seemed less a question of science, more one of commitment. For instance, three central concerns about the black second generation were the consistent underachievement of Caribbean-descended schoolchildren, their high unemployment levels and their alleged habitual involvement in street crime. Peripheral problems were homelessness and what were called 'identity problems' (presumed to derive from being caught between two cultures). One explanation of this blamed a combination of the youths themselves, their family circumstances and the disorienting long-term impact of migration. Another cited racialism – not in its conventional sense, but in its less visible guise, filtering through the routine procedures of commercial businesses, government departments and virtually any other large-scale organization in which blacks' progress was blighted. Individuals were not to blame; nor were departments, management or unions. No one was actually behaving in a racialist manner; yet blacks were still leaving school with little to show, getting few of the better jobs and not doing much to sweeten their relations with the criminal justice system. Were they to blame, or were they victims of a hidden malefactor?

A great many young blacks decided they knew the answer. What's more, they even had a name for their malefactor: Babylon. This was an elaborate political creature dating back to the sixteenth century when the colonial Europeans dominated Africa and enslaved as many as 15 million of its inhabitants to supply labour to the New World countries and extract vast amounts of profit from trade. After the abolition of slavery in the early 1860s, 'legitimate' trade continued, and the political control of the African continent (apart from Ethiopia, Liberia and Egypt) was split between the major European powers. As Pierre van den Berghe has reflected: 'The basic ideology of colonialism was paternalism and the reality was domination and exploitation' (1984, p. 5). This reality, black youths concluded, was the one they saw manifested in their everyday lives. Their dislocation was nothing to do with a lack of innate abilities, but resulted from a conspiracy to maintain blacks in subservience.

The inspiration behind rastafarian philosophy was a combination of *négritude*, Ethiopianism and reinterpreted musings of Marcus Garvey, the influential black leader of the 1920s, whose vision was to return all blacks from their diaspora to Africa. The early rastas, as adherents of the philosophy were and are known, added to Garvey's plan the idea that the 'redemption' (the intended return to Africa from exile in 'Babylon') was not only desirable but inevitable. It would be an *en masse* movement from the West Indies, executed in a moment at the will of Haile Selassie I, the then Ethiopian emperor, in whom rastas vested divine powers. Garvey made it clear that, far from seeing Selassie as a potential redeemer, he had little respect for this emperor. Some of Garvey's followers, by contrast, seized on a phrase of his – 'look to Africa when a black king shall be crowned, for the day of deliverance is near' – and connected this with the coronation of Rastafari, who took the name Haile Selassie I, in Ethiopia in 1930. Many blacks in Jamaica saw his ascension as portending an exodus to Africa, and adopted his name, Rastafari, for their cult.

The exodus, needless to say, never materialized. Even so, the vision of a cataclysmic change in which the grip of Babylon would be broken and blacks would be restored to what Garvey called their 'fatherland' stayed alive. It found its way into the imaginations of blacks in the UK in the mid-1970s, principally through the potent, jarring lyrics of reggae music. The parables of reggae combined insight with obscurity and logic with *non sequitur*; they foretold of the crumbling of Babylon, yet warned of its menace; they bade followers to prepare for Africa while insisting that 'Africa' was already within them. Out of this tangle of prophecy and liturgy young blacks constructed a history of themselves and their forebears and an ambition around which to structure their lives. Babylon had still got them trapped, but only until the messianic intervention when they would be whisked away to Africa. For many rastas this was doctrine, although the majority of youths who were attracted to the movement made their own inferences and abstractions, so there was no consensus in a technical sense about what was and what was not rastafarian. All that was agreed was that recognizing oneself to be, at source, African and using that recognition to inform one's conduct made one, in some sense, rasta. The specific interpretation of the status and role of Haile Selassie was a matter of individual taste. This contrasts with the popular and misconceived division of the movement into 'true' rasta and 'dreads', a notion I challenged in the book *Rastaman* (1983).

Bob Marley functioned, perhaps unwittingly, as a rasta prophet, providing the fledgling movement in the UK with a personal focus. An exotic character, his Medusa's head of coiled dreadlocks tumbling over his face, Marley slurred invectives against Babylon, at the same time using that same system to promote his music, which was sometimes about love and often about political revelation. The presence of rastas in Britain predates Marley by some time: Patterson, in her early research, sighted some in the Brixton area of London and noted a rastafarian organization (1963). But the huge upsurge in the 1970s suggests independent sources of influence. Marley plus reggae, when offered to young people who felt repulsed by society, was a ready mixture. The response of young blacks was to make their rejection of Babylon both visible and audible. From about 1976, rasta numbers seemed to grow daily as inner-city youths fashioned their hair into locks and clothed themselves in scarves and 'tams' (woollen hats) in Ethiopia's national colours of red, green and black. Their obscure and sometimes incomprehensible language was a style of Jamaican patois with a rastafarian lexicon. 'Jah' was God, 'I and I' referred to the spiritual cord which tied all humans together, and 'must come' meant the inevitability of Babylon's collapse.

Many writers stressed the separation of rastas and first-generation blacks. It seemed fairly obvious that young blacks were doing something of which their parents wholly disapproved: pouring vitriol on authority. There was nothing in the rasta analysis of society and history that the first generation could not recognize: racism existed, blacks were not given equal chances, whites ran society to suit their own interests. But, whereas the preferred response in the 1950s and, for many, in the 1960s was to make oneself scarce, young rastas wanted to make their discontented presence felt. They sought, in their words, to spread 'dread'. This certainly gave the impression of a distinct break with the older generation, and in terms of posture, style and invective it was. But dropping the analysis beneath the surface newness of the rastas' response, we find a deeper, underlying continuity of experience: being eased out to the margins of society, in specific kinds of jobs and in certain housing areas. In objective, measurable terms, the material conditions of ethnic minorities had improved, but expectations had also been raised. The people decrying Babylon and predicting a new beginning in Africa were no longer desperate migrants, sustained by the dream of a return to their country of origin. Growing up in the inner cities and going to school with white peers made them feel part of the UK – that is, until they reached an understanding that the sheer fact of being black was an inescapable impediment to their future. Recognizing their shared destiny and inspired by reggae, they were able to uncover an alternative vision, one rejecting the conspiracy and deceipt of whites and proclaiming new ideals. They interpreted their parents' apparent docility as the result of being 'brainwashed' into 'mental slavery'.

In fact, far from being 'brainwashed', the original migrants were vividly aware of their own position and the consequences of their behaviour. They were also aware that a more aggressive approach to their problems might be disastrously counter-productive to their progressive ambitions – for some, a prosperous stay; for others, settlement; in all cases an improvement in material circumstances. Personal humiliation and the sacrifice of some dignity were prices to be paid. As the second generation grew, the problems and conflicts remained unresolved, but confidence had increased. Children of migrants invariably see the world differently to their parents. What one generation saw as a new society with which it had only fragile links it dared not risk, the next saw as a stable and secure context in which it should develop and prosper. When it seemed to deny it the opportunities to do so, the second generation responded by denying that society its allegiance. As one youth told me in the 1970s: 'Rastas don't want no part of Babylon.'

Almost ironically, in rejecting white society and creating what amounted to a secret form of communication, rastas succeeded in conveying, in a highly articulate way, a cogent and forceful protest. Their vocabulary might have been abstruse, but the content of their messages was clear. Much of the analysis and critique was similar to that of researchers, except that rastas used 'Babylon' where academics used 'imperialism', and they used 'lies' instead of ideology. Rastas did not make the subdued moans of a discontented but hesitant group, intimidated by a frighteningly reactionary society – one in which the neo-Nazi National Front and analogous groups were operating. They were the confident shouts of people safe in the knowledge that their criticisms would be considered and their protests accepted as legitimate. Rastas' protests were also affirmations. Black youths grew up in similar circumstances to the first generation of the two decades after the war and the black power movements of the late 1960s; the common denominator was racial inequality, a powerful generator of conflict. That conflict erupted sporadically before the coming of rastas, but from the mid-1970s it became a continuing feature of British society. It was to translate into open violence in the 1980s.

The functions of rioting

On Sunday 8 September 1985, Peter Carlton Allen was celebrating in Handsworth Park, Birmingham, the scene of the area's annual carnival. Twenty-four hours later, Allen was mounting a barricade across Lozells Road, less than two miles from the park. Petrol-bombs were being thrown at police, cars were being turned over, buildings were being torched. Handsworth was ablaze, and black youths, along with a few whites, repulsed the attempts of the police to restore order. Sensing the intensity of the situation, the police cautiously withdrew, allowing a quarter-mile stretch of road to become a virtual inferno. By the middle of Tuesday, when I spoke to Allen, the violence had subsided. We looked out on the road, a strip of smouldering ruins, burned-out car shells and broken glass.

The 'Handsworth riot', as the media described it, came four years after serious disturbances in Brixton. In both cases, an incident between blacks and police officers had acted as a catalyst for a widespread, physically destructive episode in which property was wrecked and shops were picked clear – 'burnin' and lootin' '. Both occurrences set in train a sequence of violent disorders in several other British inner-city areas, invariably the poorest, least salubrious districts where there were large ethnic-minority concentrations and abnormally high rates of unemployment, particularly amongst youths. Among the areas affected in 1981 were Southall in London, Toxteth in Liverpool and Moss Side in Manchester. In 1985 Brixton again erupted, but it was in Tottenham, in North London, where events took a further turn, when a police officer was attacked and killed during a spell of especially severe violence. Some talked in terms of vengeance, referring to the fact that the day before street violence broke out a black mother, Cynthia Jarrett, fatally collapsed during a police raid on her Broadwater Farm Estate home. (In Brixton indelicate policing, culminating in the shooting of another black mother, Cheryl Groce, elicited a similar, violent response.) Rioters armed with guns fired at the police, and the police deployed (without using them) CS gas and baton rounds for the first time in mainland Britain. But while the violence at the Tottenham riot (and this time the event did measure up to the legal definition of the concept, as summarized by Joshua, Wallace and Booth, 1983, pp. 143–4) was more extreme than before, the continuities with 1981 re-established themselves.

There was another important element to the 1985 disturbances: blacks' assaults on the property and, indeed, persons of South Asians. Handsworth, in particular, saw the destruction of many Asian-owned shops, a series of attacks on Asian residents and the death, however inadvertent, of two Asians. Inter-ethnic violence in the ghetto is not novel: in the USA there have been many episodes in which, for example, blacks have turned on Cuban migrants, who seemed to be enjoying conspicuous success in business ventures – as in the Miami riots of 1981. Ethnic minorities frequently assess their own progress alongside that of other ethnics, who may or may not be outpacing them in material terms. It is as if the passengers of a slow-moving train were looking out at a faster train passing them. The other train might still be moving quite modestly, but from a certain situation it appears fast as it passes.

Despite the differences, it is possible to assess and account for 1981 and 1985 in broadly the same terms. Explanations, some hopelessly implausible, came from many sources, and by 1985 they had become repetitive. A selection of essays reflecting on the 1981 'riots and their aftermath', edited by John Benyon, considered many of them (1984). They included, in order of credibility: racialism; poor police-community relations; mass unemployment; the physical deterioration of the inner cities; the media; left-wing political agitation; drug abuse; and the innate criminality of black youths. To these we might add the dietary explanation of Dr G. Taylor, who argued in the *Daily Mirror* (2 October 1981) that vitamin C deficiency had resulted in misbehaviour amongst undernourished youth! The prescriptions, some coming before Lord Scarman's official inquiry, some after, were rather unimaginative: democratize the police force; impose stiffer sentences on the convicted rioters; spend more money on the inner cities; give the CRE more investigative power; and, according to Dr Taylor, provide oranges through the National Health Service. Most of the explanations and the 'solutions' offered were based on 'liberal determinism', meaning that material deprivation was the prime cause of the violence and that, once this was removed, then the unrest would cease. Yet there were at the time a great many other places in the UK just as stricken by deprivation and these showed no murmur of trouble. In fact, the mood of such places, particularly in the north of England, was apathetic rather than rebellious, even in areas where class solidarity was traditionally strong.

This leads to the ethnic component. Racialism, as I have argued, has remained more or less constant since the war, yet the first-generation migrants, who lacked the shield of anti-discrimination laws, did not take to the street. Why did so many of their sons and daughters do so? But is this a reasonable question? Given the persistence and scope of racialism since the war, the inequality to which it has contributed and the conflict it has inspired, we might ask: why has there not been *more* rioting? After all, through the eyes and the ambiguous loyalties of an unemployed black youth with few or no qualifications in an area such as Brixton where unemployment was well over 50 per cent for black youths in 1985, the advantages of not rioting may not have been too apparent. He or she may well ask, what there is to lose? The answer might be: very little. Once approached in this way, the prolonged *absence*, of open conflict, rather than its presence, cries out for explanation.

There are even constructive aspects to the disturbances for those who choose to look for them. Four stand out: the catharsis effect; the heightening of public awareness; the catalyst for educational reform; and the prompting of an economic revitalization of the inner cities. The cathartic function of rioting was in providing a spontaneous outlet for built-up emotional energies. By 1981, the rastas' use of the term 'Babylon' was no longer a bizarre reference to the ancient capital of Mesopotamia, but a convincing description of life in Britain for young blacks. The riot was an occasion for symbolic revenge against a system they despised; the youths, in burning the property of their own neighbourhood, were attacking symbols of their entrapment in ghettos. 'Riots' also brought with them the chance of some material gain, although those like Douglas Hurd, Home Secretary in 1985, who suggested that predation and greed were the main motives would have been hard-pressed to convince anyone that the prospect of a free video from Rumbelows' store was sufficient stimulus for a full-scale riot. (It is worth recording that Hurd was pelted and jeered when visiting the site of the Handsworth incident, showing the community's scepticism about his, or his government's, commitment to solving its problems.)

After the 1981 riots, the government ordered an inquiry under Lord Scarman. The eventual report set up an agenda for what should be done about the police and deprivation in the cities. The report highlighted the social and economic problems experienced by blacks and, to a lesser extent, working-class whites: poor-quality housing, a paucity of recreational facilities and high (and rising) unemployment. It criticized heavy-handed policing which had contributed to the outbreaks, especially at Brixton, where the notorious Swamp '85 initiative commissioned stop-and-search procedures in the district. It resisted accusations that racism was widespread in the police force, a finding that was repudiated by a later PSI report (Smith and Gray, 1985). The Scarman Report was embarrassingly clichéd in its analysis of the social conditions and processes behind the outbreak and concentrated its recommendations on the police: their role in the disorders, their accountability and their strained relationship with ethnic minority youth. Limited though the proposals may have seemed and fruitless as many felt they were, they did at least have the side-effect of drawing public attention – not necessarily sympathy – to the specific issues confronting inner-city residents. For months after the report the media seemed to have an inexhaustible supply of panellists rhubarbing platitudes about life in the ghetto. Not much action came out of it all; but it did dramatize the inner cities as problem areas in need of attention. The dramatization of obvious causes may have no palpable value. Just like a sane reaction to expected chaos, the Scarman debate was more an attempt to preserve order without resort to forceful control. Violence could not be condoned, perhaps it could not even be understood; but it could be discussed, puzzled and argued over. It *did* register. Only the Grunwick dispute approached the 'riots' in terms of fall-out. This in itself – widespread recognition – was a gain, even if it was of an intangible kind.

In the late 1970s community activist groups such as the Black Students' Action Collective and the Black Parents' Movement had tried to heighten interest in the problems of black schoolchildren and their persistent underachievement. Community-sponsored schools independent of the state system were a response. There were threats of the withdrawal of the 'ethnic vote' from local councillors who refused to attend to the particular grievances of their black constituents. Yet none of these brought results of the scale of those achieved by the 1981 disorders. 'Such an interpretation can be inferred from the fact that before 1981 only the Inner London Education Authority and Manchester Local Education Authority had produced policy statements affirming a commitment to multi-cultural policies,' writes Troyna. 'Since then, the majority of the UK's

LEAs have produced policies . . . the catalytic effect of the disturbances of the 1980s is not difficult to understand' (1988, p. 87).

The two major government reports on *The Brixton Disorders* and *Education for All* both recognized that the urban violence was partially the result of prolonged unemployment, which in turn was linked to poor school performance. This effectively limited a school-leaver's chances of finding a job, increasing his or her frustration and possibly combining with other factors to produce aggression that could be expressed in violence. The school seemed a sensible sphere in which to work, where violence born of underachievement and frustration could be nipped in the bud. Scarman and the others saw greater interest and motivation among young blacks coming from a more culturally 'relevant' curriculum. Questionable as the assumption might be, it did signal an attempt to restore the faith of blacks in the state education system and strengthen their commitment to that system as a means to a worthwhile occupation. While critics scoff at the attempt, the indisputable fact is that education is being reformed, if too slowly for many tastes. The direction of the reform, principally towards multicultural curricula, is clearly influenced by the problems of ethnic pupils – at least, the problems as they have been officially recognized.

Efforts to revitalize Britain's inner cities have taken several forms, some adopted wholescale from the USA. One of the ways the Nixon administration responded to the Kerner Report (1968) on the US riots of the 1960s was by promoting ethnic-minority business support through the Office of Minority Business Enterprise (later, the Minority Business Development Agency). The UK disorders did not prompt such direct action, but they did shift into focus the debate over the role of government in facilitating ethnic entrepreneurship by reducing the effects of racism on access to business resources. The UK's first Ethnic Minority Business Development Unit (EMBDU) was launched in 1986; it was modelled on the US prototype (by this time the USA had thirty special units helping minorities break into business). Funding for EMBDU came from the Inner London Education Authority, the government Department of Education and Science and the Home Office. After the 1985 unrest, sympathy was in short supply. There was no official inquiry on the Scarman scale; no one saw much point. Consistent with Conservative philosophy, the causes of the problems were sought in individual propensities: pathology, indiscipline, criminality and greed. The government's attitude seemed to be something like, 'We've bent over backwards in the past; now people have got to start helping themselves.' EMBDU embodied the Conservatives' encouragement of individual initiative in small businesses and, at the same time, stimulated economic activity in the inner cities, where most ethnic businesses were located.

The inner cities had been under inspection since the mid-1970s, and various inner-city redevelopments had been under way for some years before the Brixton outbreak. But the increased attention paid to such projects after 1981 had the effect of creating work, not just for local residents, but for local businesses. Construction firms retained to improve specific areas were also made to comply with government regulations, to employ or subcontract work to local companies or to ensure complete equality of opportunity. All of these measures had potential advantages for ethnic minorities – *potential* advantages only; so far, the tangible effects are not absolutely clear. One could suggest, for instance, that the main beneficiaries of contract compliance are the main contractors which charge local authorities extra for operating under restrictive conditions – and justifying this in terms of additional training expenses, etc. – and central government, the image of which is enhanced by its apparent concern with inner-city deprivation.

Searching for buried gold in the smoking rubble of Railton Road, Brixton, or in Handworth is a futile task, although we can find a few worthwhile trinkets. For all their alleged mindlessness and irrationality, the rioters forced public recognition of their plight, and that in itself, from their angle of vision, might have been worth fighting for. Difficult as it is to accept where loss of life was involved, the riots did produce results (there were three deaths in the 1985 disturbances and one immediately preceding them). The attention given to both sets of disorder made all citizens of the UK aware, however uncomfortably, that ethnic-minority youth, often unemployed and disenchanted, actually shared the same society – at least in a civil sense. The open discourse that followed this awareness may not have produced automatic reforms, but it did help create a climate in which policy reforms and projects could be accepted without severe opposition.

As potential beneficiaries of reforms, ethnic groups had entered into copious negotiations, and to do so without some kind of internal unity would have been ineffective. One of the anticipated longer-term effects is more federation and internal organization in ethnic-minority groups. Credibility and bargaining strength will be enhanced, I suggest, as ethnic groups press for reform, possibly citing the alternative scenario of more violence to support their claims. Martin Luther King once told his followers: 'To accept passively an unjust system is to cooperate with that system.' It seems reasonable to suppose that those who either participated in the riots, sympathized with the rioters, or even just understood why they rioted would be satisfied that they at least were not co-operating with injustice.

A careful adherence to rules and a willingness to submit to consensus are often a recipe for nullity and inertia. Confrontation and open conflict in the form of civil disorder at least guaranteed some action, some change, however negligible cynics may find it. For many, young Asians, with their fidelity to established formulae (such as hard work at school + qualifications = success), will have much more impact on the character of British society. The problem with this view is that it is based on a stereotype of the parvenu Indian, ignoring the fact that the vast majority of South Asians have material conditions and prospects much the same as Caribbeans. Some studies do show Asian schoolchildren faring better at school than their contemporaries, and Asian youth were not nearly as visible as blacks in the riots. But there is no evidence at present to indicate that educational performance and qualifications lead to occupational success in a society where non-meritocratic forces like racism and class make the system less than perfect.

All this assumes that Asian children are as diligent, industrious and respectful as the caricature suggests, whereas empirical accounts, such as those of Pratibha Parmar (1982) and Parminder Bachu (1985), project alternative images. Here we find Asians, particularly females, often struggling but defiant and unexpectedly militant when forced into confrontations. They do not, as Parmar stresses, 'experience the racism from which they suffer in a passive way' (1982, p. 239). Asians have not suddenly acquired the fibre needed for confrontation. It was evident at Grunwick, Mansfield and many other sites of industrial dispute where they have been involved. Similarly, the impulse to protest can be traced back lineally from 1985 through the black power response of the 1960s. There seems no reason to suppose it did not exist before this; it was merely displaced into other areas as migrants avoided acting out their feelings. As the decades passed, ethnic minorities began to see themselves not as transient or migrants, but as fully fledged members of society. Having nothing to fear or lose, they openly expressed their frustration at the barriers raised by racialism, barriers some thought were sure to fall. Asian youth especially were optimistic about the long-term future of race relations, despite being the greatest recipients of racialism, according to research undertaken by *New Society* (February 1986, pp. 312–15). Contrary to the view that the open challenges of the 1970s and 1980s were a symptom of 'alienation' from society, they indicated a sense of membership. 'We are here and parts of this society; we want a bigger stake in it!' was the resonant reminder.

One of the many posters that adorned the street walls of Handsworth after the 1985 episode read: 'From riot to revolution.' This misleading promise, or perhaps prescription, confused the imperative to protest with revolutionary energy. Those who insist that racism and racialism are deep-rooted in capitalism believe they will be eliminated only by a total transformation of the system. The people involved in the riots were certainly not negative about change; but the change they sought was the kind that would allow them more investment in the system rather than change the system itself. Far from being a struggle to overturn society, the uprisings and all the industrial protests that preceded them were attempts to maintain an active interest in it.

Opinion on the lasting value of the riots is split. Some, like Peter Alexander, see such 'street movements' as 'volatile and temporary phenomena exploding spontaneously and unpredictably into violent confrontations with the state, but dissolving just as suddenly into the apathy and isolation which preceded them' (1987, p. 108). Trevor Carter, by contrast, argues: 'The events were totally predictable' and 'must be interpreted as a positive development' (1986, p. 123).

In the 1960s, disorders in the USA led to a major redefinition of the way civil rights should be approached. Some argue that the riots achieved more in two years than the non-violent civil rights movement had in the previous ten. There is also the tempering view that all the policy reforms that followed benefited only a small minority of qualified and relatively well-off blacks. Attempts to reduce inequality and accommodate democratizing demands were largely symbolic in impact. The same view could be argued in relation to reforms in the UK. Also, there is the prospect that what might be given in one hand is not so much taken back but smashed with the other. New Right populism combines venerable principles like a respect for authority, a mistrust of state intervention and a defence of traditional morality with a call for the restoration of 'law and order'. The stepped-up use of force to repress inner-city unrest and the encouragement of ethnic-minority entrepreneurship were seen as conveniently compatible in the late 1980s. This involves no repudiation of ethnic minority problems, protests and demands. But it advocates a conservative egalitarian approach to solving those problems, absorbing those protests and meeting some of those demands. Social questions were recast in individual terms, the obsession with individual responsibility meaning that the answers were to come through initiative rather than welfare. Individualism, market-based opportunity, the minimization of state intervention: these were the mainstays of a government ostensibly opposed to racial discrimination yet unwilling to base policies on collective principles. For this reason, the violence, which was very much a collective response, may return as if as a reminder that racialism and the inequalities it generates are not the creation of individuals but of collectivities. The 1980s upsurge stimulated reforms and the modification of certain norms, but it did not alter the fundamental inequality that underlies ethnic relations in the UK.

GENDER

CHAPTER 8

Out of the ideal home

Home-making as a career

Beauty contests have extravagance, glitter and fantasy, but not recognizable human beings. They present tableaux of swimwear-clad female torsos, scrutinized, evaluated and ranked by judgemental males whose job is to select the ultimate identikit 'beauty queen'. The Mecca Organization started its Miss World Competition to coincide with the Festival of Britain, held in 1951 on the centenary of the Great Exhibition. It was very much part of the effort to break free of the austerity of the postwar 'reconstruction' period, pandering, as it did, to the British male's pursuit of pleasure. Mecca boss Eric Morley's box-office opportunism saw him draw together aesthetically pleasing, available young females (married women were ineligible) from all corners of the globe and pitch them against each other in a survival game in which the 'fittest' emerged to be crowned.

While it was seen as a marvellous spectacle in the 1950s and well into the swinging 1960s, by 1970 at least some saw Miss World merely as a *folie de grandeur*, designed by and for males. The hidebound sexism and machismo of the contest had become as visible as the backs and legs of the contestants.

The 1971 contest, at London's Royal Albert Hall, was the most significant in Miss World's history; it was notable less for the performances of the women title aspirants, more for the performances of women in the crowd. They chose the event to publicize what was then a four-year-old movement, women's liberation. As master of ceremonies Bob Hope amused the audience, the demonstrators hurled smoke-bombs, stink-bombs and bags of flour at him. They blew whistles, screamed, circulated leaflets and fought with police officers who tried to eject them. Despite failing to stop the show completely, they disrupted it enough to make their point: women were being used by men for their bodies and little else. In bed, or in factories, the end-result was unmistakably the same: women's bodies were *used*.

Miss World did not actually symbolize this – it caricatured it, even celebrated it. It boasted men's ability to induce women to undress themselves before a 'live' audience and television cameras for no purpose other than to amuse and titillate men and perhaps make less 'glamorous' women envious. In 1951 such a spectacle was an occasion to appreciate woman in her semi-naked glory; by 1971 it had become an insulting and dehumanizing offence to many of the female half (51 per cent actually) of the population, a reminder of the utility men had made of women's bodies. The demonstration was intended to be a healthy warning to all those gawping males who rarely or never questioned their instrumental relationships with females. The warning was: times were changing, and women were no longer content with the script men had written for them; some rewriting was to be done.

The script in question was much older than the Second World War, but in 1945 it was edited, and women were reminded that their place was quite properly in the home – that is, *not* in the factory. Just how they were reminded will become clear in this chapter, in which the changes affecting women and their seemingly unbreakable link with the home will be chronicled. The link is itself an instance of sex inequality, a subject that was to reach public visibility in the period between the inaugural Miss World and the 1971 episode. The full extent of sex inequality and the reasons for its persistence will be assessed in the final section of the chapter.

The war was an exceptional historical event and it required exceptional action. So the recruitment of one-quarter of the married female population to the wartime workforce was permissible, indeed necessary. Following the war, however, there was concern over the numbers of returning soldiers seeking work. Many would want to drive buses, operate cranes, work assembly lines, deliver letters – all jobs done ably by women in the war years. Now men wanted those jobs back. Women were exhorted to leave their jobs voluntarily to make way for the home-coming heroes. Few doubted that full employment for men was an important priority, and in any case there were murmurs of concern over the future of the family. What kind of mother was it who worked all day instead of tending to her children?

The reminders were fairly blunt. Social child care was abandoned as wartime nurseries were closed down. Despite a public commitment to economic renewal and social reform, the Labour government allowed public child-care provision, which had been so necessary in releasing women from the home, to decline drastically. One immediate consequence of this was that many women were obliged to give up their jobs and return to their homes. If this persuasion was insufficient, thousands of working women simply lost their jobs, employers thanking them for their efforts in substituting for men during the war whilst pushing them aside to make way for the 'rightful' occupants of the jobs. Yet by 1947, as Beatrix Campbell points out, 'there were still 300,000 vacancies for women, and government sponsored research showed that if childcare and part-time work were offered them the employment of another 900,000 women could be envisaged' (1987, p. 71). The message was clear enough: women's first responsibility was to work in the home. This was the first principle in the family's sexual division of labour – an arrangement that held the key to women's utility – in the postwar period and one that will receive careful attention over the following chapters.

The ambitious Beveridge Plan was intended to initiate an assault on the prewar social deprivations. The concept of social security and a National Health Service introduced the state into areas that had previously been controlled by the market. For millions of working people, substantial changes in welfare services were implemented. The basic idea was to dissociate benefit from wages, so that even the most poorly paid would not suffer inordinately and would be taken care of by the state in times of stress.

One of Beveridge's central themes was the condition of the housewife in the aftermath of war. Strained by the exertions of the previous five years, women were to return to the tiresome grind of housework and child-rearing. Drudgery concerned Beveridge; he suggested several schemes for eliminating it, including collectivized cooking, nurseries and sewing centres. Beneath the schemes lay a supposition, as Elizabeth Wilson detects: 'the *drudgery* must be removed so that the more stimulating and rewarding aspects of child care and beautification of the home would have a higher priority; the theme of "the housewife's home is her factory" was *part* of the broader theme of "homemaking as a career" so popular after the war' (1980, p. 22). The plan did not depart from prevailing notions about women's quintessential role in the scheme of things: workers, yes; but workers in the home, a private sphere unconnected with the more public occupational world. The idea was that women not only belonged in the home, they *wanted* to belong in the home, a point observed by Stacey and Price: 'The Beveridge reforms were based on the assumption that women should be and wanted to be first and foremost wives and mothers' (1981, p. 151). Not until the late 1960s was there an earnest questioning of this assumption, which informed many subsequent policy developments.

Although it hardly qualifies as a feminist movement by 1980s standards, the Housewives' League was established in 1947, claiming 100,000 members bent on resisting the increasing state control and welfare planning favoured by Attlee's administration. The organization opposed employment for women, but encouraged its members to strive for political power, while preserving what they felt to be autonomy in their own homes. It was essentially a rebellious middle-class, conservative movement set fast against the welfare reforms and insisting on a free-enterprise society. Its philosophy was that women are wives and mothers by nature and not waged workers. What free time they had away from the home should be spent politicking against Labour government.

The movement grew out of cold postwar temperance, with food and clothes rations compounding fuel shortages, and wage rises of 5 per cent barely keeping pace with prices. The Housewives' League was organized around the observation that women were the group suffering most the after-effects of war. Women, that is, as homemakers and mothers, not as workers. Concern centred on women at home.

'The worthy husband and father is proud to support a family and the respected wife and mother is happy to care for the home and family,' announced the Housewives' manifesto. The League recognized that women had interests and grievances unique to themselves and needed to promote their cause quite separately. The notion of a woman's place being in the home was preserved, with a proviso that efforts should be made in the public sphere of politics to improve that place. No reference was made to the underlying subordination of women which was to become a feature of British society.

Architects of oppression

In 1949, at the height of the Housewives' campaigning, a Royal Commission on Population recommended that contraceptive advice should be available to married women. Here was the glimmer of acknowledgement that for many women the alleged joys of sex and reproduction were not joyous at all. From 1948 the Family Planning Association (FPA) began a national expansion of clinics (there were 400 by 1963). They catered for married women until 1966, when pressure forced the FPA to adjust its policy in alignment with changing public perceptions of sex and morality. (FPA clinics were not part of the National Health Service, set up in 1948, but were incorporated in 1976.) The absence of women's control over their own fertility was, at this stage, quite complete; under the 1861 Offences Against the Persons Act, all abortions were statutory offences (up till 1938, even when a woman's life might be endangered by childbirth). Again, public perceptions were to change, and legislation in 1966–7 was to reflect these. Further legislation changes in 1988 reflected what amounted to a rethink of women's abortion rights.

Between the Royal Commission's recommendations in 1949 and the crucial changes of 1966–7, which were to affect women's status in many different ways, women continued to enter employment in increasing numbers. They grew confident as workers and became secure enough to articulate a series of specific demands. A report on equal pay published in 1946 failed to anticipate the sharp rise in working women and was reserved in its judgements. It argued that those women choosing careers, other than just jobs, should receive salaries equal to those of their male counterparts; women in manual work, however, should not suppose to be as able as men and should therefore not receive comparable pay. The report's assumption was that some women would opt for a career instead of marriage and a family. Those (the vast majority) who would simply work would do so merely to supplement household income; their working lives were of secondary importance, because they would surely be interrupted by spells of pregnancy. Married women especially fell into this category. There was also the fear that equal pay could serve as a deterrent to motherhood at a time when population growth was needed to refresh the future labour force. Give women equal pay, it was argued, and it would induce them to continue working in preference to raising families. Dependence on the man's wage was encouraged; this facilitated women's economic exploitation as cheap, flexible ancillary labour and their subordination at home.

But a certain ambivalence in women's position became apparent by 1951. Economic renewal quickly produced a demand for labour, and women began to seep back into the job market. Six years after the end of the war, one in five women were back at work, mostly, as Hilary Wainwright notes, 'at lower levels of the job hierarchy' (1984, p. 203). Women comprised 32 per cent of the UK's total workforce. And this was just a beginning; women's contribution kept increasing.

Women's earnings were at this stage about 53 per cent of men's. Part of the Labour government's logic in its opposition to equal pay was that it would disadvantage married women, whilst improving the conditions of unmarried women who were employed full-time. Dissatisfied with this, a Conservative, Irene Ward, in 1951 organized a demonstration in support of equal pay. It set in train a steady campaign mobilized through various feminist factions. By 1954, with personal consumption figures showing steep increases (reflecting economic improvement), the campaign reached fruition, and the Conservative government began implementing equal pay policies in areas like the civil service and the teaching profession. It was another sixteen years before the concept of equal pay was legally enshrined in the Equal Pay Act.

The trade unions' position on women's pay was as contradictory as it was in regard to race relations and immigration control. The unions were constitutionally obliged to take the problems of women workers seriously, yet at the same time they were mindful of the suspicions and views of the majority of their members, men, who saw in women potential competitors as well as 'brothers' (as they were in those days). The unions had their hand forced in the 1960s as women continued to pour into employment. After 1959 women's membership in unions rose sharply, and most of the large unions were compelled to attend to their women members' interests. In 1963 the large Engineers' Union began a major investigation into equal pay, a technically important event, but also one with symbolic significance. The Labour government of 1964–70 accepted the principle of equal pay; this again was of symbolic significance, although without much practical application.

Labour's posturing on equal pay had the effect of pumping up expectations. So when the goods were not delivered, an element of frustration appeared. It took the form of a string of industrial actions in the late 1960s. Harold Wilson's govern-

[167]

ment had won re-election in 1966, and, as we saw in Part One, for a while the unions were brimming with bargaining power. But if the government was delivering shy of its promises, then so were the unions, and events in 1968 emphasized this. Women sewing-machinists at the Ford motor works at Dagenham staged a three-week strike, at first over sex discrimination and then over equal pay. Anna Pollert points out that the women's victory led to the formation of the National Joint Action Committee for Women's Rights and 'was among the factors which led to the passing of the Equal Pay Act in 1970' (1981, p. 12). On each side of the Act there were 'landmarks', as Pollert calls them, cases of women drawing together to confront problems that affected them as workers, specifically as women workers. These are worth looking at in more detail.

Office cleaners are mostly invisible to white-collar workers, save for those who work late or arrive very early. In late 1970 May Hobbs changed all that. She mobilized a group of London cleaners, all women, many of them from ethnic minorities, into what she called the Cleaners' Action Group. Hobbs' argument was simple enough: office workers work when they do because their domestic commitments occupy their days. They work, she said, 'for little luxuries . . . like food, rent and clothes for their kids'. She realized that office cleaners, being poor, female and in many cases black, were vulnerable, so she set about trying to affiliate them with the Transport and General Workers' Union. The London Women's Liberation Workshop strengthened the cleaners' picket lines, although the campaign itself was greeted with mixed responses. Many of the cleaners themselves, as working-class women, were suspicious of 'women's libbers', popularly seen as middle-class busybodies. The other response from male union officials, was equally muted: the Cleaners' Action Group was not officially recognized and stayed out of the union movement despite over a year of arguing. The major unions were about as accommodating towards women's issues as they were towards ethnic minorities. Their focal concern was with the problems of white working-class males and they gave little practical support to the spate of conflicts that followed the office cleaners' dispute.

Nineteen seventy-one saw London telephonists in dispute and Cumberland thermometer factory workers on strike. In 1972 and 1973 there were outbursts at Fakenham, Hull and Coventry, all involving women workers. At Coventry the strikers had to contend with sabotage from their own union convenor. 'And when Asian women at Mansfield Hosiery Mill took the lead in fighting racial discrimination, they suffered both sexism and racism from their own union,' writes Pollert (1981, p. 13). Grunwick, as we saw in Part Two, became a shop window for these issues. Thousands of women threw their weight behind the struggle, which revolved around their exploitation as (in the main) ethnic minorities and their being denied the right to unionize. But in this as in many other episodes, 'for men to champion the women's cause whole-heartedly required a degree of altruism that had no part in the tradition of British trade unionism', according to Coote and Campbell (1987, p. 165). They argue that women have been reluctant to confront the fact that working-class men have actually impeded their progress as women despite periodic shows of support. There has been a more fundamental 'conflict of interest' smothered by 'an assumption of common interest'.

'Women themselves were affected by "family wage" propaganda,' suggest Coote and Campbell, even though it 'diminished their status as workers, undermined their claim to equality and contributed to a feeling that the trade unions were not primarily for them' (1987, p. 165). This is a crucial remark and needs some expansion, for the changing position of women in the labour force since the war has been influenced not just, on the one hand, by a desire or necessity to work and, on the other, a demand for labour. Right from Beveridge's statement about minimizing drudgery, assumptions about the sexual division of labour, ideologies of the home and 'propaganda' have affected women's involvement in the workforce. The steady flow of sometimes unsensational disputes were only emblematically linked, but they showed the willingness of women to mobilize in order to solve problems that affected them as workers, specifically as women workers, whose presence in the labour force continued to increase, but whose contribution was never fully appreciated.

By 1968, women constituted 35 per cent of the total workforce and, by 1974, 37 per cent (half of all married women were involved in some kind of work at this stage). In 1980 over 10,000 women worked and they made up 43 per cent of the total labour force. The triumph of the postwar economy, if we can call it that, was in drawing women back to the workplace, paying them generally less money than men for the equivalent jobs *and* maintaining the sexual division in the home. The set-up was almost 'ideal'. The sexual division of labour and the ideology that justifies it ensure that women are not dependent for their subsistence on their wage labour, Wainwright points out. 'Among workers in a capitalist society they are unique in having access to a means, or a partial means, of livelihood on the basis of social relations other than economic exchange relations' (1984, p. 233).

Viewed like this, we see the political sphere intrude into the personal and vice versa. The capitalist economy, on Wainwright's account, found an 'ideal workforce' in women, especially married women, who were quite used to the discipline and rigours of work, but had 'initially low wage expectations, negligible traditions of organization' and, crucially, 'an alternative life to return to'. The alternative life was, of course, at home – their real domain. Work was not central, but peripheral to their lives; theirs was not usually the main income in the household, but an auxiliary supply.

Three further features of this arrangement strengthened its expediency. First, women were able to meet demands for new types of labour, for example service and clerical work created by the expanding welfare state. Routine and semi-skilled work that required only limited training attracted women. There was also a demographic change that enabled women to enter, or perhaps re-enter, the job market; they began marrying younger, having fewer children and at earlier stages in the life cycle, enjoying better health and living longer (thanks, in part, to the welfare state). So a married woman with two or three children might be in her late thirties by the time her more burdensome rearing duties were at an end and still be physically fit enough to go back to work.

A third point concerns the role of women as consumers, rather than producers. Consumerism, as we have seen, surged in the affluence of the 1950s and 1960s. In particular, the Conservative administrations of 1951–64 elevated the position of women as consumers. It was reasonable economic theory to suggest that, if women earned money, then that money would very quickly be injected back into the economy and continue circulating. Consumption was necessary to sustained economic recovery, and women were logically the targets for advertisers' campaigns.

The arrangement had a certain rationality to it. No violence was done to the ideals of family life, while a possible crisis over the shortage of labour was averted. Women served the needs of the system and were able to add to their families' income without neglecting their duties at home. It was an unfair, unequal arrangement, but it worked. Women, especially younger women, wanted to work; the dual role that offered them a stake in the public as well as the private sphere was a mutual accommodation. 'Architects of the reproduction of their own oppression' is how Stacey and Price describe women for accepting the dual role and not seeking to upend the social arrangements that ensured their subservience – certainly not until the late 1960s, when some women at least recognized that their own personal circumstances reflected political circumstances. Gender became an important issue in postwar Britain precisely because women ceased being architects and became demolition agents.

A decade of release

The 1960s were Britain's decade of release from old paternalistic restraints and controls, themselves vestiges of the war. National

Service ended in 1960, and this signified as well as anything that the postwar consensus was drawing to an end. Cultural upheaval followed. Amidst the consumer affluence and *embourgeoisment*, there emerged a cleavage to rival those of class, race and sex. This cleavage concerned age; young people emerged as a self-conscious, independent group with their own particular and frequently outrageous values and life-styles and a determination to stake out boundary markers between themselves and the rest of society.

This was a very deliberate, motivated attempt to create youth, a different order of people with their own approach to life. The approach involved, amongst other things, spending inordinate amounts of money on leisure, dressing in distinct, recognizable outfits and reformulating moral standards. 'Permissiveness' became a key concept. In constructing the permissive society, young people were very amply abetted by a whole new industry geared to youth. Records, motor scooters, boutiques, magazines, radio stations – all products for the expanding youth market – were items that symbolized the 1960s. This period witnessed a blurring of sexual boundaries: young men wore make-up; women wore cropped hairstyles; both wore 'unisex' clothes signifying the moral re-evaluation that was taking place, especially amongst young people. An active sex life was one of the prescriptions of the time. At the close of the 1950s the film *Room at the Top* marked the degree of change. Critic Nigel Andrews comments: 'That film's steamy sex scenes (which now seem about as steamy as a vicar's lightly boiled egg) had critics gasping, audiences flocking and British cinema switching track virtually overnight into the Swinging Sixties' (1987, p. 23). The impact was 'seismic'.

Another movie just six years later in 1965 had the punchier parable of an acquisitive young woman manipulating men sexually and often dispassionately to further her own schemes. Yet John Schlesinger's *Darling* was, by that time, considered provocative rather than liable to get a Richter scale reading, a reaction that indicated the rapidity of change in mores. Liberalization of statutes reflected the changes of the decade. Integral to these were attitudes towards male homosexuality. The Wolfenden Report proposed reforms in 1957, but it was ten years before the Sexual Offences Act decriminalized homosexual acts between two consenting adults in private in England and Wales. Changes in mores and attitudes and the efforts of politicians were thrust together in an ideological constellation that was independent of any women's organization. There was a sexual revolution of sorts, even if it relied more on people like Liberal MP David Steel than feminist writer Germaine Greer.

Nineteen sixty-seven was something of a sexual *annus mirabilis*. The National Health Services (Family Planning) Act authorized local authorities to give contraceptive advice and appliances to anyone in need, if necessary, free of charge. The contraceptive pill, developed in the USA, was commercially available, although there was much scepticism about oral contraception after the thalidomide episode in 1961. That sedative drug was found to cause malformation of the limbs of the embryo when taken by a mother early in pregnancy. Assurances of the harmless affects of 'the pill' could not crush feelings of doubt about its long-term consequences to mother and child. The thalidomide scare actually assisted a sympathetic Labour government in passing Steel's Abortion Law, also in 1967. Prior to this, abortion was illegal under section 98 of the 1861 Offences Against the Person Act, except that legislation in 1938 permitted abortion when a pregnant woman's life or health was endangered. The Abortion Act made it legal for a clinical doctor to terminate a pregnancy if two other registered practitioners agreed that a continuation of the pregnancy would be a greater risk to the life or health of the woman or her existing children than an abortion would be, or if it was thought the child would be born handicapped, physically or mentally. This widened the scope of abortion appreciably and brought it within grasp of a great many women; for example, in 1973 there were almost 120,000 legal abortions performed in the UK. The figure suggests that a substantial number of women had probably resorted to illicit, back-street abortions prior to the legislation. The Act carried no financial provision, so abortions

[173]

were available but not freely to all – only to those who could afford to pay privately, or raise the funds from charitable institutions (even in the late 1980s the charitable sector underwrote the costs of about half of all abortions).

Ostensibly, both pieces of legislation gave women greater self-determination concerning their own bodies by providing the means to control some areas of fertility. 'Women have been given the initiative, and often the whip hand, in deciding when to have children and how many,' wrote Maureen Green enthusiastically (1984, pp. 18–19). David Bouchier was equally convinced of the potential of freely available birth control: 'This was something infinitely more revolutionary than any philosophical notion of liberation or equality because it offered women an elemental power which only celebacy or age could previously have given them: the power to control their own bodies' (1983, p. 27).

But the *ultimate* control lay with men. Doyal and Elston make the point: 'Like other fields of medical and scientific activity, research and development in the area of contraception continues to be dominated by men . . . Women's interests and feelings are not taken seriously . . . the "side-effects" of particular methods are often ignored in a way in which they would not be if men were the users' (1986, p. 184).

The Act did not significantly alter the existing arrangement whereby fertility control was defined as a male prerogative. While 'the pill' seemed to give more responsibility to women, its administration was structured by men. A further issue that detracted from 'the pill's' advantages was its side-effects. Questions about its safety were raised virtually from the date of the Family Planning Act; and for the next twenty years evidence mounted, particularly relating continuous use of 'the pill' to heart disease. Control over their own bodies was bought by women at a costly price.

Abortion carried with it less qualifying factors. It removed the dreadful spectre of illegal and self-induced termination, replete with images of knitting-needles, turpentine-dipped goosequills, wire hangers and all manner of purgative preparations. As US pro-abortion lobbyists said: 'Women of the world unite. You have nothing to lose but your coat-hangers!'

From 1970 to 1979, the number of legal abortions grew by 40 per cent. The abortion rate (i.e. per total number of women of child-bearing age) rose by 13 per cent, due largely to the population growth. By 1988 about 18 per cent of all pregnancies ended in abortion. There have been two easily identifiable upswings in abortions, both inspired by scares about the safety of 'the pill'. The first followed reports in 1977 of a possible link between the contraceptive and heart disease; the second, at the end of 1984, came after well-publicized research relating 'the pill' to cancer of the breast and cervix.

Figures in the twenty years following the 1967 Act showed a wide regional variation in the availability of abortions. For example, in the mid-1980s, 80 per cent of abortions performed in Merseyside and the North-west were on the National Health Service (NHS), whereas in the West Midlands 80 per cent were conducted privately. The variations serve as reminders of the discretion allowed under the law to medical practitioners in controlling women's access to abortion. Applying for a legal abortion has always put women in a submissive role *vis-à-vis* the medical authorities, the latter being 'dominated by men', as Doyal and Elston reminded us. Decisions about whether or not a woman should have an abortion have been taken not by the woman involved, but by personnel of a medical profession traditionally influenced by and organized in the interests of men.

The response evoked by the passage of the 1967 Abortion Bill suggested the legislation was out of alignment with public and medical opinion. There were already powerful opposition lobbies to the Bill, including the medical profession, and pressure to limit the terms under which abortion could be obtained continued. Some women's organizations polarized the issue by demanding an extension of the legislation to permit free abortion on demand. The whole issue was, in a sense, of great service to feminism; it provided a focal point about which to organize. Being a strictly 'women's issue' in so far as it was based in the female's capacity to bear children, it held an emotional appeal. 'A woman's right to choose' was the slogan of early campaigns to resist the backlash.

There was success and failure: success in terms of uniting women in a legitimate cause and establishing an agenda for future campaigns designed and executed by women; failure in terms of the attempt to subdue the reactionary forces led by James White, William Benyon, John Corrie, Cora Robertson and others, all of whom had Bills defeated but, at the same time, maintained the anti-abortion momentum. In 1981 the Department of Health and Social Security instructed doctors to refrain from allowing either 'medical' or 'social' grounds for abortion and use only 'medical' as their criterion. Over a million abortions had been performed on social grounds since 1967.

The fight against reactionary tendencies had an enormous effect on women's organizations. In particular, the National Abortion Campaign (NAC) managed to capture the sentiments of an inchoate women's movement and involve many disparate groups over the best part of a decade. It promoted a 20,000-strong demonstration in 1975. There had already been a reduction in the abortion time limit from 28 to 24 weeks of pregnancy, and the forces of reaction were gathering strength, especially in such organizations as the Society for the Protection of Unborn Children and LIFE. The women's movement became a useful 'auxiliary resource', as Gelb calls it, for politicians trying to defeat such organizations. But perhaps more importantly for the unity of the women's movement, the backlash groups provided a recognizable enemy. Women's groups coalesced, defined boundaries and asserted their unity in defiance of the new threat.

Women have had mixed fortunes since the war. New mores and standards of sexual conduct have combined with advance in medical science to give them a greater role in the determination of their own bodies in general and their own fertility in particular. Medical evidence from the USA prompted the suspicion that contraceptive technology might have almost boundless potential in enhancing women's role. Legislative changes both reflected and structured changes in sexual behaviour and moral codes. Those directly concerning women gave further proof of the probability that women could take control of their own bodies. The contraceptive hardware was becoming available, as was the legal software. In industry, women have had an important presence in the full-time and part-time labour force. But they have been used as a relatively cheap, expendable and flexible convenience. As we have seen, women have responded vigorously to this situation. Industrial conflicts featuring women in unity fighting on issues that affected them *qua* women gave substance to the idea that there were experiences and problems unique to women that only they were prepared to fight for.

The phrase 'women are their own worst enemies' exempts men from responsibility, but it is much more than a convenience. A great many women expect and accept (or act as if they accept) subordinate roles and status in society. Just as racism works on its victims' mentality, so sexism penetrates the consciousness of women, and many of them have arranged their own needs, goals and perceptions so that they fall within specific limits.

'Women as well as men continue to believe that political and public affairs are male domains,' Stacey and Price remind us in their analysis of *Women, Power and Politics*: 'In the roles they adopt in the family, in their differential upbringing of their boy and girl children, women help to perpetuate a gender order that ensures a subservient place and a secondary position in public affairs for women' (1981, p. 153). The argument follows that social arrangements have been so affected by the family ideology that women have rarely been permitted the opportunity as Stacey and Price put it, 'to imagine alternatives, let alone invent them'. They have been provided with a cultural template for themselves. Success in commerce, the professions and politics is not a feature of the template's design; a life at home, bearing and rearing children is.

Important equal pay and anti-discrimination legislation in

the 1970s certainly removed many of the technical barriers to women, in much the same way as race relation laws in the period 1965–76 brushed away the obstacles to ethnic minorities. In neither case was anything but the symptoms tackled. Causes, like sexism and racism, run much deeper; they are reinforced by ideologies shaped by victim and offender alike. Sexism is not to be confused with misogyny. It permeates as much as it envelops, operating at all levels from the political to the personal, and this has produced a qualitative difference in material circumstances and life-styles between men and women – in a phrase, sex inequality. For the rest of this chapter I will look in detail at the extent of sex inequality and consider some answers to the question of why it exists.

The gender gap

How come there are so few women in top jobs and so many in service occupations? *Well, because they're the gentler sex.* Then, what are they best suited to do? *Work in the home where their natural, nurturant skills, their supportive tendencies and their caring gifts are best deployed.* Then, what is woman's essential role? *To serve her husband, bear and rear his children and make his home comfortable.* Presumably, the old saying, 'a woman's place is in the home', is still a correct one, then? *Absolutely: domestic activity is the woman's forte; history proves it.*

Actually, history does not prove this; it proves something rather different. It proves that this charmless theory about 'woman's nature' has been one of the most outrageously inaccurate, yet most influential, techniques used by men for their own convenience. Men have used the myth of 'woman's nature' to disburden themselves of what would otherwise be an uncomfortable fact: that women have been consistently relegated to poor-paying jobs, largely excluded from spheres of political influence and repeatedly had their unity undermined in a world dominated by men. Both sexes have been enmeshed in a family ideology which purports to explain and justify women's attachment to the home in the sexual division of labour. The basic assertion that women's central – one might say primal – duty is to children and the domestic environment in which they must be raised leads to a whole series of pretexts for women's exploitation in other contexts, particularly employment.

It could be argued that women as a group are worse off than ethnic minorities. The respective experiences of both groups suggest comparisons. Both are subject to '-isms': for ethnic minorities, racism; for women, sexism. Both are deemed to be disabled by what are, at source, biological properties. And both have had limitations placed on their progress in society. As a result, neither group has enjoyed much access to positions of prestige or power, nor developed a great deal of income-earning potential.

Some would want to halt the comparison there. Others would push it further, arguing that, while women have not been lynched nor manacled, they have been harnessed in a kind of slavery. They have been 'enslaved' in the home for generations, working, frequently without credit, at rearing children and maintaining domestic comfort. The tyranny they have lived under is of a less visible kind than that endured by blacks. Yet its effect has been to subjugate women and restrict their mobility in society. Men have dominated women as consummately as whites have exploited blacks and oppressed other ethnic minorities. Also, in both cases, the subordinated groups have become unwitting accomplices to their own social exclusion. Sexism, like racism, prospers best when the group being kept out does not try too hard to get in; the gatekeeper's job is vastly simplified.

Somehow, sexism fails to evoke the same intensity of emotion as racism. It has not prompted spectacular riots, nor commanded the media's attention; until quite recently it had not established itself as a social problem worthy of serious academic inquiry. The suffering of victims of sexism is often inconspicuous. A typical sufferer may be an ordinary, anonymous housewife living with her family in Coventry, quietly rearing her two children and adding a modest income from a part-time typist's job to the household income, the major part of which is supplied by her draughtsman husband. This is hardly the sort of person likely to take to the streets with petrol-bombs.

Yet it is still possible to argue that women suffer more than ethnic minorities. If, for example, we took just one index – earnings potential – and in measurable terms assessed the impact of sex and ethnic origin, we would be drawn to the conclusion that sexism has greater consequences than racism. Being a woman 'costs' more than being black. Statistical studies by Christine Greenhalgh (1977), who compared men's and women's earnings, and by McNabb and Psacharopoulos, who published a paper on 'Racial earnings differentials in the UK' (1981), reveal that the gap between men and women is rather wider, in absolute and percentage terms, than that between white and ethnic minority workers. US research cited by Michelle Stanworth (quoted in Beechey and Whitelegg, 1986, p. 129) tried to isolate the weight of different factors affecting pay differences and found that a hypothetical white, male, unionized employee would be likely to earn three times as much as a black, female, non-unionized employee performing the same work. The difference was due 36 per cent to 'sex differences' compared to only 17 per cent to 'racial differences'. Anthony Heath calculates that the gender gap leaves single men with 23.5 per cent more than single women, whereas white workers earn only 17.2 per cent more than their ethnic counterparts. And, when we add to this what Heath calls 'the enormous gap [in earnings] between married and single women and the substantial gap between married and single men', we might conclude, as Heath does, that the problem of gender differences 'seems to be of quite a different order of magnitude from the ethnic differences' (1981, p. 186).

On this account, gender divides more sharply and decisively and with more powerful effects than race – although the account is purely one-dimensional and fails to encompass the multiple and often immeasurable ways in which racism systematically disadvantages its victims. As well as being inadequately renumerated for their labours, furthermore, women have been allowed fewer educational opportunities than males and have been consigned to marginal positions in society, all this justified on dubious biological grounds. Such facts support the view that, since the war, women have been ravaged, albeit less conspicuously, than ethnic minorities.

There are some revealing figures to record. Women are a numerical majority in the UK, yet in the mid-1980s only 41.4 per cent of the total workforce was female. In all, 10.9 million women worked in some capacity – that is, 1.1 million more than in 1975 – although most of the increase is accounted for by the growth of part-time work. Women have very different kinds of jobs to men. For example, they are much less likely to own their own businesses; only 20 per cent of all businesses are owned by women, according to Goffee and Scase (1985, p. 20). By contrast, females are over-represented in seasonal or temporary jobs, particularly in hotels and catering. A handful of occupations, especially those with a need for part-time workers, account for most working women. More than 40 per cent of full-time women workers are in clerical and related jobs and almost 20 per cent in education. Two out of five part-time women work in catering, cleaning, hairdressing and other personal services that have traditionally been regarded as 'women's jobs'. Clerical jobs account for one out of five part-time women workers.

In 1983, 38 per cent of working women had dependent children, and over two-thirds of these were working part-time. Only a quarter of women with children aged 4 or under were at work and in only 5 per cent of families with children of this age were both parents working full-time. Clearly, then, whether a woman has children or not influences the hours she is available for work and therefore the nature of work she can do. Also, the more children in the family, the less likely it is that a mother will be working.

Equal pay legislation since the war should have paved the way for an equalization for men and women, but this has been far from the case. Across the board, women's hourly earnings are still only about three-quarters of men's. In some jobs the gender gap is small – for instance, a female police officer earns almost 92 per cent of her male colleague's pay – but elsewhere the difference is more pronounced; a female sales supervisor earns just 67 per cent of her male equivalent.

Women do rise to managerial positions, but not in great numbers, nor with any regularity. And, when they do, they are more likely to land in junior and middle management jobs, rather than positions that carry decision-making weight. Stacey and Price give two illustrations based on empirical research (1981, p. 136). At one large engineering firm employing 15,000 women, of a total workforce of 50,000, there were 4,784 managerial posts; women occupied 35 of them. Nearly one-third of a national insurance company's staff were female, yet less than 1 per cent of them were in managerial positions, compared to 17 per cent of the male staff.

In the professions, women also fare badly, as the portraits in the volume by Spencer and Podmore show so vividly (1987). In the civil service, women hold only 10 per cent of the 5,000 Assistant Secretary and Principal posts, while in grades at the top of the higher civil service there are only 21 women as against 700 men. In the legal profession, despite steady increases in the recruitment of women, females represent only 12 per cent of both barristers' and solicitors' branches of the profession; this is a staggering increase on the proportion thirty years ago, when, according to Spencer and Podmore, 'only two or three per cent of practising lawyers were women' (1987, p. 113). The pattern is replicated in virtually all the professions and prestigious occupations, so that, as the title of Spencer and Podmore's book puts it, high-achieving, success-hungry women compete *In a Man's World*.

There is little cause for enthusiasm either in the sphere of national politics, despite the rise of Mrs Thatcher to No. 10 in 1979. This feat tended to obscure the fact that, in the same year, only nineteen women were elected to Parliament – the lowest number of females in the House since 1951, and six less than the twenty-four elected in the 1945 general election. Since the war, women have occupied between 2.7 and 4.6 per cent of the available seats. All this makes women's impact on local government and the European Assembly, where their percentage representation has been well into the teens, seem very impressive. Stacey and Price, however, make the sobering point that this can be seen as either a 'feminization' process or an indication that the elected bodies in question may be lightly regarded and not seen as 'prestigious or influential' (1981, p. 142).

Even in the trade unions, where women's membership has increased with the number of females in paid employment since the war, there is a lack of female representation at full-time official, executive member and delegate levels. The story repeats itself time and again: women have become more involved in various spheres of employment but have proportionately failed to make the decisive breakthrough at the highest levels. At the other end of the spectrum, women are concentrated in specific types of employment, popularly characterized as 'women's work' – like waiting tables, cleaning and 'temping' – which usually command comparatively small earnings; hence, as we saw earlier, the incomes gap between women and men.

One area, perhaps *the* area, in which women seem to hold their own is the ownership of capital. In 1980 they owned about 40 per cent of all private wealth. But this figure diminishes in significance once it is realized that women are given ownership 'on paper', mainly, as Hilary Wainwright detects, 'for reasons of tax and inheritance'. Further: 'This property is rarely controlled by the women; it is family property, invested by the husband' (1984, p. 202).

Other patterns are just as revealing. Women are divided by gender from men; they are further subdivided by class and racism. There is a much lower proportion of women than men in professions and managerial and skilled occupations, although the contrast between black and white women is less marked than the very vivid contrast between black and white men. A tiny 2 per cent of black women are employed in professional or managerial jobs; this compares with 17 per cent of white women and 20 per cent of Asian women. Occupational segregation also exists at this level. Asian women are disproportionately concentrated in textile and clothing industries, black women in the NHS. Both situations are legacies of early postwar migration tendencies. Because of a variety of economic and cultural factors, black women have been very active in the workforce; around 65 to 70 per cent of black females of working age have been in the job market. This compares with about 37 per cent of Asian women, who, according to Pratibha Parmar, are 'over-represented in the lower paid unskilled and semi-skilled sectors' (1982, p. 247). This relects the different status of black women in the family. As Hermoine Harris points out: 'Although Asian women do largely fall into the category of dependants, the reverse is true for West Indian women, many of whom are household heads, solely responsible for their children' (1972, p. 171).

Whilst the vast majority of ethnic-minority women have working-class origins, they have slightly different experiences in the job market. As well as being more likely to be looking for work, they will find themselves at the mercy of forces within the occupational world, forces that will press them into specific sectors. As Veronica Beechey concludes: 'Overall, black women are employed in more highly segregated occupations than white women and many of them work in the least desirable jobs' (1986, p. 91).

In male hands

Explaining women's general position in the labour force is a relatively straightforward matter and one that elicits further parallels between women and ethnic minorities. Whilst the number of women in the labour market has grown since the war, their earnings level has generally, as we have seen, remained lower than that of men. In effect, women have acted

[184]

as a supplementary army of labour – flexible, relatively unorganized, inexpensive and convenient. They have also shown a marked tendency to stay in segregated areas of the job market, what some writers have described as a secondary labour market in which career prospects are few, as are opportunities for high salaries. Adding to the convenience is the fact that women have become important as consumers.

All this hinges on the sexual division at home. If women were not convinced of the 'rightness' of their primary duty and their subordinate position to men, their whole relationship to the occupational system would be in doubt. So we need to explain why women remain subservient to men, why they accept the traditional family ideology, which affords men dominance. The skeleton key here is *patriarchy*, which expresses the totality of men's power, not only in the family, but in all major sectors of society. Kate Millett asks us to recall that 'the military, industry, technology, universities, science, political offices, finances – in short, every alliance of power within the society, including the coercive force of the police – is entirely in male hands' (1971, p. 25).

Specifying the origins of patriarchy has been the task of many writers, some of whom suggest a biological source, others citing economic processes. While some writers like Millett and Shulamith Firestone (1970) analyse patriarchy as independent of capitalism, others have combined the two. Vicky Randall, for instance, has formulated an account based on the assumption that 'biological differences between the sexes were the root cause of and to a lesser extent continue to underpin male dominance':

> Women's greater physical vulnerability enabled men to dominate them; their reproductive role gave men a motive for doing so . . . The institution of the family, and women's mothering role within it, are cultural phenomena which reflect and reinforce, especially through the separation of domestic and public spheres, male chauvinist attitudes and practice. Culture in its turn is significantly shaped by economic forces. It may well be that the emergence of an economic surplus encouraged man's more systematic domination not only of other men but of women.
>
> (1982, p. 33)

[185]

Patriarchy may have its source in the biological differences that allowed the possibility of physical domination. But cultural factors (such as a widespread belief in the woman's role in the family), bolstered by the economic imperatives of capitalism (to maintain a pliable supply of labour), have superseded biology in helping sustain male dominance. The convenience of patriarchy is that it dovetails so snugly with the requirements of capitalism, at the same time giving the appearance of being independent of any economic or political system. Women's position in the family is seen as the product of natural forces, not *man*-made ones.

This is no more than a general statement on the subordination of women and needs some qualification. For instance, it would be absurd to maintain that all women are equally subordinated. Women from ethnic minorities, as we noted earlier in this chapter, are, in sheer material terms, worse off than their white counterparts. This can be accounted for partially by the effects of institutional racism, but also by the fact that the vast majority of ethnic women come from working-class backgrounds. Contrasting the position and earning power of ethnic women with those of the white female population, then, is hardly comparing 'like with like'.

There is also a problem in lumping ethnic-minority women together in the family ideology argument. Asian women, especially Muslims, are tightly bound to their home role and are less likely to appear in the labour market than other women; they also seem disinclined to accept docile roles, as their bitter resistance in various industrial disputes suggests. By contrast, black women are much more likely to be working full-time, or seeking full-time work, than others (recall Harris's point about black women's bread-winner role and their sole responsibility for their children); this indicates a cultural norm that allows for a female bread-winner in the home – a norm perhaps born of necessity.

The question of class is never far away from such analysis. A woman's progress in the class structure will inevitably be influenced by her dependence on men in many areas of life.

Even wealth-owning middle-class women have, as Michele Barrett expresses it, 'a simultaneous ownership of, yet lack of control over, capital' (1980, p. 139). No one can escape the effects of class, yet Anne Phillips has a strong point when she argues that 'class when experienced by women is unlikely to be the same as class when experienced by men' (1987, p. 28). This in no way denies that middle-class women do not feel the effects of dependence and subordination in the same way as working-class women. Anna Pollert's study of Bristol women factory workers found them to be in 'partial collusion' when it came to their own subordination, and it seems likely that middle-class women are also. Yet Pollert's workers were additionally 'self-effacing . . . about the triviality of their work' (1981, p. 135). It is doubtful whether middle-class women denigrate themselves and their labours in quite the same way.

Ethnic background and class add filters to the female experience, so that, as Phillips sums up: 'No one is "just" a worker, "just" a woman, "just" black' (1987, p. 12). She illustrates her point:

> Working-class women, and even more so, *black* working-class women, would find themselves more threatened by pressures to abort [despite] medical resistance to abortion. For where a white, middle-class married woman can experience great difficulty in persuading her doctor to recommend a termination, a woman living on social security in an inner-city slum can face the opposite problem. 'Abortion, fine, but why not have yourself sterilized at the same time?'
>
> (1987, p. 7)

This is not to suggest an image of women as lifeless characters pushed into 'middle class', 'working class', 'white' and 'ethnic minority' boxes. Women are, like all other members of society, active contributors to their own position. But they act *within* the objective limits set by class, race and gender and *because* of the subjective experiences towards which those factors will incline them. This assessment takes us some way towards understanding the scale of the gender divide and the way it has affected women in postwar Britain. We still need to explain two things, however: first, how the patterns of sex inequality have been maintained and, secondly, what attempts have been made to break them. Women's attempts to promote change will be considered in Chapter 10. The factors working to inhibit change are dealt with in Chapter 9, where we will discover how education and the family encourage in women a particular type of outlook whereby life is seen to revolve around the home rather than the workplace, child-rearing rather than career-building.

CHAPTER 9

Shaping moulds

Sex in the classroom

Educating Rita describes a young working-class woman's climactic journey to an Open University (OU) degree and personal independence. It strings together episodes of varied hue – some comic, some violent – which suggest the problems faced by women in higher education. The gawky, aspiring student has unsympathetic and incomprehending peers, a husband who continually discourages her efforts and puts her under pressure to have children and low-budget housing circumstances hopelessly ill suited to academic study.

In 1977 OU applicants who did not take up the places offered them were surveyed to find out the reasons for their refusal. Sixty-two per cent of women compared with 44 per cent of men gave 'non-work demands' as the reason; these included domestic duties, care of children, moving home and having a new baby – some of the problems that playwright Willy Russell's resilient Rita had to overcome. Work-related problems affected 43 per cent of men who refused places but only 27 per cent of the women. Forty-seven per cent of the housewives (or 35 per cent of all women) isolated a lack of financial independence as an important factor. While Rita succeeded, ditching her domineering husband into the bargain, many other women do not even get to open a book. Domestic and family commitments weigh heavily against women's chances of educational success, even in the OU, an inexpensive institution specifically designed to encourage those who may not have had

[189]

opportunities earlier in life. Clearly, women, particularly working-class women, fall into this category.

The Robbins Report on higher education was published in 1963 and disclosed what it considered an untapped pool of ability amongst working-class children, in spite of the effects of the 1944 Education Act. Far from being irrelevant to educational achievement, class, Robbins found, was a major determinant of a child's chances of continuing into higher education. Forty-five per cent of young people with fathers in the 'higher professional group' advanced to higher education, whereas only 4 per cent of those from manual working-class backgrounds followed them. 'The link is even more marked for girls than for boys,' the reported argued. If you had working-class parents you had only a slim chance of going to university, and if you were a woman with working-class parents your chances were even slimmer.

The provisions of the 1944 Act which provided free secondary education regardless of class were found to have had no effect on the patterns of entry into higher education (especially universities), patterns which were class-related. Fifteen years after Robbins, research reflected on the expansion of higher education in the 1960s and the availability of student grants from the government. The figures tell us that in absolute terms the number of women entering higher education rose. But relative to men the proportionate rise was insignificant – from about 1 in 4 to just under 1 in 3 – and the increase was mainly accounted for by students from middle-class backgrounds. A substantial 15.5 per cent of female independent school students and over 30 per cent of female direct-grant school pupils went to university, while under 3 per cent of female comprehensive pupils made similar progress.

Part of the results indicated that women were less likely than men to have reached degree level and more likely to have no qualifications at all, although women who had fathers from the highest social class had marginally better chances of gaining a degree than similar men (Reid, 1981). Women were taking advantage of the new chances of higher education, but they were mostly middle-class women. Only 19 per cent of female graduates had fathers in manual work.

Scanning the statistics on women's educational achievements since the war, one realizes not so much what is wrong with the education system as what is right with it. It reflects almost perfectly the class and sex divisions in society generally. It is geared precisely to the position of women in the economy. This has been made possible by a series of state policies which have held fast to traditional assumptions about the rightness of the sexual division of labour and have made further assumptions about the unique educational needs of women in contrast to men. Education, then, has not simply reflected broader inequalities; it has assisted them.

Madelaine Arnot argues that two of the major education reports since the war (the Crowther Report of 1959 and the Newsom Report of 1963) shared with one of their earlier counterparts (the Norwood Report of 1943) a set of assumptions about women's education (1986, p. 151). The first of these concerned the alleged differences of interests: girls would become wives and mothers, while boys would become wage earners, so their interests would be fundamentally different. The Crowther Report, for example, presumed a female interest in 'dress, personal appearance and human relationships' and suggested that the prospect of marriage be integrated into girls' education. Second, each report uncritically accepted the nuclear family set-up and the sexual division of labour. Newsom's report was notorious in this respect, anticipating that all girls should be educated for motherhood. Finally, all reports took hardly any account of women's changing position in the employment market. Here we should recall how ever-increasing numbers of women were going to work and thus making an important contribution to the economy in the 1950s and 1960s. The reports implicitly endorsed women's position as marginal, underpaid workers with an auxiliary function only.

Tying all the above reports to the 1963 Robbins Report was the concern with social inequality and educational opportunity.

All uncovered evidence of the consistent underachievement of children with working-class origins. None, I might add, demonstrated any interest in the functions of independent schools in perpetuating privilege and inequality. Attention was concentrated, instead, on alleviating the problems of the deprived. The Plowden Report on *Children and their Primary Schools* (1967) drew on J. W. B. Douglas's research (1964) to highlight the crucial relationship between social conditions and performance at school. Plowden proposed educational priority areas into which extra resources and effort could be channelled. The publication of the Plowden Report coincided with several other key events affecting women, as we have seen.

At this stage, only 5 per cent of women in the UK were entering universities and polytechnics. The conventional wisdom was that this minority were the exceptionally talented few and that the other 95 per cent would be better off learning the more domestic skills which they could apply in the home. Like barnacles clinging to a sunken rusting hulk, ideas about the propriety of women's domesticity stayed fixed to the educational system. These ideas and the attitudes they fostered ensured, as David Bouchier, observes 'that most girls learned almost nothing which might be of use to them in the competitive world outside, and that those who made it into college would be steered towards the gentle but relatively useless fields of the arts and the humanities' (1983, p. 34).

This 'steering' began not at some late secondary school stage as the pupil prepared for the prospect of work (or lack of it, as we might properly say nowadays) but from the word 'go'. Burgess writes of sex-dividing strategies employed in nurseries, infant and junior schools (1984, p. 76). Looking closely at nurseries, Sara Delamont reported that the toys and games given to girls were passive, home-centred, non-scientific and non-technical compared with those on offer for boys: 'beautifully dressed, soft-bodied doll, who sucks her thumb' versus 'home workshop with drill, hammer, wrench and blueprints' (1980, p. 41).

Classroom organization, such as single-sex work groups and

sex-allocated registers, established a basis for division, and curricular materials reinforced this. Education serves as a shaping mould, and in the 1970s it turned out boys who generally ended up selecting studies in science and technological subjects and girls who either chose or were gently persuaded to study subjects such as needlework, cookery and sociology. (Arnot, 1986, p. 158, provides a statistical profile of subject choices.) The selection patterns held for GCE O- and A-levels, CSEs and higher education courses. For example, 43 per cent of male sixth formers took science A-levels as against 18 per cent of females; females comprised only 23 per cent of physics candidates at O-level, a pattern repeated at A-level.

Arnot believes that subject choices reflected the pupils' 'image of themselves and their future' and were also 'crucial to their eventual training and placement in the occupational hierarchy' (1986, p. 158). Predictably, the types of further training girls received were different to those of boys; courses in science, engineering and technology, for example, attracted very few females, whereas education tended to be popular with them. One consequence of this, apart from the entirely expected fact that many women are now found in service industries, is that even women who did receive advanced training (perhaps at a university or a polytechnic) in the 1970s were in the 1980s concentrated in a limited range of occupations, especially teaching.

By the mid-1980s the report was not so much 'could do better' but 'could do *different*'. Female achievement across the board improved, but the improvement came in subjects such as art, domestic science and sociology (which would be fine if all women wanted to be artists, cooks, or unemployed teachers). In 1984 girls gained 53.6 per cent of all GCE O-level passes and 47 per cent of all A-level passes. Nearly 49 per cent of the grade one CSEs in maths were achieved by girls, compared with 36 per cent in 1970. A major initiative designed to encourage girls' interest in craft and science subjects was Manchester's Girls Into Science and Technology (GIST), which, Coote and Campbell believe, failed in terms of stated ambitions but had a ' "ripple" effect, raising awareness and interest' (1987, p. 199).

A further encouraging trend was the greater number of women who continued into further or higher education, although, again, there is a qualification: many chose vocational studies such as secretarial courses or nursing. Six times as many women as men opted for teacher training. Women in the 1980s established a firm presence in polytechnics; they accounted for 48 per cent of all full-time students. In universities, too, women had a 41.5 per cent stake at undergraduate level, and they commanded a third of postgraduate places. So those wishing to see the glass just under half full instead of just over half empty could take solace from the statistical trend. Those taking a different view would point to the continuing minority of females specializing in science, technology and business courses – the ones that provide the best guarantee of jobs. Whatever one's view, the trend was undeniable. The demand from women for more education gained impetus, especially from the mid-1970s.

At the turn of the century, accessibility was women's primary problem in education. They were simply not admitted to many universities; and at the other extreme, primary education was not freely available anyway. Post-1944, the doors were thrown wide open (even though Cambridge refused to award degrees to women until 1948). Yet education has been of an uncertain value to women. On the one hand, it has offered opportunities equal to those of males. On the other, it has guided women towards domesticity as effectively as if it had dumped them on a number 8 bus to Tesco's. Sure, the opportunities were widened, but always within a framework. Policy documents were laden with preconceptions about the role of women and their ultimate destination in life. Such preconceptions were shot through the entire system, right down to the classroom practice of primary schools where girls were encouraged to splash about with toy washing-machines 'just like Mummy's' while boys exercised their imagination on spy kits (Delamont, 1980, p. 14). As they progressed through school, classes and subjects were differentiated by sex, and syllabuses were suffused with sex-role assumptions; one dreads to think what advice careers masters offered even the intellectually promising girls. There was little odd in all this: education was reasonably well regulated with the rest of society. Women were not expected to excel academically, Yet, from the early mid-1970s, that is precisely what they did and in all probability will continue to do: excel.

After struggling for so long in education, women began to seize the opportunities it offered. Have they succeeded? The answer is 'yes', but with a rather important proviso. The reservation is that the majority of women who have made progress in tertiary education are from middle-class backgrounds and mainly white. Also, the subject areas in which women command a majority are education, language and literature. So there remains a problem of academic 'ghettoism', women congregating in certain subject areas.

Education has been as vital to the subordination of women as it has been to their attempts to break free of traditional roles, and this is precisely the reason I have dwelt on its functions and impact. It has turned out women primed for motherhood or a fringe position in the workforce. As such, it has worked as a perfectly tuned machine – perfectly tuned, that is, for the postwar economy. But, while education has a kind of mechanical quality, in the sense that it can be (possibly quite openly) used for political and economic purposes, there are other areas of society that have contributed to women's position without appearing to be anything but totally 'natural'. I am thinking of the family, an institution held dear to the hearts of many, yet despised by others as a curse on all women.

Work and marriage as alternatives

In 1900 a 20-year-old woman would expect to live, on average, another forty-six years and spend about one-third of that time bearing and rearing children. Richard Titmuss compared this with the position of another hypothetical woman of the same age, this time in 1960. She would expect to live a further fifty-five years, but would spend only 7 per cent of her remaining time child-bearing or involved in maternal care (1976, pp. 1–2). The shrinking family has been a feature of British society since the beginning of the century, a result of economic circumstances and an awareness of the deleterious medical consequences for women of having many children. Having fewer children has weakened women's ties to their homes. From 1944, with the coming of free education, children spent less time at home with their mothers.

Elizabeth Roberts, in her oral history of working-class women between 1890 and 1940, argues that before the war women were 'disciplined' and 'conforming' and 'placed perceived familial and social needs before those of the individual'. Women 'did not seek self-fulfilment at the expense of the family . . . they saw little distinction between their own good and that of their *families*' (1984, p. 203). The prewar working-class household, Roberts points out, was dominated by women, whose lives would be centred on 'their homes, families and neighbourhoods'.

Six years of war effort in industry and the long periods of enforced separation caused momentous disruptions with incalculable consequences for family life. So after the war there was widespread concern over the impact on family stability generally and on the woman's role in the family in particular. Women's spell at work came to an end at the war's conclusion; we have seen how they were shunted out of industry and back into their homes. The dissolution of state-run nurseries and the introduction of maternity benefits and child allowance reflected the mood, and Beveridge, in his report, underscored the point that women had primary duties as mothers and housewives. The later expansion of professional social work, with a focus specifically on the maintenance of family stability, and marriage counselling services sponsored by the Home Office, deepened the state's involvement in supporting the traditional family structure. The welfare reforms of the 1940s and 1950s indexed married women's circumstances to those of their husbands, assuming that they would be provided for by the 'man of the house' and, in the process, weakening the economic independence-of-sorts they had established during the war. Despite this, the postwar refluence ensured that a substantial number of women took on two roles.

While there may have been some initial male hostility to the idea of women's resuming paid employment and possibly neglecting home responsibilities, this seems to have faded, certainly by the 1950s when the consumer boom and the thirst for higher living standards brought strains on the family budget. A married woman's earnings, in many cases, became an essential part of the family's income. Houses, cars and holidays abroad came within reach of the working-class family thanks to women's incomes.

Family building in the sense of child-bearing and -rearing and investing time and money in making a home became, as Jacqueline Burgoyne describes it, 'a major national preoccupation, gathering momentum in the affluence of the fifties' (1987, p. 13). Consumer advertising both encouraged and reflected this. It focused not so much on individual buyers, but on families. A 'family car', a 'family restaurant': these were products of the time, as was the holiday camp, purpose built for family vacations. The graphics on the cornflakes boxes supplied a kind of blueprint for the 'ordinary family', while the ultimate model for the 'perfect' set-up was the Royal Family. Despite fears that the war would cause serious disruptions, family life soon returned to a state of 'normality', although some interesting changes lay beneath the surface continuity.

A substantial body of research provided evidence that family relationships were changing. With rising salaries and standards of living, husbands and wives came to share incomes and to plan household purchases, they divided up household tasks more evenly and both undertook child-rearing duties. The shape of the family became more 'symmetrical', as Young and Willmott were to describe it (1973). Complementary studies by John and Elizabeth Newson (1965) and Ronald Fletcher (1973) documented a decline of the sprawling authoritarian patriarchies that were thought to characterize prewar families and their replacement by smaller units with more balanced power relations between spouses. Research on the emergent family proliferated in the 1950s and 1960s.

Birth control for married women was freely available from 1947. Besides relieving some women of the burden of unwanted pregnancy and child-rearing, this introduced the element of democratic choice. Couples could, in principle, deliberate about and decide upon the size of their family (the 1967 Family Planning Act extended the state's provision of contraception). The whole effect of contraception was beneficial for married women, not only in reducing physical strain and allowing them a greater say in their own reproductive functions, but also in releasing them to pursue other endeavours, especially paid employment. The emancipatory effect of contraception was heightened by the ability of partners to dissociate sex from reproduction and indulge in sex simply for its own sake.

Improvements in the efficiency of birth control methods, greater availability and more public awareness of them contributed to the diminishing size of families. Despite a 'baby boom' in the early 1960s, the birth rate fell steadily in the postwar period, most markedly after 1964. By the 1980s the average family had two children. The trend was for women to have fewer children at younger ages, most births occurring when the mother was under 30. One consequence of this was that many mothers were still under 40 by the time their youngest child had reached school age. Still being physically active, many married women, their child-bearing over, returned to work. This posed no immediate problem until the late 1970s when rising unemployment and job scarcity converted married women into unwelcome competitors in the job market in the eyes not only of men, but of resentful, job-hunting single women with no other means of financial support save for the state.

Combining work and child-bearing has been a target for many women, who have seen continuous employment as the key to their independence but do not wish to deny themselves the gratification of having children. Available figures suggest that it has not been a particularly successful combination, for the married women least active in the job market since the war have been those aged between 25 and 30, while the most active have been aged between 45 and 49. The implication of this is that child-care responsibilities effectively cut mothers out of the job market. (Even so, in 1981, 21 per cent of mothers with children under 3 went out to work, 5 per cent of them on a full-time basis.) The motivation for mothers going to work is not difficult to find. Research by Karen Dunnell (1976) and Martin and Roberts (1984) indicated that between 50 and 69 per cent of married women went to work just for the money and not for companionship, job satisfaction, or anything less tangible. (The percentages of black and Asian women who worked because of the money motive was even higher.)

The cash nexus would seem to apply, in the main, to working-class wives who wanted or needed the money a job brings. But the trend for mothers to work has not been an exclusively working-class phenomenon; for since the war more middle-class mothers have broken away from the home, presumably for different reasons. It has become quite acceptable for middle-class wives to work, although, as Mary Farmer notes, only in specific high-status occupations, such as journalism, the arts and the professions (1982, p. 74).

Regional variations, while not noticeable in the immediate postwar years, became apparent much later, especially in the 1970s. For example, in areas traditionally dominated by textiles, married women's employment has been a virtual norm; whereas, in heavy manufacturing areas, working wives were something of a novelty after the war. It is possible to read these trends as reflecting a satisfactory accommodation of home and work for women. Compared to the prewar situation described by Roberts, this was a deliverance. Women were able to break loose from their homes and advance into the new areas of work that were opening up in the postwar period. Wage packets relieved women of some of their former dependence on men. Vacuum-cleaners, refrigerators and those domestic icons washing-machines simplified and reduced the number of household chores. Combined with smaller numbers of children and increasing educational facilities, these developments helped detach women from their previous home-locked situation. Or so it might seem.

Women's relations with their homes did change, but not in such a way as to permit a complete integration of the two roles. 'Work and marriage were still understood as *alternatives*,' Elizabeth Wilson reflects on an equal pay report of 1946 which gave a 'guarded welcome' to the idea of married women at work. As we have seen, welcome or not, married women did work and continued to do so, but without ever divesting themselves of their domestic responsibilities. The boundaries of a woman's ambitions were thought properly to end at becoming an ancillary or acolyte, a point expressed in Susan Maughan's popular song of the 1960s, in which she announced her aim to become 'Bobby's Girl': 'That's the only thing I want to be. And if I was Bobby's girl, what a grateful, thankful girl I'd be.'

Work or, more accurately, a career remained an 'alternative' to family life. A woman who wished to pursue vocational work in, say, the professions or the civil service was not, it was supposed, going to marry and raise a family. Women who were intending to build families would have to assume principal responsibility for the home while their husbands went to work. If these women did wish to go to work, then they would have to be content with jobs that were transient, usually unskilled, invariably underpaid, often part-time and generally inferior in status to those of men. And, while household appliances improved some of the less pleasant aspects of housework, higher standards of child care and home management added to women's domestic burdens and so tended to counterbalance some of the advantages of technology.

It would seem reasonable to project that, as more and more women of all class backgrounds joined the labour force, there would be some shift in the fulcrum. The family studies of

Fletcher and others appeared to give empirical backing to this. But whatever changes there have been in the distribution of household duties since the war, they have not damaged the basic sexual division of labour; the female role has stayed inviolably in the family. Even after the mid-1970s, when unemployment began its climb to 13.5 per cent (in some regions as high as 30 per cent) and many women took over from their husbands as the household's principal or only money earner, the traditional female role remained. Studies found that the majority of women in paid employment continued to perform two sets of duties, earning a wage and running a home. Lydia Morris explains why working women with out-of-work husbands were unable to divest themselves of their domestic jobs: 'Male unemployment is likely to carry with it a resistance on the part of the man to any suggestion that he should take over domestic chores. His identity, already threatened by job loss, will be further threatened by "women's work" ' (1987, p. 18). This is the situation in the 1980s, the implication being that there has been great continuity in gender roles since the war. Changes have affected family patterns but have not dislodged the woman from her central position in the home. In profile, the family structure seems not to have altered appreciably from prewar times, when women's lives, to repeat Roberts, were centred on 'homes, families and neighbourhoods'. Watch any television soap opera for confirmation of this. Even in progressive dramas, like *Brookside* and *EastEnders*, families form foci of interest, and women characters tend to be associated with rootedness and domestic values.

Stability in marriage has been empirically associated with male dominance (witness Japan's low divorce rate), and what shifts in family power balances there have been have proved subversive. Loss of their primary economic function has threatened (but not destroyed) men's previously absolute authority, and instability has resulted. Not surprisingly, divorce rates can be taken as a litmus test of this; they have risen sharply amongst the unemployed. This leads to the question of the family's possible 'disintegration', a question that has troubled policy-makers since the war. The grounds for divorce have been progressively widened, and predictably divorce rates have risen consistently, particularly among the working class, leading many to the conclusion that the family is in crisis, as we will now see.

Wedlocked?

There was a steep rise in divorces in the two years following the end of the war, as one might expect after such an event. A tapering off followed, and stability held until 1965, after which there was a dramatic upswing, amounting to a 600 per cent rise in the overall divorce rate (up till 1987). In 1961 there were over 27,000 divorces; by 1971, this figure had increased to just under 79,000. In 1981 the total number of divorces was 157,947; or, put another way, one in every three marriages ended in divorce.

Legal and financial obstacles to divorce were removed by the Legal Aid Act of 1960 and the Divorce Reform Act of 1969, which made 'irretrievable breakdown' the sole ground for divorce and so introduced much more flexibility for both partners. Court procedures were shortened and simplified. Legal aid brought divorce within reach of many more working-class couples. Generally, having fewer resources than men, women qualified for legal aid and took advantage of this. Once the prohibitive financial cost of divorce was removed, a far greater number of women filed petitions. The 1960s witnessed new kinds of strain on marriage; it became an arrangement in which both partners searched for meaning, identity and personal fulfilment. Indeed, sexual satisfaction became a culturally prescribed goal. The concept of a constantly stimulating, challenging, even experimental sexual life made couples strive for more than they had in bygone years when sexual satisfaction might have been a coincidence rather than something to be assiduously worked at. 'Orgasm', argued Germaine Greer in 1984, 'is everybody's right and bounden duty' (1984, p. 201). A great number of marriages ended because one or both partners fell short of achieving their sexual goals. Greer believed that many couples virtually commended each other to adultery.

Sexual intercourse with a person other than one's spouse may still be regarded as sinful, but research tells us that about six out of every ten married men under 40 and four out of every ten married women have disregarded the message inscribed by the finger of God on the tablets of stone. Couples may have been inhibited about dissolving marriages prior to the 1969 Act, but the terms of the legislation were such that irreconcilable differences could be widely interpreted.

The questions revolving around issues of morality and intimacy did not automatically translate into an attack on marriage. In fact, during the 1960s young people, themselves products of the postwar baby boom, married in unprecedented numbers. Pregnancies prompted this trend: one-third of all teenage brides in this decade were pregnant, and over 40 per cent of births conceived maritally were to teenage mothers. This has had consequences for divorce patterns. Hypothetically, the woman most prone to divorce was married before she was 20, was childless or had one child only and had been through between four and six years of married life. But, whatever the duration of the marriage, the divorce rate among early brides was double the rate for women who married later, between the ages of 20 and 24. When both spouses were under 20 at the time of their marriage, the chances of divorce were three times as great as for marriages overall.

By the 1980s unemployment had become an ingredient in the recipe for divorce. Rates shot up amongst couples in which the male was out of work for long periods. The economy seems to play as large a part as emotion in marital break-ups, a view supported by the fact that the highest overall divorce rates have been amongst the unskilled, manual working class – a group with low incomes, irregular earnings and frequent over-commitments to hire purchase.

Rising divorce statistics tell one story, but there is a different side to the picture that supplies little comfort to those wishing to hasten the end of marriage as an institution. Consider the

following: in 1971 about one in every thirteen divorces involved
a partner who had been previously married (and, of course,
divorced); by 1984 about one in every five divorces involved a
person who had been divorced before. Second marriages are
more precarious than first: a considerable 40 per cent end in
divorce. This is an interesting, though perhaps not important,
point. Less interesting but more important is the fact that in the
1980s one out of every three marriages involved at least one
partner who had been married before. People who divorce have
a tendency to marry again. This tells us something about the
peculiar value placed on marriage and, consequently, on family
life in general. Remarriages seem to indicate that divorcees can
'write off' previous mistakes without questioning the validity
or propriety of marriage. Taboos about divorce might have
faded, and divorces may have become practically easier to
attain, but this has not loosened people's commitment to
marriage. 'Wedlocked Britain' is how David Clark has described the situation. 'The divorce revolution *has* happened, but
the marriage rites go on, largely unchecked,' he observes (1987,
p. 15).

Despite spiralling divorce rates, the institution of marriage
has proved its toughness and remained central to family life.
The nuclear family of man, woman and children living together
has diminished in size, but its structure has lasted. Interpreted
this way, the family's durability is an arrow in the quiver of
those who insist that it is, in the words of Peter and Brigitte
Berger, 'a natural unit of parents and children united by love,
mutual respect, trust and fidelity, based on religiously inspired
values and giving a distinct moral quality to this basic unit of
moral life' (1983, p. 107). Proponents of this view would need
to look no further than the Bible for support; at the beginning
of the Scriptures, there is an account of the origins of the
heterosexual relationship in the 'rib' scenario. For those who
are not convinced by the Scriptures, there is always the tax
incentive to marry.

Marriage has, then, proved resilient and shows few signs of
decline. It is, of course, the basic bond of the nuclear family,

both an emotional tie and a legal contract, linking the average man and woman together for 85 per cent and 75 per cent of their adult lives respectively. Nine out of ten married women have at least one child within the first ten years of marriage, and 75 per cent have two or more children. Marriage and kin relations affect most people's domestic arrangement for most of their lives. Yet there is an alternative interpretation.

The darker side of family life

The Bergers contrast their first depiction of the family with a second:

> A narrowly constraining cage, turning its members into mere instruments of production, profoundly destructive of the personalities of women and children (and, perhaps to a lesser degree, of men), and generally cutting off its members from participation in the larger concerns of society.
>
> (1983, p. 107)

In this perspective, the stable monogamous life has worked against the best interests of both sexes, but particularly women. Two systems of exploitation have been propped up by the family. The sexual division of labour at home has perpetuated unequal relationships in which men have inevitably carried the power and used it to dominate women. In an economic sense, capitalism generally benefits from women's divided loyalties; encouraged to see their real responsibilities as with their families, women accept their marginal position in the labour force in the belief that their paid employment is not central to their lives. The idea here is that the family has many more qualities than those idealized in popular images.

In Part One we recognized the vital role of wealth inheritance in sustaining class inequality. The family is the vehicle through which wealth and, therefore, power is transmitted, via direct and indirect methods (the principal indirect method being, as noted, the education system). Wealth passes from one generation to the next through lines of descent, and in this sense the family can be seen as an economic unit of transmission. Not merely an economic unit, however: it is also an important agency of socialization, an enclosure in which children learn values and principles, roles and statuses. At a political level, children are taught to believe in prevalent ideologies; at a personal level, they are persuaded to accept behaviour, characteristics and roles 'appropriate' to their sex. These are two fairly unexceptional observations about the functions of the family in the political and economic system and in the construction of gender.

Exactly how the family constructs gender identities is a subject of debate. It seems clear nevertheless that, during socialization, conceptions of femininity, maternity and subordination are imparted to girls. The family encourages not only heterosexual tendencies but other supposedly natural proclivities, such as mother–child bonding and breast-feeding. The desirability – indeed, rectitude – of such practices is never in doubt. And only a short step away are ideas about women's passivity, their dependence on men and their primary responsibility in household organization. The family expresses men's power – not their direct material power, as Randall points out, but 'their indirect ability to make women feel inferior and unaware of alternative ways of living' (1986, p. 26). This is a generalization to which there are many exceptions, and the rise of the women's movement itself confirms that the family is not universally perfect in churning out successive generations of obedient 'house slaves'.

Once again, there has been in the family an undeniable tendency towards continuity rather than change. Girls have had limits imposed on their horizons. Domesticity and motherhood, they have been led to believe, are their primary concerns. Their material dependence on men has not been regarded as problematic, just part of the natural order of things. Their *independence*, on the other hand, *has* been problematic. It is by approaching the family in this way that we learn much about those aspects of male–female relationships that have often been taken for granted and allowed to pass unquestioned: the idea that 'that's the way things are because that's the way they've always been'. Feminists have asked painful questions, specifically about the family, some, like Michele Barrett, identifying it as 'the central locus of women's oppression' (1985). Material produced since the war has chronicled the destructive effects of the family, particularly on women. Laing and Esterson compiled case studies to illustrate how some forms of mental illness are induced by the tight intimacy of family circumstances (1980). Familial violence against women and children became recognized as a serious social problem (see Borkowski, Murch and Wacker, 1983, for an overview). And, at a less dramatic level, the physical stresses and sheer grind of housework were made a topic of academic inquiry by Ann Oakley (1974) and Allen and Wolkowitz (1987). Critical studies disclosed hitherto ignored aspects of marriage and family life. In the late 1970s and early 1980s, unemployment introduced further unpleasant features, as men's traditional bread-winner status was called into doubt, and family tensions resulted.

The irony is that most women actually choose to get married and to become mothers and housewives. This is one of the points addressed by Michele Barrett: women are socialized into accepting their subordination. In her book with Mary McIntosh, *The Anti-Social Family*, she argues that women's choices are largely illusory ones: 'What they can seldom choose are the social circumstances and pressures that would enable them to resist being swamped by motherhood' (1982, p. 61). Women may be their own worst enemies, but the problem is to understand the conditions under which they fail to recognize the fact. Being brought up in the unquestioning environment of a nuclear family is one of them.

Since the war people have continued to marry and have children; and their children have also married and had children. The solidity of marriage and the family has been confirmed continually. Yet, as Barrett and McIntosh observe: 'Marriage is a form that is sanctified by tradition, not justified by rational social debate. The tradition is one that carries with it the whole historical baggage of male power and patriarchal authority'

[207]

(1982, p. 55). The family has a self-perpetuating facility that closes off possible questions about itself. 'For even to *mention* the darker side of family life can make people blind to the rest of the message, so resistant are we to seeing *our* marriages, *our* relations with *our* fathers, mothers, spouses and children, in any except the best light,' write Leonard and Speakman (1986, p. 21). 'The implications are so dreadful, we do not want to think them through.'

One of the implications, and not such a dreadful one, was explored by a great many women (and a smaller number of men) in the 1970s and 1980s. From the mid-1970s the number of families headed by one parent only grew at a rate of approximately 6 per cent per year, so that by 1987 there were over one million lone parents with dependent children under the age of 16 (who totalled 1.6 million). One in eight families in the UK were headed by a lone, or single, parent, women outnumbering men by nine to one. Many feminist authors wrote enthusiastically about the trend, the one-parent family being depicted as a positive, liberating innovation with a potential for flexibility not possible in two-parent set-ups. Epitomizing this view was Catherine Itzin, who argued that the one-parent alternative 'challenges fundamentally many of society's fervently held beliefs and values; sexual role conditioning . . . marriage, nuclear family values . . . basically the whole role of women and men in society' (1980, p. 9).

My own work on this subject drew me to rather different conclusions. Whilst applauding the vigour and determination of a great many parents who had struggled, often against severe opposition, to manage a family without detriment to their children, I also found that one-parenthood can be, in the Bergers' phrase, 'a narrowly constraining cage'. Some parents make a conscious decision to become lone parents, but the vast majority are compelled by a combination of personal and social circumstances. As suggested in the title of my book, being a lone parent is frequently a case of *Having To* (1985).

Given the 'darker side of family life' and the unseen ways in which the nuclear unit serves 'male power' rather than the interests of women, the idea of parents breaking free of marriage and raising children single-handed has its appeals. One-parenthood 'may be the grounds of a real independence for some women, with much more complete responsibility for their destiny', Paul Willis speculates (1984, p. 14). But being a lone parent often involves the individual in another relationship of dependence – this time with the state. This generates a different set of problems: low income, poverty, restricted access to decent accommodation, limited nursing and child-care facilities. Lone parents do not need a partner so much as a partner's income. Children do not suffer inordinately through the absence of a parent, and most instances of child disturbance or deviance are the result of material and not emotional deprivation. It scarcely needs to be stated that the majority of one-parent families are of working-class origin; amongst the working class there tends to be more suspicion of contraception, more proscription about abortion and more resistance to adoption than in the middle class.

The one-parent model is the most significant alternative to the nuclear family, although many lone parents remarry and become part of a 'reconstituted' nuclear family. There are also homosexual liaisons, heterosexual de facto partnerships, ménages, communes and a variety of other deviations from the 'two plus two' norm. Such impulses away from the nuclear family standard will undoubtedly raise more questions about its potential destructiveness, its reproduction of sex roles in the family and its perpetuation of sex inequalities in society. The single prevailing norm about what the family should be like is under some pressure, and the UK may now be in transition to a society in which a plurality of family forms will be recognized as legitimate or even desirable. If so, the UK could become 'unwedlocked', and women would have one of the sources of their subordination removed.

Yet social trends rarely conform to particular interest groups' requirements. The appearance of a new malevolent force in the late-1980s strewed the path of sex with deadly traps, threatening with dire consequences anything other than stable, monogamous, heterosexual pairing. The pursuit of alternative family arrangements will, it seems, be curtailed by the panic surrounding Aids.

Changes since the war have ensured that women can now compete academically with men. They have been discharged from many of their former family obligations and released to explore their independence in the job market. Women have a lot to be grateful for, yet there is an exasperating ambiguity in this 'success'. We can angle our lenses another way and see women trudging through an endless assault course. The educational system and the family may be seen as devices in a larger, perhaps subtler process that keeps women entirely marginal to all the key positions in society. Education and the family do not merely reflect, validate, or seal women's marginality; they actively create it – even if not uniformly. Women have had success in the postwar years, but success drawn not wholly from education, nor from the opportunities permitted by smaller families. What seems to have happened since the 1970s is that many women have studied carefully the rules and prescriptions for female success and, as if infuriated by their onerous nature and sheer prolixity, tossed them away and formulated their own alternatives. The results will be examined in Chapter 10.

CHAPTER 10

The feminist solution

Governing body

No issue has aroused more passion, controversy and crisis amongst women than the *body* – more specifically, the abuses of the body. Barrett describes it as 'a central political concern of the women's movement' (1980, p. 44). Prior to the war women had only limited redress against rape and domestic violence and virtually no control over their fertility. Their bodies were, in a real sense, not their own. Biological differences do not explain inequalities but, as we noticed in Chapter 8, they lie at the source. Women, being biologically equipped to reproduce and physically less powerful than men, have in a way been appropriated by men, who have sought some degree of control over reproduction: in itself, a political motive. Women's vulnerability has been continually compounded by their inability to control their reproductive processes. What control there was came from the medical profession, the church and the state, all male-dominated institutions. But developments in the postwar period made it at least technically possible for women to capture some influence over their own reproductive functions, and to protect themselves more effectively, if only in a legal sense, from violence.

Gender was created as a social question not just by the availability of contraception and abortion, nor just by legislation relating to sexual offences. The developments were catalysts. Once added to a solution of sexual inequality, relative

[211]

affluence and social democratic beliefs about the progressive improvement of women's status, they produced a set of ideas and a movement known as 'second-wave feminism'. The term suggests a continuity with a 'first wave', but this is rather misleading, since the original feminism was quite different organizationally and ideologically. Immediately after the war, Elizabeth Roberts writes, 'Feminists fully shared the general optimism of the progressive sections of society and many had great expectations of the welfare state' (1984, p. 164). Roberts quotes Vera Brittan, a feminist of the 1940s and 1950s who identified three stages of the first wave: the original pioneers who had begun by demanding equality and rights; those who, in the war years, had valued the idea of self-support and independence; and those who emphasized the special values women could bring to a society menaced by destruction. The thrust was not to elevate women to a position of equality with men, but to educate men to adopt and respect women's values.

The early movement shared in the emergent consensus and in general placed its faith in a widespread improvement, rather than concentrating on the specific case of women. Roberts believes that the orchestrated consensus imposed on the position of women resulted in a 'false harmony'. Many of the issues which were to become central – rape, violence, sexual orientation, etc. – were not recognized. The received wisdom about women was that they were part of society; their position would improve with society's progress and not independently of it. Later feminists were to challenge this notion and suggest another view whereby women as a group were seen as effectively detached from many processes and institutions in society. Although both movements were feminist in the sense that they were concerned with morally and materially upgrading women, the early wave lacked the critical impulse so important to the later developments.

There is often special providence in the timing of a social movement's inauguration. Although it was actually its second national conference, the meeting of the United States National Organization for Women (NOW), under the presidency of

[212]

Betty Friedan, in November 1967 drew publicity from all quarters in its attempt to create an agenda for women's issues. News of the conference reached Britain at a time when legislators were dancing on hot coals over the liberalizing reforms. Among the eight-point 'Bill of Rights for Women' there were demands for the enforcement of laws banning sex discrimination in employment, more day-care centres, equal educational and training opportunities and the right of women to control their reproductive lives. This final demand effectively called for greater contraceptive facilities and for the repeal of laws limiting abortion – demands that were already satisfied, at least partially, in the UK.

The US campaign had drawn sustenance from a revolutionary coalition of black groups that was challenging traditional principles and institutions and demanding major changes to accommodate the interests of the USA's black minority. Women were not a minority in a numerical sense, yet they shared a similar awareness of their powerlessness and others' prejudice. David Bouchier believes that 'working-class women served the same liberating function for British feminists as did blacks for the Americans' (1983, p. 57). He means that the industrial action of women in the 1960s had brought public recognition for women's grievances and, in the process, gained them some legitimacy. In this way, they made it possible for other women, not necessarily working-class women, to identify with them.

The women working in the Ford machine shops at Dagenham and those demonstrating at the Albert Hall Miss World contest may not appear tangibly related. Neither do an exhaust system and a windscreen wiper until fitted to a fully assembled motor car – then the purposes they serve in a larger design is recognizable. Basically, that is all the feminists did: connect together what seemed singular, separate events. Not being in control of the body meant not being in control *period*.

A gift-wrapped smoke-bomb

The 1970 Women's Liberation Conference was held at Oxford and attracted six hundred delegates. It officially constituted the beginning of a movement that issues challenges to the political Left and Right. It was no coincidence that the first set of demands for women's liberation in the UK was abstracted without much revision from the US agenda. Equal pay was the first demand; this had been agreed in principle, although the Equal Pay Act would not be completed for another five years. Equal education and opportunity were technically established by the 1944 Education Act, but, as we saw in Chapter 9, patterns of sex inequality stayed entrenched. The call for 24-hour nurseries recognized the burden that child-rearing placed specifically on women and pushed for a dissolution of the home-centred role. Finally, the women's conference argued for an extension of the contraception and abortion reforms. The demand was for free contraception for all women and abortion on demand.

One could argue that the demands were so unrealistic as to have no effect on public policy. In contrast to the USA where the statute books were targets, Britain had already enacted major changes that were directly to affect the material position of women. Equal pay was, in a legal sense, on its way, and contraception and abortion were legal in clinically prescribed circumstances. To push for more was like having your cake, eating, it, complaining about its taste and then asking for more. Yet some analysts, such as Joyce Gelb, have argued that this view betrays a misunderstanding of the purposes and motives of the movement, which was unlike its US counterpart from the outset: 'British feminists have, in the main, been concerned more with changing consciousness than with public policy' (1986, p. 117). The movement chose to operate often independently of party or pressure-group politics.

The first public demonstration by the women's liberation movement was in 1971 when a petition was presented to Prime Minister Heath. Publicity for the event secured widespread interest; and within months there was an astonishing increase in awareness of, and identification with, the movement's aims, both in numbers and regionally. What made the movement's growth more remarkable was the fact that it was accomplished without any organization of note, no effective communication system, nor any systematic ideology, save for the general feminist impulse and the four principles. Neither did it have the kinds of legislative target of its US forerunner – which is why the reactionary anti-abortion lobby was so important in providing an enemy that symbolized the worst features of a male-dominated society by attempting to deny women 'the right to choose'.

Having – or, conversely, not having – the ability wilfully to determine one's own fertility was the issue that gave feminism its dynamism in the late 1960s. 'The physical basis of women's oppression' is how Randall describes the preoccupation of the movement; in contrast: 'Socialist feminists have been more prepared to campaign for equal pay and the advancement of women in trade unions, so long as these are understood as transitional objectives' (1986, p. 181). Without suggesting a clear demarcation between the radical and socialist wings, it seems fair to follow Randall's distinction and recognize two imperatives in the movement. One was to dismantle the structure of male domination which has its source in a physical control and manifests in patriarchies. The other was to challenge the economic system that permits, even facilitates, the exploitation of women's labour. Interestingly, while in Oxford six hundred women were attending the official launch of women's liberation, seven thousand textile workers went on strike at Leeds clothing factories, where the workforce was 85 per cent female. Any issue that uniquely affects the material conditions and experience of women has to be seen as legitimately feminist.

It is difficult to gauge the tangible success of either wing of the movement, particularly if we accept Gelb's point about the priority of changing consciousness rather than policies. It may be that the movement hastened or assisted policy changes rather than forced them. The Equal Pay and Sex Discrimination Acts of 1975 were hailed as products of feminist campaigns, yet equal pay, as we have noticed, was already in gestation by the end of the 1960s; its pertinence was emphasized by the Dagenham dispute of 1968 when women sewing-machinists won a battle over equal grading for both sexes.

By 1969 both government and opposition were in agreement over the issue. The Sex Discrimination Act began life as a Private Member's Bill in 1967 and attracted growing support in both Houses until in 1973 the House of Commons established a Select Committee. The Conservative government announced legislative proposals in 1974 and created the Equal Opportunities Commission (EOC). That same year, the Labour Party, now back in government, published a White Paper on *Equality for Women*. On assuming power later in the year, Labour widened the terms of reference of the White Paper by introducing a Bill designed to deal with direct and 'indirect' discrimination.

The Sex Discrimination Act outlawed the unequal treatment of women in all educational institutions, including training programmes, in employment (including vacancy advertising, recruitment, pay, promotion and redundancy) and in trade unions. Financial and public services were not allowed to exclude women on grounds of their sex. In a way, the Act paralleled the race relations legislation in that it outlawed a set of practices without making additional provision that might aid the disadvantaged group to improve its position (like free child care or greater access to abortion). Neither this nor the equal pay legislation was a response to feminists' demands, even though women's organizations' campaigns persisted up till 1975.

The legislation came as a gift-wrapped smoke-bomb. It brought feminists what they wanted, but it filled the air with enough dense cloud to obscure the purpose and direction of the movement. Uncertainty and confusion over whether the day had actually been won, or not, robbed the movement of its drive. Riddled with faults as many critics believed the legislation to be, it did at least deliver a legal end to sex inequality and the promise of a palpable improvement in the condition of women.

While some women celebrated victoriously, others chained themselves to railings outside Parliament to signify the insufficiency of the legislation. Between 1972 and 1976, when both major laws went into effect, women's earnings compared to men's increased from 59.5 per cent to 68.9 per cent. Bouchier notes how a 1976 opinion poll found that 48 per cent of women believed they had gained equal job opportunities (89 per cent thought they had equal educational opportunities). For many who had thrown their weight behind the early women's liberation campaigns, there were no further laws to be fought for, no areas of society befouled by sex discrimination: just a residue of prejudice that would surely disappear. Many anti-racist campaigners must have felt similarly after the 1968 Act. As we have seen, both racism and sexism have an immanent stubbornness, and legal measures have been unable to shift them. Those who thought the battle against sexism in employment won were rudely awakened by the news that, although women's earnings rose to 71 per cent of men's in the two years after the Acts came into operation, they stayed static thereafter. This was possible because, as Angela Coyle points out, 'The fact of the matter is, that women do different jobs from men, cannot be directly compared with men, and women's [work] is persistently undervalued' (1984, p. 139). The European Economic Community found that the Equal Pay Act did not comply with European law in this respect and called for an amendment, which duly came in 1984. This stated that work of 'equal value' must be rewarded at equal rates. It remains to be seen whether the long-term effects of this will be offset by unemployment, which disproportionately affects women.

There were two independent pieces of legislation which, while not direct answers to feminists' prayers, certainly effected some change in the required direction. Much less publicized than the other major Acts of the 1970s were the Employment Protection Act, which contained the first statutory entitlement women had to maternity leave, and the Social Security Pensions

Act, which abolished some of the more obvious areas of discrimination against married women within the social security system. The original women's liberation charter, as we have noted, included a demand for maternity leave. However, the main impetus behind the 1975 changes came from the Trades Union Congress.

Nineteen seventy-six saw another two pieces of legislation designed to afford women more protection, this time from the physical violence of assailants rather than the more abstract and anonymous violence of institutions. Before the Sexual Offences (Amendment) Act, rape, while universally recognized as a grave offence, was not a statutory offence but was governed by common law (prior to 1840 it was punishable by death). This made convictions rare, a situation compounded by the reluctance of victims to report the crime for fear of the stigma, the dubious interrogation techniques employed by the police investigating reported rapes and the prohibiting problem of producing corroborating evidence (although this is not technically required). The precise effect of rendering rape a statutory crime is impossible to assess, principally because of what is suspected to be gross under-reporting. (US studies suggest that between 6 and a staggering 44 per cent of women sampled have been subjected to at least one completed or attempted rape.) Such statistics as are available indicate that the number of rapes reported in England and Wales between 1973 and 1983 increased by 33.7 per cent from 998 to 1,334. The twelve-month period immediately following the 1976 Act saw a leap of 22 per cent in notified rapes. It could well be that the actual number of offences committed remained stable, but women, urged by feminists and encouraged by the Act, became less anxious about the problems of reporting. While this has been the trend, under-reporting remains a problem. One wonders how many women simply remain silent or maybe seek the kind of vengeance taken in Robert M. Young's film *Extremities* (1986), where the victim sprays insecticide into her male predator's eyes, wallops him with a shovel, kicks him in the groin and cages him up in a fireplace. Not many, one imagines – unfortunately!

[218]

While rape is a shockingly vivid offence that draws widespread public disapproval, violence against women and children within marriage is an altogether more private affair. The subject was considered by a Parliamentary Committee on Violence in Marriage in 1974. One of the committee's admissions was that, like rape, an unknown amount of marital violence goes unreported. The Domestic Violence and Marital Proceedings Act of 1976 made it possible to institute injunction proceedings without assuming that divorce would follow, effectively acknowledging that wishing violence to end is not necessarily the same as wishing a marriage to end. The intention was to help 'battered' wives minimize their stress without plunging them into an insecure or even homeless situation. Neither piece of legislation fully satisfied the women's liberation movement, which in 1978 added to its list of demands a call for an end 'to all laws, assumptions and institutions that perpetuate male dominance and aggression towards women'.

While it is not always easy to ascertain the degree of influence that the women's movement had on the legislation of 1976, there can be little doubt that the women's issue had been etched on to the official scroll of social problems after resolute campaigning from feminist quarters. The message was clear enough and that was that women have had their bodies misused by men: their labours have been insufficiently rewarded, their fertility has not been completely in their control and their physical vulnerability has been violently exploited. In employment, actions over pay and conditions have not been specifically 'women's issues' but rather 'bread and butter' ones. Yet the way women have, in practice, defended their positions has forced into public focus the unique personal problems of working women. The issues of the body and of work have been the two great rallying points for the women's movement generally and have brought diverse numbers of women together. But the same two issues have also introduced strains in allegiance, as we will see next.

Sisters

In 1984–5 Britain witnessed its most historic period of industrial unrest as miners stoutly attempted to resist pit closures and the unemployment they brought. Significantly, women were extremely active in the resistance, organizing such groups as Women Against Pit Closures to focus attention on the experiences of working-class women in the context of industrial action. This was an example of women's unity within a class unity. In the opening phase of the strike, women were active, but essentially as back-ups for their husbands. They cooked in collective kitchens, distributed food parcels, washed clothes – tasks associated with the traditional woman's role. Over time, many women began travelling throughout the country, staging rallies to generate funds, speaking at meetings and leading marches. Broadening their role in the strike further, they made links with women's groups with totally different origins and purposes: black activists, lesbians, Greenham campers.

This was a case not of women supporting their husbands but, in some cases, of actually leading and encouraging them 'from the front'. They stood on picket lines and harangued police and those who crossed the lines to work. Even after the strike had ended, the Women Against Pit Closures staged a conference attended by about one thousand. There is a story that, at a meeting during the strike, a miner from Kent asked the chair if he might have his wife back when the strike was over. 'Not this one,' he added, 'the one I had before.' Some men clearly appreciated the comradeship of their wives at the height of the conflict; yet many, it seems, still wanted a housekeeper to return home to once the strike was over.

One criticism faced by the other current of feminism is that it has a pronounced middle-class orientation. Its campaigns have usually been guided by idealistic rather than pragmatic concerns (wages for housework, abortion on demand), and this has tended to remove it from grass-roots considerations. The Greenham Common campaign provides an illustration. In 1982 thousands of women converged on the cruise missile base to protest *as* women, but *for* humanity. They cut through the base's barbed-wire surrounds and hung children's garments on the fences to symbolize their concern for the future. Over the next several years, the women established camps and prolonged the protest, living without electricity or sanitation – or, for that matter, men.

The campaign was actually started by women who, in August 1981, with four men and some children, walked from Cardiff to Greenham Common, the planned British site for cruise missiles. They delivered a letter to the RAF base's commander. 'The greatest threat ever faced by the human race and our living planet,' is how the Women for Life on Earth (as they called themselves) described nuclear arms. 'We want the arms race to be brought to a halt now – before it is too late to create a peaceful, stable world for our future generations' (quoted in Coote and Campbell, 1987, p. 48). No reference was made to specifically 'women's issues'; but, by February 1982, after much disagreement, it was decided to establish a 'women's camp'. In the interim, the campaign had attracted publicity and support. At this stage, the majority of campaigners were women, but not all. Coote and Campbell believe that the decision to block men was that non-violent protest was favoured, and 'women feared men would more readily engage in violent confrontation with the police' (1987, p. 48). Contentious as the belief might be, it gave the campaigners the opportunity to suggest new aims for the women's movement, at that stage losing some direction and momentum as widely recognizable causes (like abortion and equal pay) disappeared.

In December 1987 about 30,000 joined hands and encircled the entire nine-mile perimeter of the Greenham Common base. Eleven months later, the missiles arrived, prompting another mass demonstration, this time of 50,000. The camp surrounding the base remained, drawing together particularly those women who, as Coote and Campbell put it, 'missed out on the high tide of discovery and invention that launched women's liberation in the seventies' (1987, p. 50).

Worthy as this campaign might have been, a working-class riposte might be that the typical camper had the time, resources and propensity to carry out her task, in contrast to a working-class woman who was too preoccupied with making ends meet to divert her energies to issues that left her day-to-day circumstances unaffected. Also, men, to the same woman, were not enemies beyond redemption but rather required – irritatingly, perhaps – in order to make life more satisfactory in a heterosexual relationship.

Even within the feminist current concerned specifically with the position of working-class women, there has been ample scope for discord. In the mid-1970s, for example, feminists from the Communist Party initiated a 'working women's charter' relating to women's employment. It was envisioned as a healthy alternative to the women's liberation movement, which seemed too quixotic and ignorant of the practicalities of working-class life. Also designed as a vehicle for working women, yet in sharp opposition to the charter, was the Wages for Housework Campaign (WHC), an organization whose title captured the premiss of its argument: working women performed two jobs, one of which went completely unpaid. The proposal to introduce a national wage for domestic labour was regarded as so unrealistic as to provoke ridicule and so undercut the legitimacy of all feminist groups. The organizers of the charter, in particular, tried to ostracize the WHC. Yet both were allegedly promoting the interests of working women and offering what they considered working-class antidotes to the strong bourgeois medicine of women's liberation. As Anne Phillips comments with regard to the charter and WHS:

> The first could say it expressed the needs of working-class women, for where pay and conditions were appalling, surely improvement at work was the major concern? The second could equally claim to be the authentic voice of working-class women, for without the qualifications and opportunities that might delude others into 'liberation through jobs', these were the women who were housewives first and wage workers second

. . . When the movement so decisively rejected wages for housework, did this, at bottom, reflect its middle-class nature – a lack of interest in those who were working at home?

(1987, p. 116)

The question could be asked of the entire women's movement and all the factions it has spawned since its early years. Despite attempts to integrate philosophies and campaigns, the feminist movement has remained exactly that – a movement and not a social organization. In other words, feminism has been a form of collective action, not highly institutionalized, nor backed by rigorous theory, but arising from protest that has been directed at both specific and widespread grievances. Splinters, even splinters of splinters, may have bedevilled the movement; yet the very nature of feminism has virtually guaranteed this. Social issues do not have a uniform quality that strikes all women similarly. Even issues about which there has been extensive agreement amongst feminist groups, like abortion, have elicited a range of reactions. This has been because, as Phillips argues, 'Abortion on demand could be presented as a *class* issue', rather than as a women's issue: 'Those with money could always turn to a private clinic; the rest depend on the vagaries of their NHS consultant, and if they lived in the wrong area, they had no choice at all' (1987, p. 118). All women are in some way affected, but working-class women are most adversely affected. This type of analysis can be applied to most alleged women's issues. While most 'class issues' and 'race issues' also have to be seen through several prisms, the problem has been especially punishing for the women's movement.

'The notion of priority', as Phillips calls it, has been hard, if not impossible, to avoid. Women's energies have been dissipated instead of concentrated. Those miners' wives who mobilized so effectively to oppose pit closures in 1984–5 actually dissociated themselves from the Greenham Common protesters. Yet, each in its own way, these two efforts present the most impressive and forceful displays of unified female enterprise in the 1980s. Both elicited genuine feelings of 'sisterhood', while also illustrating that feminism has two distinct aspects that are only loosely coupled.

One aspect is based on a demand for equality of consideration as women but as members of a class of people. The purpose is that the experience and preoccupations of women should be taken as seriously as those of their male counterparts, whether in industry, the professions, or any other sphere in which gender has been used as a criterion for separate treatment. Women have, in other words, tried to play down differences and play up their indisputable capability for performing tasks as well as men.

This contrasts with the other aspect, whose purpose is not to show how women can enrich, modify, or add to traditional arrangements, but to pursue a complete alternative to them. Its orientation, like that of the Greenham campaign, has been separatist. While it does not rule out the possibility that men can respond positively, it does tend to exclude them from any central role. The justification for this is that women, because of their unique experiences – social and biological – are the only people equipped to assert values, stake claims and precipitate the relevant conflicts.

After the rabbits are caught

For many working-class women, Greenham Common triggers images of lesbians rearing children in squalor. And lesbianism is a subject that plunges even feminists into uncertainty, let alone working-class women trying to reinforce their husbands' stand against the National Coal Board. It has estranged working-class women and deepened divisions within feminist ranks. To many in the movement, lesbianism was 'the solution', as Jill Johnston put it, to the problems posed by feminism (1973). A logical conclusion to the argument predicated on the assumption that the personal is political, lesbianism was seen as the ultimate sign of repudiation of and withdrawal from male-dominated society. Others saw in the claim a new provincialism, a tendency to attach oneself to groups on the basis of sexual preference rather than acting on women's wider concerns.

Any social movement that seeks legitimacy has to confront the problem of simultaneously satisfying all tendencies; the task is like trying to keep plates spinning atop poles. The women's movement in the 1980s has had to agonize over how to resolve the issues raised by lesbian groups, without completely losing public approval. Hostility towards lesbians – 'lesbophobia' as some are wont to call it – has been absorbed into culture. Singer Diana Ross, reasonably aware, intelligent and independent in most people's estimation, allegedly walked out of a part in the American television soap, *Dallas*, when told she would have to perform a lesbian scene. It is difficult to assess the strength of anti-lesbian feeling in British society, but film director Neil Jordan seems to have captured the essence in his *Mona Lisa* (1986), the central character of which is delegated the task of chauffeuring and minding a prostitute. Soft-hearted custodian George, at great risk to his own life, helps his protégé track down her lost 'sister', only to find that she is, in fact, her lover. 'I've sold myself for a pair of dikes,' curses George, vengeful after discovering the relationship. He instantly cuts dead a friendship that had grown with kindness during the previous weeks.

Lesbian schisms grew out of a 1977 debate over the scope and purposes of women's demands, although as early as 1974 a demand for an end to all discrimination against lesbians was added to the women's liberation agenda. The dialogue was between, on the one hand, those who pushed for reforms to pay structures, abortion legislation and legal independence and, on the other, those who believed no solution to the women's problem could be found within existing institutional frameworks, nor within any institutional framework dominated by men. 'You can't trust another . . . take our advice and keep looking after number one,' singers Mel and Kim told women in the 1988 song, 'That's the Way It Is', the lyric of which contradicted a Dusty Springfield counsel of the 1960s: 'You've got to show him that you care just for him, do the things he likes to do. Wear your hair just for him. You won't get him wishing and hoping' ('Wishing and Hoping').

Men were the enemy, and to develop freely women must separate, argued lesbian groups. The debate had echoes of the US black nationalists' disagreement with gradualist, civil rights campaigns; more radical in the whole approach, nationalists believed the ideal of integration to be a mirage, a product of whites' connivance to deflect the advances of blacks. The defining feature of black nationalism was its implacable refusal to allow validity to any effort to negotiate within existing political arrangements. Similarly, lesbian groups insisted that women could not win their fight whilst continuing to have sexual relations with their enemies. The alternative was to withdraw from heterosexual activities. This was a political as well as a sexual statement, and its practical implication was to isolate the women's movement so that it could develop as independently as possible from the rest of society. By 1978, Angela Weir and Elizabeth Wilson reflected, 'almost every campaign threw up issues which provoked disagreement . . . Effectively the women's movement had fragmented' (1984, p. 78).

Class and sexual orientation have been two sources of disunity within the women's movement and have raised the problem of competing philosophies. Some women, for instance, simply do not believe men to be the root problem; it just so happens that men control the political and economic system, that system itself being the problem. The attempt to incorporate political lesbian into a socialist analysis has not been at all convincing, and the breach has yet to be healed. Black women have contributed a further argument, pointing out that they uniquely have been made to swallow an unsavoury cocktail of sexism and racism and want this recognized in campaigns. Revolutionary feminists accuse others who would describe themselves as sisters of collaborating with the enemy because of their involvement with community projects and women's service organizations. Causes of disunity seem to multiply.

Only on occasion have all factions of the women's movement congregated around focal concerns. They stood four-square against Victoria Gillick's attempt in the 1980s to stop girls' access to contraception without parental consent. The movement was almost as resolute in its support for Wendy Savage, who in 1985–6 was suspended from her post as consultant obstetrician and subjected to an inquiry on her natural childbirth methods. These cases helped the women's movement reconstitute itself, strengthening group consciousness and issuing reminders about group boundaries. Solidarity, as we have seen, results from the apprehension of a common enemy; it is unlikely to occur when the enemy is so anonymous as to be virtually undetectable. It was not due only to good fortune that the movement coalesced in the late 1960s with one of its concerns being the defence of the Abortion Act. The coalescence was a response to the backlash against abortion. As the reactionary threat receded, more ideological goals replaced pragmatic ones, and the movement tended to lose some of its purpose. Such purpose may return after the moral U-turn of 1988 and David Alton's Bill to reduce the upper time limit for abortions to eighteen weeks.

In general, the opposition, or enemy, is now less identifiable (but more pervasive). Institutional sexism operates rather like institutional racism; it does not reveal itself but has to be discovered with painstaking research, such as that commissioned by the EOC into British Rail (BR) in 1986.

Out of the BR workforce of 17,000, only 6.5 per cent were women, most of whom were confined to clerical posts and cleaning jobs. Only 82 women guards and 12 women footplate staff were employed by BR. The management was found to have sex-stereotyped ideas about the natural unsuitability of women for what was regarded as 'men's work'. Also, the National Union of Railwaymen and the drivers' union, Aslef, were found to have done nothing constructive for their minority of women members and, on occasion, actually hindered their progress. If this was the position in BR, ostensibly an equal opportunity employer subject to all legal conditions, then it hardly strains credibility to believe that sexism still exists in other major institutions in the UK. Employers will not readily admit to such practices, which tend to become exposed only after investigation. No one, however, attempts to defend such practices. This suggests that there was a revolution of sorts in the late 1970s and 1980s: at the level of perceptions. No serious consideration was given to arguments about the inferiority of women. Male supremacists in the late 1980s resembled Ronald Relf in the 1970s. (Relf advertised his house for sale to an 'English family' only and was subsequently gaoled for refusing to take down the sign outside his house.) Obstinate and occasionally threatening as they might have been, they were dwindling in numbers and lacking in credibility by the late 1980s.

After all the wild rabbits have been caught, the hunting dogs will be cooked. The import of this Chinese saying is that the fate of predators is always linked to that of their prey: one becomes obsolete as the other perishes. Whereas in the late 1960s and 1970s the feminists' prey was a palpable reality, in the 1980s it became, for many, rather nebulous. The old male chauvinist pigs became figures of fun; sex-structured pay inequalities were a thing of the past (despite continuing differentials); and equal opportunities were provided by employers—if only technically. Personal feelings of hatred, which had served the movement so well in focusing concerns and distilling energies, were diffused as a result both of legal changes and of innovations in anti-sexist educational policies. The peculiar sharpness of conflict characteristic of the early movement was replaced by duller, less passionate internal conflicts about heretics and apostates. It might be argued that what the women's movement of the 1990s will really need is a few more Gillicks, or Savages, or even a renascent Mary Whitehouse!

Schismatic breakaways do not threaten the unity of the women's movement because there is little unity to threaten. A continuing, vital movement must search for enemies to remain effective, to keep its members conscious of their essential unity. Mindful of this fact, the women's movement can be expected to attract or provoke enmity. But will it attempt to force crises, or be content to claim small victories? Most probably the latter. The movement seems to have left its most volatile period behind. Even then, it seems, the conflicts it hastened, while reflecting a razor-edged dissatisfaction, did not betray any fundamental lack of confidence in society. Women have been unafraid to express disagreement over sex inequality precisely because they have felt secure in society's ability and willingness to accommodate their interests. Fundamental values were not necessarily questioned in the late 1960s. Reversing the logic, we can also maintain that the relative absence of overt conflict in the postwar period did not necessarily mirror firm stability. Despite the pressure of some feminist groups, women for the most part avoided acting out hostile feelings, perhaps because of the suppressing effects of the postwar consensus, or perhaps because of a lack of certainty in their own ability to bond together as a force.

I have identified the broad social changes that underlay the emergence of second-wave feminism. From a woman's perspective, the feeling of confidence in her own power was enhanced by the greater ability to control her own fertility. This in turn signalled society's apparent sensitivity to women's experiences and its willingness to absorb their interests. Laws were created and modified that changed the position of women in employment. New rules were drawn up for structuring women's opportunities in work and education, and new agencies were established for enforcing these rules. Disregarding their effectiveness for now, we can observe that their very existence served an integrating function and tied in women more firmly with the established order. The conflict catalysed by the women's movement did not directly produce these changes, but it certainly reminded society of the impossibility of *not* changing in a progressive direction. The resistance to the abortion backlash illustrates this.

While, in some lights, the women's movement might be seen to have arisen from a widening divide between women's groups and society, the argument offered here is that it actually developed out of security, a security women felt in society. At the crucial stage at the end of the 1960s, women felt a strong allegiance to society and grew confident of its ability to satisfy new demands within existing institutional structures. While many might insist that the movement's ultimate project was – and still is – the transformation of the power relations underlying women's subordinate status, its actions and their effects to date have not moved significantly towards this. One of the major consequences of the movement, it could be argued, has been not in transforming power relations, but in confirming their effectiveness. Similar judgements can be made of the impact of virtually any social conflict inspired by the quest for more equality. Even finely drawn visions have a habit of descending abruptly into piecemeal reforms in a conservative society that is well practised in handling struggle. What implications does this type of judgement have for British society in the future? I will draw out some of them in the Conclusion.

CHAPTER 11

Conclusion: Potential and prohibition

The changing state

If you were a miner in Cortonwood Colliery, South Yorkshire, in March 1984, you would have been told that your pit was to close in five weeks. It is probable that you would have attended a meeting of the local branch of the National Union of Mineworkers and voted, along with your fellow workers, to strike in an attempt to halt the intended closure, a closure that threatened not only your livelihood but that of the whole community. Your action would have implicated you in the longest industrial strike in the United Kingdom's history.

If you were in your fifties at the time, you might recall a National Coal Board recruiting advertisement from just after the war, which read: 'Coalmining gives you a job for good.' Images of the strikes of the early 1970s would be reasonably fresh. Since then, you might have changed your car three times or more, each time buying a newer and better model; you might have added a video-recorder to your home, maybe moved home completely. You could have invested some of your savings in the privatized British Telecom. In fact, it would be possible for you to reflect on how comfortable life had become since the 1950s, when many domestic staples were regarded as luxuries and before the mechanization of the coal industry had removed some perilous aspects of work. The buoyancy that accompanied such 'affluence' and eventually assisted Labour's election to government in 1964 would awaken memories of better times. Such times were not always as good as some people think: when racial conflict opened a sore that seemed impossible to heal; when women joined unions in growing numbers and insisted they were being treated unfairly; when, for a four-year period, the collieries were closed at the rate of one per week.

After the strike, you might have moved south in search of a job, or signed on the dole. Embittering and demoralizing as the defeat of the miners was, your resolution might still be sound. The experience would no doubt help shape your answer to the question posed in this book. You might point to the policing of the strike, indicating the willingness of the government to use force. The sight of police deploying CS gas in the riots of 1985 and women peace campaigners being dragged by police and army officers would influence your judgement – as would the unemployment statistics. Not only would you see actual and potential conflict all about you, but also a more forceful role for the state in controlling that conflict. There is some support for this view that the flexibility of the British system, especially in its conserving strategies, is disappearing.

Many speculate that the UK is in the midst of a large-scale political change that will incline it towards a prohibitive authoritarian rigidity. The undermining of local governments and appropriation of its powers has centralized Westminster's control over key resources. The argument gains further strength from the episode at the General Communications Headquarters (GCHQ), where employees were obliged to sign away their rights to join trade unions in the interests of 'national security'. A similar justification informed the government's widely unpopular attempt to suppress the publication of Peter Wright's book *Spycatcher* in 1987. 'National security', like 'law and order' and 'individual freedom', is a convenient emotive subterfuge used to ease the passage of policies weighted in favour of state control. If this argument is correct, then conflicts may accumulate and eventually be channelled along one major line of cleavage.

Some think that 'the great strike', as Callinicos and Simons call it, was a breakthrough, when miners 'began to make political connections': 'They met black people and discovered they too were persecuted by the state. Their views about sexuality began to change when they came across lesbians and gays who supported their strike' (1985, p. 252). This resonates with the view of Trevor Carter, quoted previously, who believes that the miners' strike 'awakened a level of solidarity with the black community's daily experience' (1986, p. 143). There will continue to be loose coalitions of frustrated and possibly isolated groups, such as in the strike itself or on the 'march for jobs', but their interests may not extend beyond immediate purposes. In other words, such alignments are unlikely to evolve into more permanent forms of mass unification. The reasons for this were investigated in the previous chapters, and here I will redraw the broad outlines of the argument.

The UK has many social inequalities; but they are neither putrescent nor fecund, in the sense that they will not cause society to rot, nor produce a fresh revolutionary change. All forms of structured inequality create conflict. Almost by definition, conflict is endemic in unequal societies. Yet, beneath the British conflict, there has been agreement over the nature and types of conflict and its acceptable limits. The issues, objectives and *modus operandi* of conflict have rarely been in dispute. Conflict has usually taken place over specific issues and within particular settings. Principles and values have not been questioned, making the UK's institutional arrangements and values amongst the most secure in the Western world. What conflict has flared openly has been assimilated, institutionalized and, often, acted upon. Saying that conflict has functions is more than a cliché; it is a persuasive fact in the context of modern Britain. It is also an affront to conservatives and a giant brake on revolution. The fact remains: institutionalizing conflict has encouraged faith in and commitment to the openness of society. The UK is united *because* of social conflict.

Gathering clouds

A question remains about the future: is the UK undergoing the most significant change since the war, a change that will perhaps damage the underlying unity? Events since 1980 have created uncertainty and a pervasive sense of insecurity about the future. The more the state's dimensions of control expand, the more unsure dissenting groups will become. Where does legitimate protest end and criminal behaviour begin? Confusion is compounded by the persistence of unemployment, which, despite aberrant statistics in the late 1980s, has left a workless group as a kind of social residue, an underclass, populated overwhelmingly by young people and ethnic minorities. Their life in the British cities was described euphemistically by Scarman as one of 'enforced idleness'. Educational failure, illiteracy, poor-quality housing, broken homes, criminality and shameless poverty are features of this underclass. Its members have a kind of scavenger existence, scrabbling for work in the informal economy, mixing petty theft with signing on as unemployed, wasting away, their ambitions paralysed by the prospect of no future.

There is little resemblance between this residual group and the wealthy or the rising sections of society, the prospering, shareholding, high income earners. Mobile groups are hardly the raw material of future challenge; their expectations are on an upward curve and are often met by economic improvements. New Right policy in the 1980s has held clear attractions for many sections of the working class. Even those who have not benefited economically have attitudes towards race relations and immigration, the women's movement, homosexuality, defence and nationalism that have been adequately catered for by recent government policies.

The gap between what the dispossessed poor want and what they get is wide; the gap between what they actually *expect* and what they get is much narrower. The poorest see all the videos, cd players and computers the advertisers have been exhorting them to buy as unlikely to come within their grasp. Their main concern is with surviving at the outer edges of society, keeping alive a fragile stake in the job market and a claim to citizenship – a claim that has arisen out of what Daniel Bell has called 'a revolution of rising entitlements' (1976, p. 232). Since the war, Western populations have been encouraged to think in terms of their legitimate rights – be they social, political, or civic – and to expect or even demand them. One of those expectations has, for long, been a lifetime of work. But this has changed. At the end of the 1980s more than a million Britons had been without a job for a period of twelve months or more. They are, as the phrase goes, on the outside looking in. But they want to be *in*; an interest in society, however small, is the extent of many people's ambitions.

'Why is society not exploding?' asked United States journalist Robert Gibson, after looking at the British unemployment statistics (*Financial Times*, 11 August 1986, p. 13). 'Is there a secret siphon?' The answer is that there does not need to be. Conflict will arise, but it is likely to be stirred by remanent groups and will be of a defensive nature, the underlying concern being self-preservation in a culture that emphasizes pragmatism, instrumentalism and independently achieved success. The reasons for the presence of an underclass are so complex as to defy its easy banishment. It is attractively simple to advocate more jobs, but this is virtually impossible to achieve. And, in any case, it cannot be certain that more work would be an automatic solution. Yet this social residue, strictly speaking, will not become a permanent under*class* in that it will not solidify into a unified amalgamation of similarly deprived interest groups united in the face of common adversity. The emergence – or, more accurately, submergence – of these groups should not be misinterpreted as a fourth great divide in the UK's structure of inequalities; it does not represent another cleavage to rival class, race and sex, but rather crystallizes and caricatures all three.

In Britain there are around three million people unemployed and a group of about one million others in part-time or low-paid jobs, 'moonlighting' in the informal economy, engaged on Youth Training and associated schemes, or scratching around to put an income together from various sources: that is, in all over 7 per cent of the population. The distribution and composition vary, of course, but the greatest concentrations are north of a bisecting line drawn from Norwich to Holyhead, and the majority of these dispossessed are aged between 16 and 25. Within the group there are disproportionate numbers of blacks and South Asians. Female single parents also figure prominently, making the underclass a dense body of disadvantaged women, ethnic minorities and white youths with a penumbra of various other constituents. In this way, the residue actually embodies the other main divisions in modern Britain. It is a class phenomenon in that its members are *déclassé*: from a working class whose bottom has dropped out. But its existence also owes much to the forces that work virtually to exclude women and ethnic minorities from the 'official' labour market.

And so to a prognosis. Will the expansion of the underclass prompt more conflict? Will it lead directly and inescapably to further violence? Or will it work in catalytic conjunction with other factors, such as an iron-clad state and politically committed organizations, to incline the residual groups to violence? It is highly probable that there will be more open conflict that will concern issues, goals and interests; it will be sectional, identifying the special problems of, say, unemployed mothers or black school-leavers. The impact is, of course, unknowable, but it will at least increase the probability of new norms, freer dialogue and changes in policy. It seems doubtful whether any burst of conflict will contradict the basic assumptions of British society or the values on which its legitimacy rests. The conflict will be disruptive, but will eventually be contained or suppressed by a state bent on increasing its control – in which case it will resurface. One effect of this might be that the goal or ambition of the conflict could become obscure and so the behaviour will no longer be directed at reaching a solution to an unsatisfactory situation, but merely at releasing the tension which arose from it. I believe this is already happening, and inner-city events in 1985 (as distinct from 1981) seem to confirm the view.

This type of sporadic, violent conflict that breaks formal bounds, undesirable and sickening as many may find it, seems set to become part of the character of modern Britain. Whether one finds this acceptable or not is largely a matter of political hue. The social, political and industrial conflict that emerges will not be of a scale or intensity to threaten the consensual basis of society. But then again, conflict that does threaten seems to arise within societies of such rigidity that hostilities cannot be played out at all. Whether those who speculate that Britain is headed towards such rigidity have made rash prophecies, or whether they have a sensitive measure of an emergent trend, remains to be seen.

What does seem beyond doubt is that the great structural inequalities of class, race and gender will endure, at least for the foreseeable future. So will the conflict those inequalities engender; for, as Coser observed: 'As long as there are large inequalities among human beings, as long as there exist sharp asymmetries in power and structurally induced discrepancies in access to resources, it seems unlikely that the potential for conflict will be successfully minimized' (1984, p. 20).

The unfathomable question is: how long will this last? Toleration and management of conflict and dissent are currently (and have long been) achieved without unacceptable cost. Disparate forces are tamed, for the most part without bloodshed. But one wonders how long such a society can preserve itself, especially with governments favouring control rather than accommodation or negotiation. The divisions remain and in some cases deepen; and while this book has been an oblique, if grudging, tribute to Britain's democratic adaptability, it also shows the harsh, debilitating inequalities and squandered energies. This has, in a sense, been a chronicle of unmitigated gloom. Each spell of conflict may clear the air temporarily, but, as Coser has pointed out, such spells can never prevent the recurrent gathering of clouds.

[237]

References and Bibliography

Abrams, M., and Rose, R. (1960), *Must Labour Lose?* (Harmondsworth: Penguin).

Abrams, P., and Brown, R. (eds) (1984), *UK Society* (London: Weidenfeld & Nicolson).

Adorno, T., Frenkel-Brunswick, E., Levinson, D., and Sanforo, R. (1950), *The Authoritarian Personality* (New York: Harper & Row).

Alexander, P. (1987), *Racism, Resistance and Revolution* (London: Bookmarks).

Allen, S., and Wolkowitz, C. (1987), *Homeworking* (London: Macmillan).

Andrews, N. (1987), 'Pre-permissive prudery put to flight', *Financial Times*, 4 December, p. 23.

Anwar, M. (1986), *Race and Politics* (London: Tavistock).

Arnot, M. (1986), 'State education policy and girls' educational experiences', in V. Beechey and E. Whitelegg (eds), *Women in Britain Today* (Milton Keynes: Open University Press), pp. 132–72.

Bachu, P. (1985), *Twice Migrants* (London: Tavistock).

Banton, M. (1985), *Promoting Racial Harmony* (Cambridge: Cambridge University Press).

Barker, M. (1981), *The New Racism* (London: Junction Books).

Barnett, A. (1982), *Iron Britannia* (London: Allison & Busby).

Barrett, M. (1980), *Women's Oppression Today* (London: Verso).

Barrett, M., and McIntosh, M. (1982), *The Anti-Social Family* (London: New Left Books).

Barstow, S. (1973), *A Kind of Loving* (London: Corgi).

Bartlett, C. J. (1977), *A History of Postwar Britain* (London: Longman).

Bauer, P. (1978), *Class on the Brain* (London: Centre for Policy Studies).

Bechhofer, F., and Elliott, B. (eds) (1981), *The Petit Bourgeoisie* (London: Macmillan).

Beechey, V. (1986), 'Women and employment in contemporary Britain', in V. Beechey and E. Whitelegg (eds), *Women in Britain Today* (Milton Keynes: Open University Press), pp. 77–131.

Beechey, V., and Perkins, T. (1986), *A Matter of Hours* (Oxford: Polity Press).

Bell, D. (1976), *The Cultural Contradictions of Capitalism* (London: Heinemann).

Benyon, J. (ed.) (1984), *Scarman and After* (London: Pergamon).

Berger, P., and Berger, B. (1983), *The War over the Family* (London: Hutchinson).

Beveridge, W. H. (1944), *Full Employment in a Free Society* (London: Allen & Unwin).

Bognador, V. (1970), 'The Labour Party in opposition, 1951–1964', in Bognador and Skidelski, op. cit., pp. 78–116.

Booker, C. (1980), *The Seventies* (London: Allen Lane).

Borkowski, M., Murch, M., and Wacker, Y. (1983), *Marital Violence* (London: Tavistock).

Bouchier, D. (1983), *The Feminist Challenge* (London: Macmillan).

Box, S. (1987), *Recession, Crime and Punishment* (London: Macmillan).

Boyd, D. (1973), *Elites and their Education* (Windsor: National Foundation for Educational Research).

Braham, P., Rhodes, E., and Pearn, M. (eds) (1981), *Discrimination and Disadvantage in Employment* (London: Harper & Row).

Brown, C. (1984), *Black and White Britain* (London: Heinemann Educational Policy Studies Institute).

Burgess, R. G. (1984), 'Patterns and processes of education in the UK', in Abrams and Brown, op. cit., pp. 58–128.

Burgoyne, J. (1987), 'Material happiness', *New Society*, 10 April, pp. 12–14.

Burnham, J. (1945), *The Managerial Revolution* (Harmondsworth: Penguin).

Callinicos, A., and Simons, M. (1985), *The Great Strike* (London: Socialist Worker).

Campbell, B. (1987), *The Iron Ladies* (London: Virago).

Campbell, M., and Jones, D. (1982), *Asian Youths in the Labour Market* (Bradford: Bradford College).

Carter, T. (1986), *Shattering Illusions* (London: Lawrence & Wishart).

Cashmore, E. (1983), *Rastaman* (London: Allen & Unwin).

Cashmore, E. (1984), *No Future* (London: Heinemann Educational).

Cashmore, E. (1985), *Having To* (London: Allen & Unwin).

Cashmore, E. (1987), *The Logic of Racism* (London: Allen & Unwin).

Cashmore, E., and Bagley, C. (1985), 'Colour blind,' *The Times Educational Supplement*, no. 3574, 28 December.

Cashmore, E., and Troyna, B. (1983), *Introduction to Race Relations* (London: Routledge & Kegan Paul).

Centre for Contemporary Cultural Studies (1980), *The Empire Strikes Back* (London: Hutchinson).

Clark, D. (1987), 'Wedlocked Britain', *New Society*, 13 March, pp. 12–15.

Coates, K., and Topham, T. (1986). *Trade Unions and Politics* (Oxford: Blackwell).

Collins, W. (1965), *Jamaican Migrant* (London: Routledge & Kegan Paul).

Commission for Racial Equality (1980), *Ethnic Minority Youth Unemployment* (London: CRE).

Coote, A., and Campbell, B. (1987), *Sweet Freedom* (Oxford: Blackwell).

Coser, L. (1968), *The Functions of Social Conflict* (London: Routledge & Kegan Paul).

Coser, L. (1970), *Continuities in the Study of Social Conflict* (New York: Free Press).

Coser, L. (1984), 'Salvation through communication?', in A. Arno and W. Dissanayake (eds), *The News Media in National and International Conflict* (Boulder, Colo: Westview), pp. 17–25.

Cox, O. C. (1948), *Caste, Class and Race* (New York: Doubleday).

Coyle, A. (1984), *Redundant Women* (London: Women's Press).

Crosland, C. A. R. (1956), *The Future of Socialism* (London: Cape).

Cross, M., Edmonds, J., and Sargeant, R. (1982), *Special Problems and Special Measures* (Birmingham: Research Unit on Ethnic Relations).

Dahrendorf, R. (1959), *Class and Class Conflict in Industrial Society* (London: Routledge & Kegan Paul).

Dahrendorf, R. (1982), *On Britain* (London: BBC Publications).

Dahrendorf, R. (1987), 'The erosion of citizenship and its consequences for all of us', *New Statesman*, 12 June, pp. 12–15.

Daniel, W. W. (1968), *Racial Discrimination in Britain* (Harmondsworth: Penguin).

Davie, R. (1966). *11,999 Seven-Year-Olds* (Harlow: Longman).

Davie, R., Butler, N., and Goldstein, H. (1972), *From Birth to Seven* (Harlow: Longman).

Davison, R. (1966), *Black British* (London: Oxford University Press).

Delamont, S. (1980), *The Sociology of Women* (London: Allen & Unwin).

Douglas, J. W. B. (1964), *The Home and the School* (London: MacGibbon & Kee).

Doyal, L., and Elston, M. A. (1986), 'Women, health and medicine', in V. Beechey and E. Whitelegg (eds), *Women in Britain Today* (Milton Keynes: Open University Press), pp. 173–209.

Dunnell, K. (1976), *Family Formation* (London: HMSO).

Egbuna, O. (1971), 'The "contradictions" of black power', *Race Today*, vol. 3, pp. 266–8 (August) and 298–9 (September).

Farmer, M. (1982), *The Family*, 2nd edn (London: Longman).

Fevre, R. (1984), *Cheap Labour and Racial Discrimination* (Aldershot: Gower).

Firestone, S. (1970), *The Dialectic of Sex* (New York: Morrow Quill).

Fletcher, R. (1973), *The Family and Marriage in Britain*, 3rd edn (Harmondsworth: Penguin).

Floud, J. E., Halsey, A. H., and Martin, F. M. (eds) (1957), *Social Class and Educational Opportunity* (London: Heinemann).

Foot, P. (1965), *Immigration and Race in British Politics* (Harmondsworth: Penguin).

Fox, A. (1985), *History and Heritage* (London: Allen & Unwin).

Fox, I. (1984), 'The demand for a public school education', in G. Walford (ed.), *British Public Schools* (Lewes: Falmer Press), pp. 45–64.

Fryer, P. (1984), *Staying Power* (London: Pluto Press).

Gelb, J. (1986), 'Feminism in Britain', in D. Dahlerup (ed.), *The New Women's Movement* (Beverly Hills, Calif.: Sage), pp. 103–21.

Gilroy, B. (1976), *Black Teacher* (London: Cassell).

Gilroy, P. (1987), *There Ain't No Black in the Union Jack* (London: Hutchinson).

Glasgow, D. (1980), *The Black Underclass* (New York: Jossey Bass).

Glass, D. V. (ed.) (1954), *Social Mobility in Britain* (London: Routledge & Kegan Paul).

Glass, R. (1960), *Newcomers* (London: Allen & Unwin).

Goffee, R., and Scase, R. (1985), *Women in Charge* (London: Allen & Unwin).

Goldthorpe, J., Lockwood, D., Bechhofer, F., and Platt, J. (1969), *The Affluent Worker in the Class Structure* (London: Cambridge University Press).

Goldthorpe, J. H. (1980), *Social Mobility and the Class Structure in Modern Britain* (Oxford: Oxford University Press).

Greaves, G. (1984), 'The Brixton disorders', in Benyon, op. cit., pp. 63–72.

Green, M. (1984), *Marriage* (London: Fontana).

Greenhalgh, C. (1977), 'Is marriage an equal opportunity?', LSE Discussion Paper No. 14.

Greer, G. (1984), *Sex and Destiny* (London: Secker & Warburg).

Halsey, A. H. (1986), *Change in British Society*, 3rd edn (Oxford: Oxford University Press).

Halsey, A. H., Heath, A. F., and Ridge, J. M. (1980), *Origins and Destinations* (Oxford: Oxford University Press).

Harris, H. (1972), 'Black women and work', in Wandor, op. cit., pp. 166–74.

Heath, A. (1981), *Social Mobility* (London: Fontana).

Heath, A. (1987), 'Class in the classroom', *New Society*, 17 July, pp. 13–15.

Hinton, J. (1986), *Labour and Socialism* (Brighton: Wheatsheaf).

Hiro, D. (1973), *Black British, White British* (London: Monthly Review Press).

Hiro, D., and Fay, S. (1967), 'Man it's beautiful – but does it work?', *Sunday Times*, 29 October, p. 8.

Hobsbawm, E. (1981), 'The forward march of labour halted', in M. Jacques and F. Mulhearn (eds), *The Forward March of Labour Halted?* (London: New Left Books).

Honeyford, R. (1983), 'The right education?', *Salisbury Review*, vol. 13, no. 1, pp. 28–30.

Horsman, R. (1981), *Race and Manifest Destiny* (Cambridge, Mass.: Harvard University Press).

Hubbuck, J., and Carter, S. (1980), *Half a Chance* (London: CRE).

Hyman, R. (1980), 'British trade unionism', *International Socialism*, series 2, pt 8, pp. 64–79.

Hyman, R. (1984), *Strikes*, 3rd edn (London: Fontana).

Itzin, C. (1980), *Splitting Up* (London: Virago).

Jenkins, R. (1982), *Managers, Recruitment Procedures and Black Workers* (Birmingham: Research Unit on Ethnic Relations).

Johnson, R. W. (1985), *The Politics of Recession* (London: Macmillan).

Johnston, J. (1973), *Lesbian Nation* (New York: Simon & Schuster).

Jones, J. (1986), *Union Man* (London: Collins).

Joshua, H., Wallace, T., and Booth, H. (1983), *To Ride the Storm* (London: Heinemann Educational).

Kapo, R. (1981), *A Savage Culture* (London: Quartet).

Kerner, O. (1968), *Report of the National Advisory Commission on Civil Disorders* (New York: Bantam).

Laing, R. D., and Esterson, A. (1980), *Sanity, Madness and the Family* (Harmondsworth: Penguin).

Lawrence, D. (1974), *Black Migrants – White Natives* (London: Cambridge University Press).

Layton-Henry, Z. (1984), *The Politics of Race in Britain* (London: Allen & Unwin).

Lee, G. (1987), 'Black members and their unions', in G. Lee and R. Loveridge (eds), *The Manufacture of Disadvantage* (Milton Keynes: Open University Press), pp. 144–58.

Lee, G., and Wrench, J. (1981), *In Search of a Skill* (London: CRE).

Leonard, D., and Speakman, M. (1986), 'Women in the family', in V. Beechey and E. Whitelegge (eds), *Women in Britain Today* (Milton Keynes: Open University Press), pp. 8–76.

Little, K. (1975), 'Performance of children from ethnic minority backgrounds in primary schools', *Oxford Review of Education*, vol. 2, no. 2, pp. 117–35.

Lukes, S. (1984), 'The future of British socialism?', in B. Pimlott (ed.), *Fabian Essays in Social Thought* (London: Heinemann).

McKenzie, R., and Silver, A. (1968), *Angels in Marble* (London: Heinemann Educational).

McNabb, R., and Psacharopoulos, G. (1981), 'Racial earnings differentials in the UK', Oxford Economic Papers.

Marris, R. (ed.) (1974), *The Corporate Society* (London: Macmillan).

Martin, J., and Roberts, C. (1984), *Women and Employment* (London: HMSO).

Marwick, A. (1970), *Britain in the Century of Total War* (Harmondsworth: Penguin).

Marwick, A. (1982), *British Society since 1945* (Harmondsworth: Penguin).

Miles, R. (1982), *Racism and Migrant Labour* (London: Routledge & Kegan Paul).

Miles, R. (1987), 'Recent Marxist theories of nationalism and the issue of racism', *British Journal of Sociology*, vol. 38, no. 1, pp. 24–43.

Miles, R., and Phizacklea, A. (1984), *White Man's Country* (London: Pluto Press).

Millett, K. (1971), *Sexual Politics* (New York: Avon Books).

Milne, R. S., and McKenzie, H. C. (1954), *Straight Fight* (London: Hansard Society).

Morris, L. (1987), 'The no-longer working class', *New Society*, 3 April, pp. 16–18.

Mullard, C. (1975), *Black Britain* (London: Allen & Unwin).

Mullard, C. (1985), *Race, Power and Resistance* (London: Routledge & Kegan Paul).

Myrdal, G. (1944), *An American Dilemma* (New York: Harper & Row).

National Youth Bureau (1986), *Black Youth Futures* (Leicester: NYB).

Newson, J. H. (1963), *Half our future* (London: HMSO).

Newson, J., and Newson, E. (1965), *Patterns of Infant Care in an Urban Community* (Harmondsworth: Penguin).

Oakley, A. (1974), *The Sociology of Housework* (Oxford: Martin Robertson).

Parkin, F. (1967), 'Working-class conservatives', *British Journal of Sociology*, September, pp. 278–90.

Parmar, P. (1982), 'Gender, race and class', in Centre for Contemporary Cultural Studies, op. cit., pp. 236–75.

Patterson, S. (1963), *Dark Strangers* (London: Tavistock).

Peach, C. (1968), *West Indian Migration to Britain* (London: Oxford University Press).

Pen, J. (1971), *Income Distribution* (Harmondsworth: Penguin).

Phillips, A. (1987), *Divided Loyalties* (London: Virago).

Phizacklea, A., and Miles, R. (1987), 'The British trade union movement and racism', in G. Lee and R. Loveridge (eds), *The Manufacture of Disadvantage* (Milton Keynes: Open University Press).

Pitts, J. (1986), 'Black young people and juvenile crime', R. Matthews and J. Young (eds), *Confronting Crime* (London: Sage), pp. 118–44.

Pollert, A. (1981), *Girls, Wives, Factory Lives* (London: Macmillan).

Ramdin, R. (1987), *The Making of the Black Working Class in Britain* (Aldershot: Gower).

Randall, V. (1982), *Women and Politics* (London: Macmillan).

Reid, I. (1981), *Social Class Differences in Britain*, 2nd edn (London: Grant McIntyre).

Rex, J. (1983), *Race Relations in Sociological Theory*, 2nd edn (London: Routledge & Kegan Paul).

Rex, J. (1986), 'The role of class analysis in the study of race relations', in J. Rex and D. Mason (eds), *Theories of Race and Ethnic Relations* (Cambridge: Cambridge University Press), pp. 64–83.

Rex, J., and Moore, R. (1981), *Race, Community and Conflict* (London: Oxford University Press).

Richmond, A. (1954), *Colour Prejudice in Britain* (London: Routledge & Kegan Paul).

Robbins, L. H. (1963), *Higher Education Report* (London: HMSO).

Roberts, B. (1982), 'The debate on "sus" ', in E. Cashmore and B. Troyna (eds), *Black Youth in Crisis* (London: Allen & Unwin), pp. 100–42.

Roberts, E. (1984), *A Woman's Place* (Oxford: Blackwell).

Rock, P., and Cohen, S. (1970), 'The teddy boys', in Bognador and Skidelski, op cit., pp. 288–320.

Rose, E. J. B. (1969), *Colour and Citizenship* (London: Oxford University Press).

Rowbotham, S. (1973), *Women's Consciousness, Man's World* (Harmondsworth: Penguin).

Rubinstein, W. D. (1986), *Wealth and Inequality in Britain* (London: Faber).

Runnymede Trust (1980), *Britain's Black Population* (London: Heinemann Educational).

Ryder, J., and Silver, H. (1985), *Modern English Society* (London: Methuen).

Sampson, A. (1982), *The Changing Anatomy of Britain* (London: Hodder & Stoughton).

Schoen, D. E. (1977), *Enoch Powell and the Powellites* (London: Macmillan).

Seymour-Ure, C. (1974), *The Political Impact of the Mass Media* (London: Constable).

Sitkoff, H. (1981), *The Struggle for Black Equality* (New York: Hill & Wang).

Sivanandan, A. (1982), *A Different Hunger* (London: Pluto Press).

Smith, D. (1977), *Racial Disadvantage in Britain* (Harmondsworth: Penguin).

Smith, D., and Gray, J. (1985), *Police and People in London* (London: Gower/Policy Studies Institute).

Spencer, A., and Podmore, D. (eds) (1987), *In a Man's World* (London: Tavistock).

Stacey, M., and Price, M. (1981), *Women, Power and Politics* (London: Tavistock).

Stanworth, P. (1984), 'Elite and privilege', in Abrams, P. and Brown, R. (eds), *UK Society* (London: Weidenfeld & Nicolson), pp. 246–93.

Swann, M. (1985), *Education for All* (London: HMSO).

Titmuss, R. M. (1962), *Income Distribution and Social Change* (London: Allen & Unwin).

Titmuss, R. M. (1976), *Essays on 'The Welfare State'* (London: Allen & Unwin).

Tomlinson, S. (1980), 'The educational performance of ethnic minority children', *New Community*, vol. 8, no. 3, pp. 213–34.

Townsend, P. (1979), *Poverty in the United Kingdom* (London: Allen Lane).

Troyna, B. (1988), 'Education and racism,' in E. Cashmore (ed.), *Dictionary of Race and Ethnic Relations*, 2nd edn (London: Routledge), pp. 85–90.

Troyna, B., and Smith, D. (eds), (1983), *Racism, School and the Labour Market* (Leicester: NYB).

van den Berghe, P. (1984), 'Africa', in E. Cashmore (ed.), *Dictionary of Race and Ethnic Relations* (London: Routledge), pp. 4–8.

Wainwright, H. (1984), 'Women and the division of labour', in Abrams and Brown, op. cit., pp. 198–245.

Walker, M. (1977), *The National Front* (London: Fontana).

Wandor, M. (ed.) (1972), *The Body Politic* (London: Stage 1).

Ward, R., and Jenkins, R. (eds) (1985), *Ethnic Communities in Business* (London: Cambridge University Press).

Weir, A., and Wilson, E. (1984), 'The British women's movements', *New Left Review*, no. 148, pp. 74–103.

Westergaard, J. H. (1972), 'Sociology: the myth of classlessness', in R. Blackburn (ed.), *Ideology in Social Science* (London: Fontana), pp. 119–63.

Willis, P. (1984), 'Youth unemployment 2', *New Society*, 6 April, pp. 13–14.

Willmott, P., and Young, M. (1957), *Family and Kinship in East London* (London: Routledge & Kegan Paul).

Willmott, P., and Young, M. (1960), *Family and Class in a London Suburb* (London: Routledge & Kegan Paul).

Wilson, E. (1980), *Only Halfway to Paradise* (London: Tavistock).

Worsley, P. (1970), *Introducing Sociology* (Harmondsworth: Penguin).

Wright, P. (1968), *The Coloured Worker in British Industry* (London: Oxford University Press).

Young, M. (ed.) (1972), *Knowledge and Control* (London: Collier Macmillan).

Young, M., and Willmott, P. (1973), *The Symmetrical Family* (London: Routledge & Kegan Paul).

Index